EX MACHINA

BOOK 1:
THE FIRST HUNDRED DAYS

Brian K. Vaughan: Writer

Tony Harris: Pencils

Tom Feister: Inks

JD Mettler: Colors

Jared K. Fletcher: Letters

Larry Berry: Design

Ex Machina created by Vaughan and Harris

Jim Lee, Editorial Director **John Nee,** VP—Business Development **Scott Dunbier,** Executive Editor
Ben Abernathy, Editor—Original Series **Alex Sinclair,** Editor—Collected Edition **Kristy Quinn,** Assistant Editor
Robbin Brosterman, Senior Art Director **Ed Roeder,** Art Director **Paul Levitz,** President & Publisher
Georg Brewer, VP—Design & Retail Product Development **Richard Bruning,** Senior VP—Creative Director
Patrick Caldon, Senior VP—Finance & Operations **Chris Caramalis,** VP—Finance
Terri Cunningham, VP—Managing Editor **Alison Gill,** VP—Manufacturing **Rich Johnson,** VP—Book Trade Sales
Hank Kanalz, VP—General Manager, WildStorm **Lillian Laserson,** Senior VP & General Counsel
David McKillips, VP—Advertising & Custom Publishing **Gregory Noveck,** Senior VP—Creative Affairs
Cheryl Rubin, Senior VP—Brand Management **Bob Wayne,** VP—Sales & Marketing

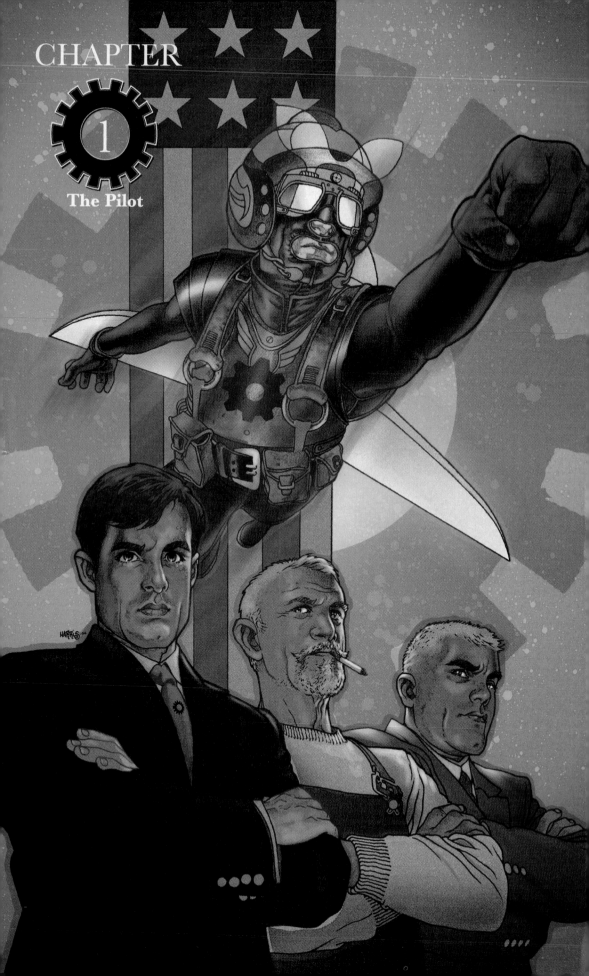

CHAPTER

1

The Pilot

deus ex machina (DAY-us ex MAH-kin-ah): Literally, "god from the machine." A person or force that arrives to provide an improbable solution to an impossible situation, named after the mechanical device used by Greek dramatists to lower actors playing deities onto the stage.

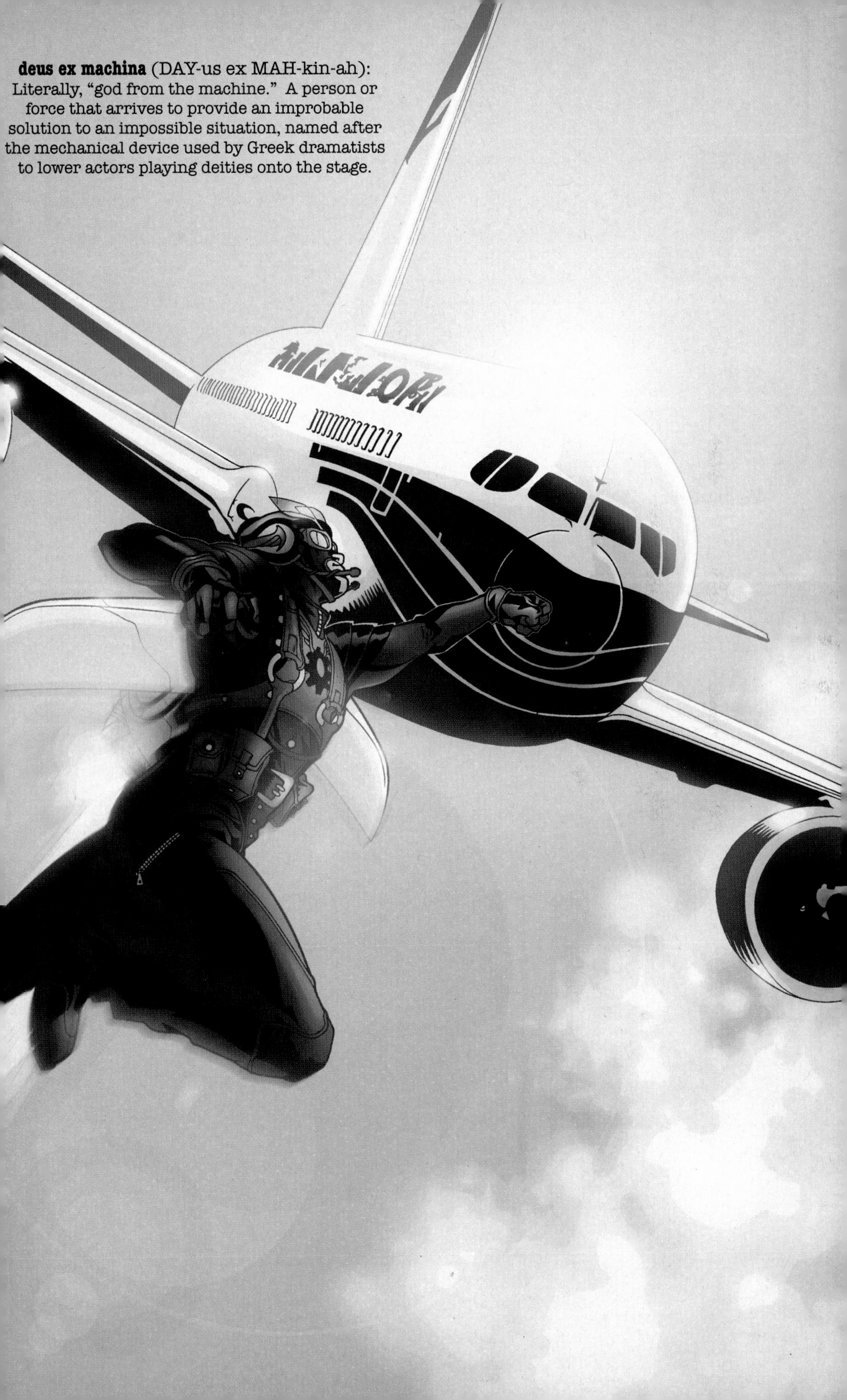

YOU'RE PROBABLY SICK OF THAT PICTURE BY NOW, HUH?

CHRIST KNOWS I AM.

PEOPLE BLAME ME FOR BUSH IN HIS FLIGHT SUIT AND ARNOLD GETTING ELECTED GOVERNOR, BUT TRUTH IS...THOSE THINGS WOULD HAVE HAPPENED WITH OR WITHOUT ME.

EVERYONE WAS SCARED BACK THEN, AND WHEN FOLKS ARE SCARED, THEY WANT TO BE SURROUNDED BY *HEROES*.

BUT REAL HEROES ARE JUST A FICTION WE CREATE. THEY DON'T EXIST OUTSIDE OF COMIC BOOKS.

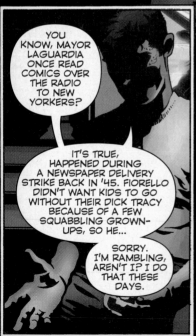

YOU KNOW, MAYOR LAGUARDIA ONCE READ COMICS OVER THE RADIO TO NEW YORKERS?

IT'S TRUE, HAPPENED DURING A NEWSPAPER DELIVERY STRIKE BACK IN '45. FIORELLO DIDN'T WANT KIDS TO GO WITHOUT THEIR DICK TRACY BECAUSE OF A FEW SQUABBLING GROWN-UPS, SO HE...

SORRY. I'M RAMBLING, AREN'T I? I DO THAT THESE DAYS.

ANYWAY, THIS IS THE STORY OF MY FOUR YEARS IN OFFICE, FROM THE BEGINNING OF 2002 THROUGH GODFORSAKEN 2005.

IT MAY LOOK LIKE A COMIC, BUT IT'S REALLY A TRAGEDY.

THAT'S LIFE, HUH?

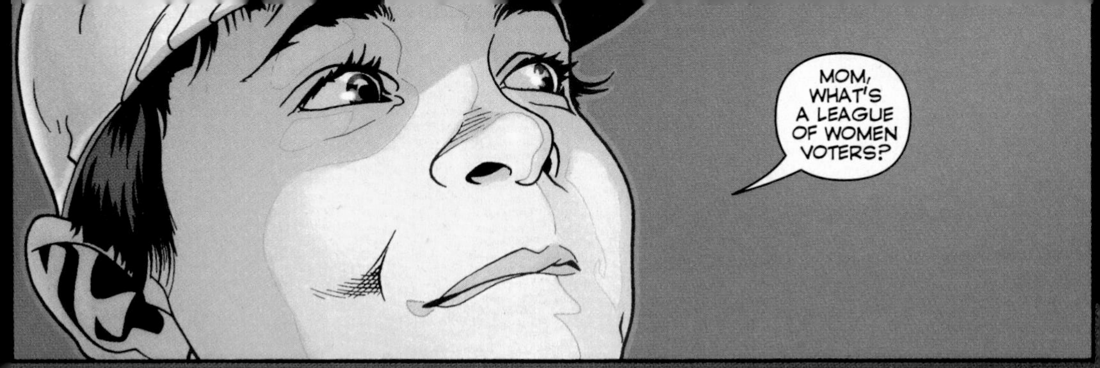
MOM, WHAT'S A LEAGUE OF WOMEN VOTERS?

TUESDAY, NOVEMBER 2, 1976

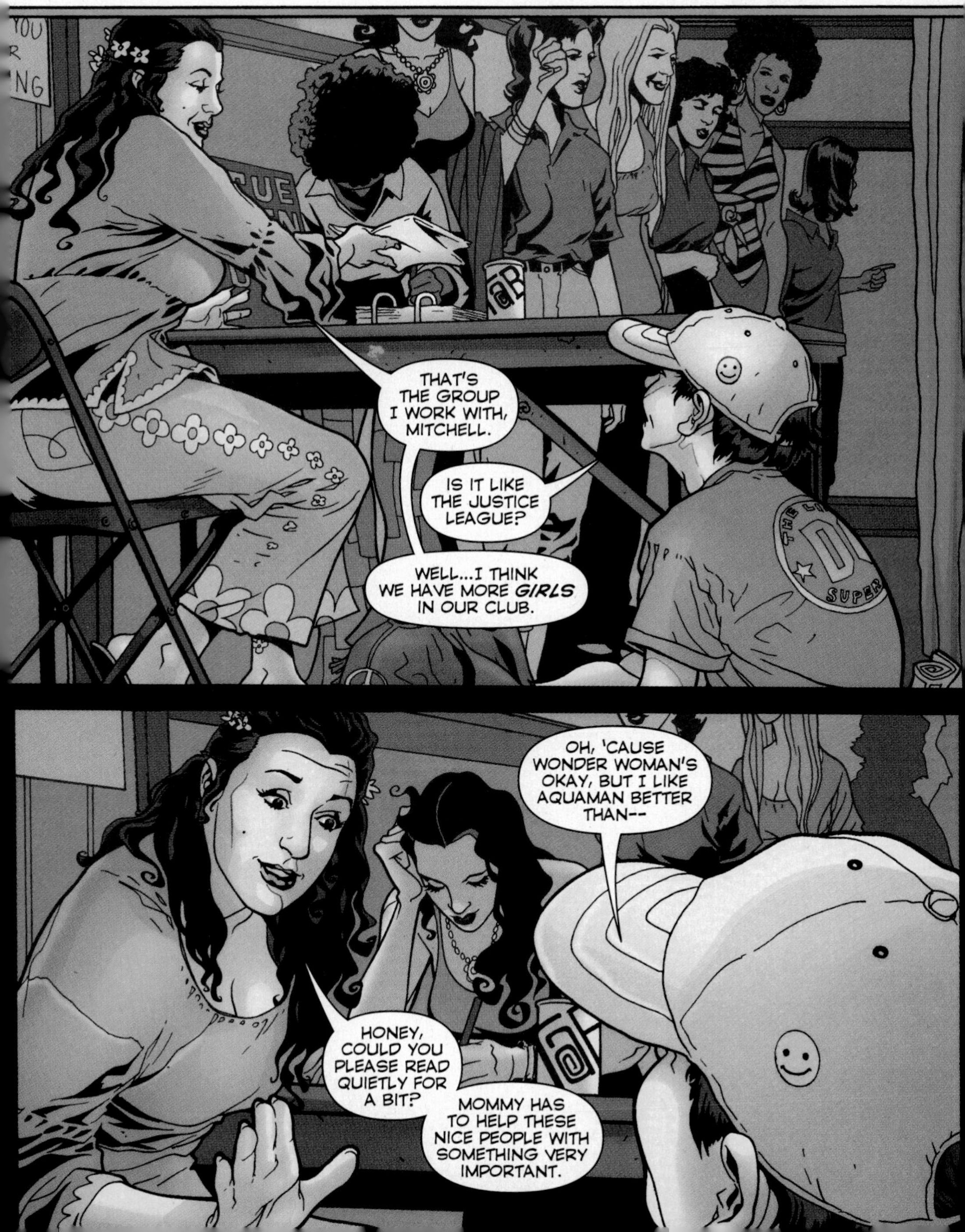
THAT'S THE GROUP I WORK WITH, MITCHELL.
IS IT LIKE THE JUSTICE LEAGUE?
WELL...I THINK WE HAVE MORE *GIRLS* IN OUR CLUB.
OH, 'CAUSE WONDER WOMAN'S OKAY, BUT I LIKE AQUAMAN BETTER THAN--
HONEY, COULD YOU PLEASE READ QUIETLY FOR A BIT?
MOMMY HAS TO HELP THESE NICE PEOPLE WITH SOMETHING VERY IMPORTANT.

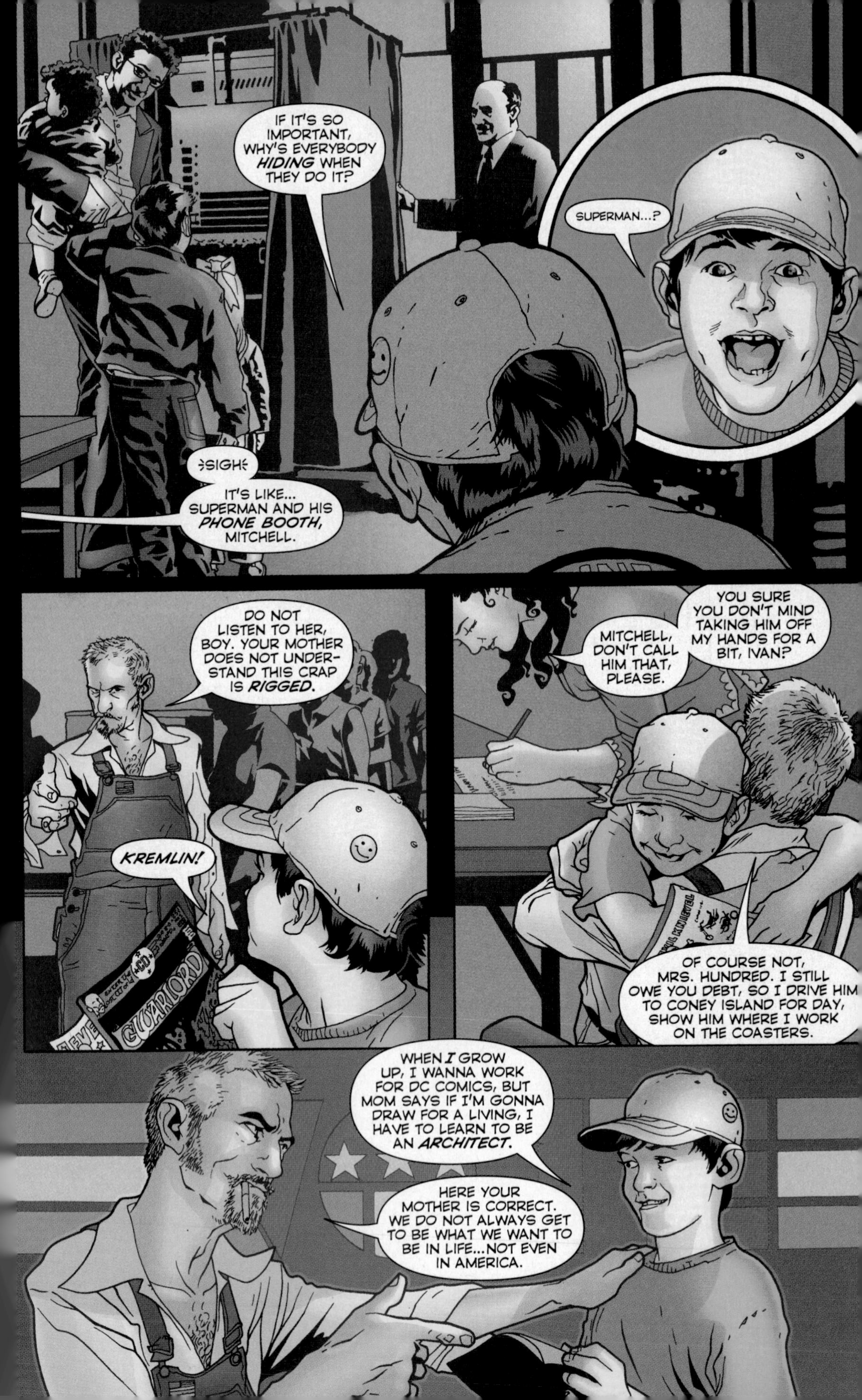

IF IT'S SO IMPORTANT, WHY'S EVERYBODY HIDING WHEN THEY DO IT?
SUPERMAN...?
SIGH
IT'S LIKE... SUPERMAN AND HIS PHONE BOOTH, MITCHELL.
DO NOT LISTEN TO HER, BOY. YOUR MOTHER DOES NOT UNDERSTAND THIS CRAP IS RIGGED.
KREMLIN!
GUARLORD
MITCHELL, DON'T CALL HIM THAT, PLEASE.
YOU SURE YOU DON'T MIND TAKING HIM OFF MY HANDS FOR A BIT, IVAN?
OF COURSE NOT, MRS. HUNDRED. I STILL OWE YOU DEBT, SO I DRIVE HIM TO CONEY ISLAND FOR DAY, SHOW HIM WHERE I WORK ON THE COASTERS.
WHEN I GROW UP, I WANNA WORK FOR DC COMICS, BUT MOM SAYS IF I'M GONNA DRAW FOR A LIVING, I HAVE TO LEARN TO BE AN ARCHITECT.
HERE YOUR MOTHER IS CORRECT. WE DO NOT ALWAYS GET TO BE WHAT WE WANT TO BE IN LIFE...NOT EVEN IN AMERICA.

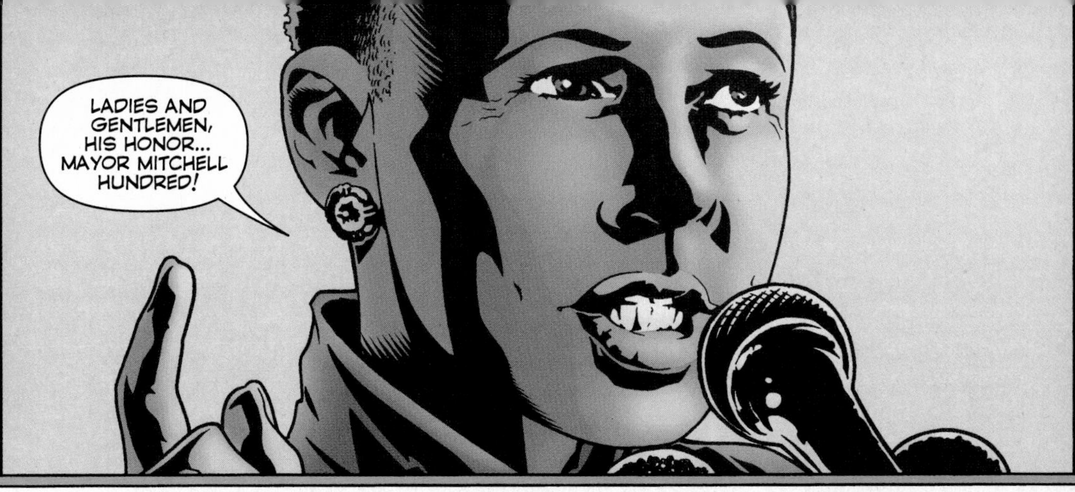
LADIES AND GENTLEMEN, HIS HONOR... MAYOR MITCHELL HUNDRED!

WEDNESDAY, JANUARY 9, 2002

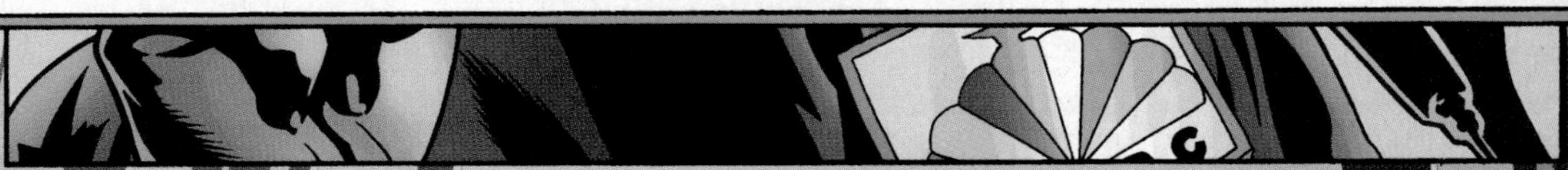

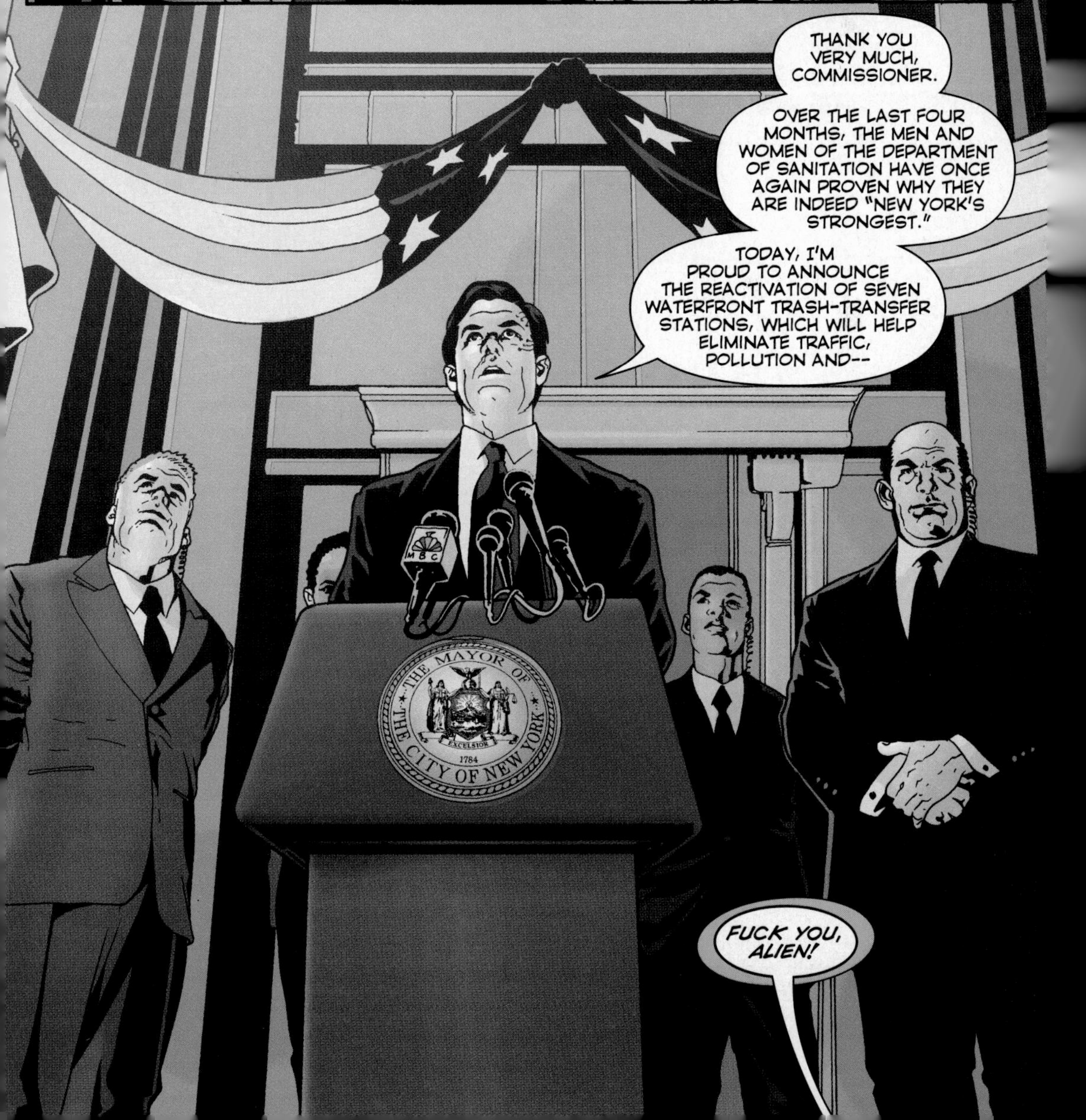
THANK YOU VERY MUCH, COMMISSIONER.
OVER THE LAST FOUR MONTHS, THE MEN AND WOMEN OF THE DEPARTMENT OF SANITATION HAVE ONCE AGAIN PROVEN WHY THEY ARE INDEED "NEW YORK'S STRONGEST."
TODAY, I'M PROUD TO ANNOUNCE THE REACTIVATION OF SEVEN WATERFRONT TRASH-TRANSFER STATIONS, WHICH WILL HELP ELIMINATE TRAFFIC, POLLUTION AND--
THE MAYOR OF THE CITY OF NEW YORK
EXCELSIOR
1784
FUCK YOU, ALIEN!

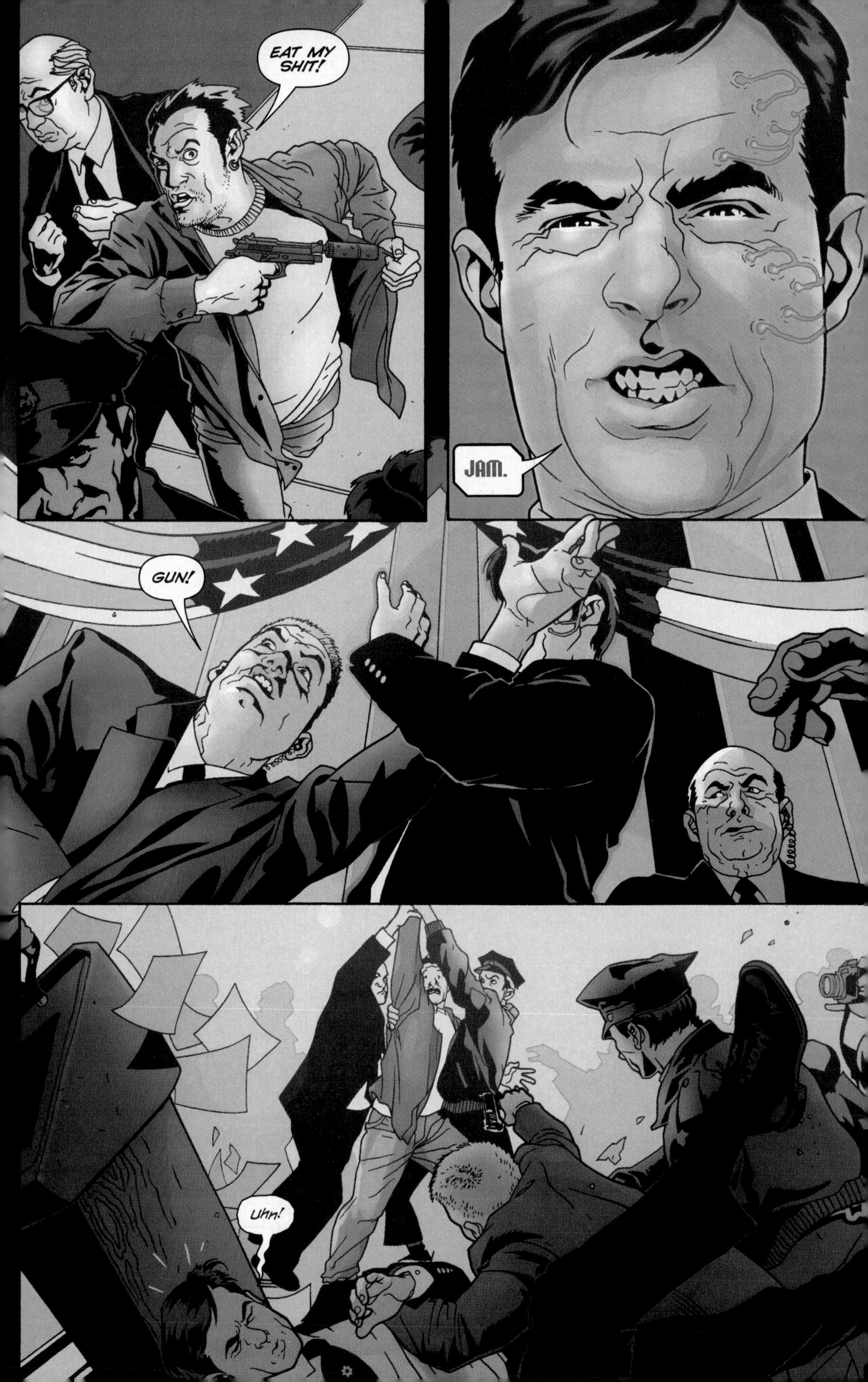
EAT MY SHIT!
JAM.
GUN!
Uhn!

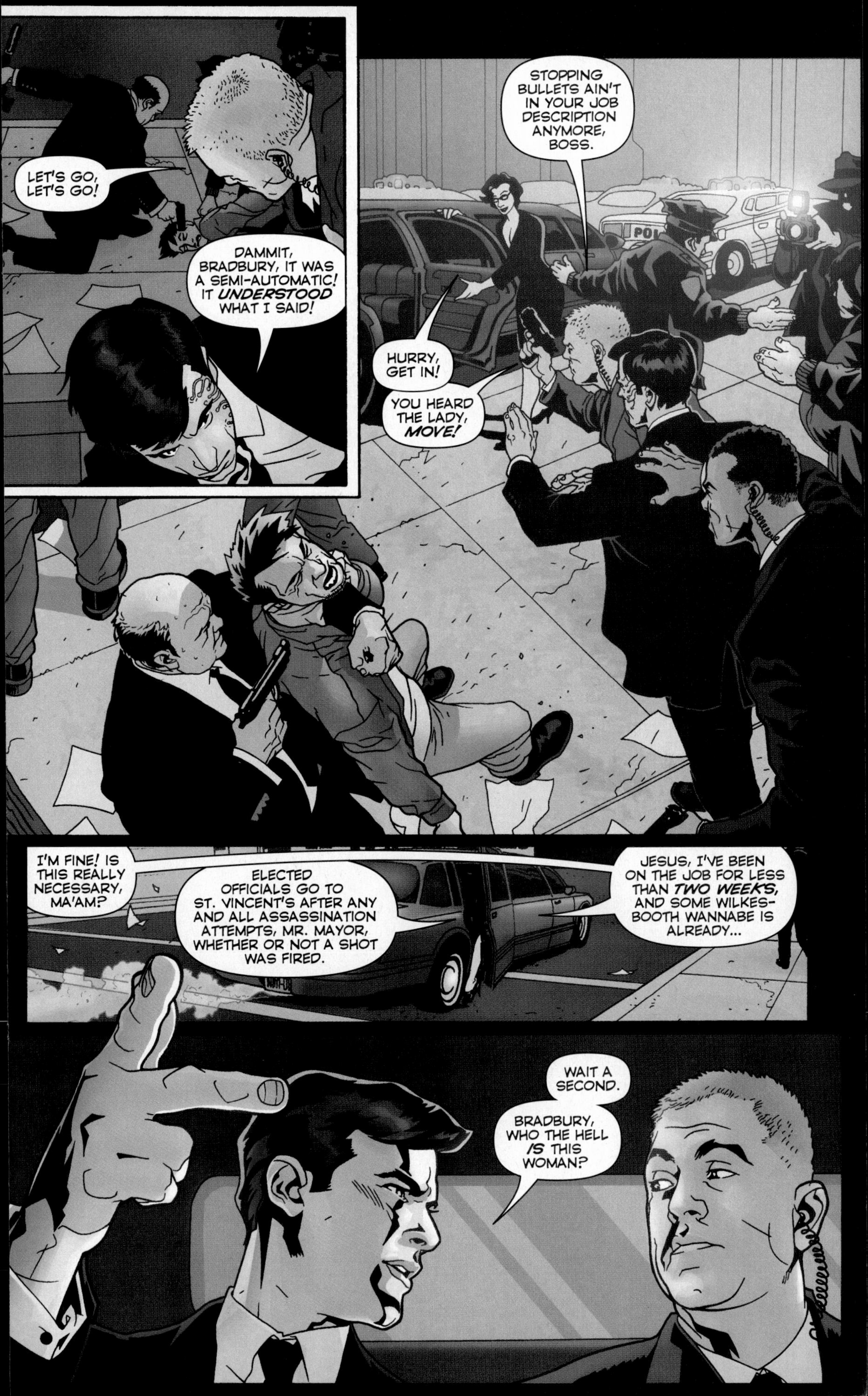
LET'S GO, LET'S GO!
DAMMIT, BRADBURY, IT WAS A SEMI-AUTOMATIC! IT *UNDERSTOOD* WHAT I SAID!
STOPPING BULLETS AIN'T IN YOUR JOB DESCRIPTION ANYMORE, BOSS.
HURRY, GET IN!
YOU HEARD THE LADY, *MOVE!*
I'M FINE! IS THIS REALLY NECESSARY, MA'AM?
ELECTED OFFICIALS GO TO ST. VINCENT'S AFTER ANY AND ALL ASSASSINATION ATTEMPTS, MR. MAYOR, WHETHER OR NOT A SHOT WAS FIRED.
JESUS, I'VE BEEN ON THE JOB FOR LESS THAN *TWO WEEKS,* AND SOME WILKES-BOOTH WANNABE IS ALREADY...
WAIT A SECOND.
BRADBURY, WHO THE HELL *IS* THIS WOMAN?

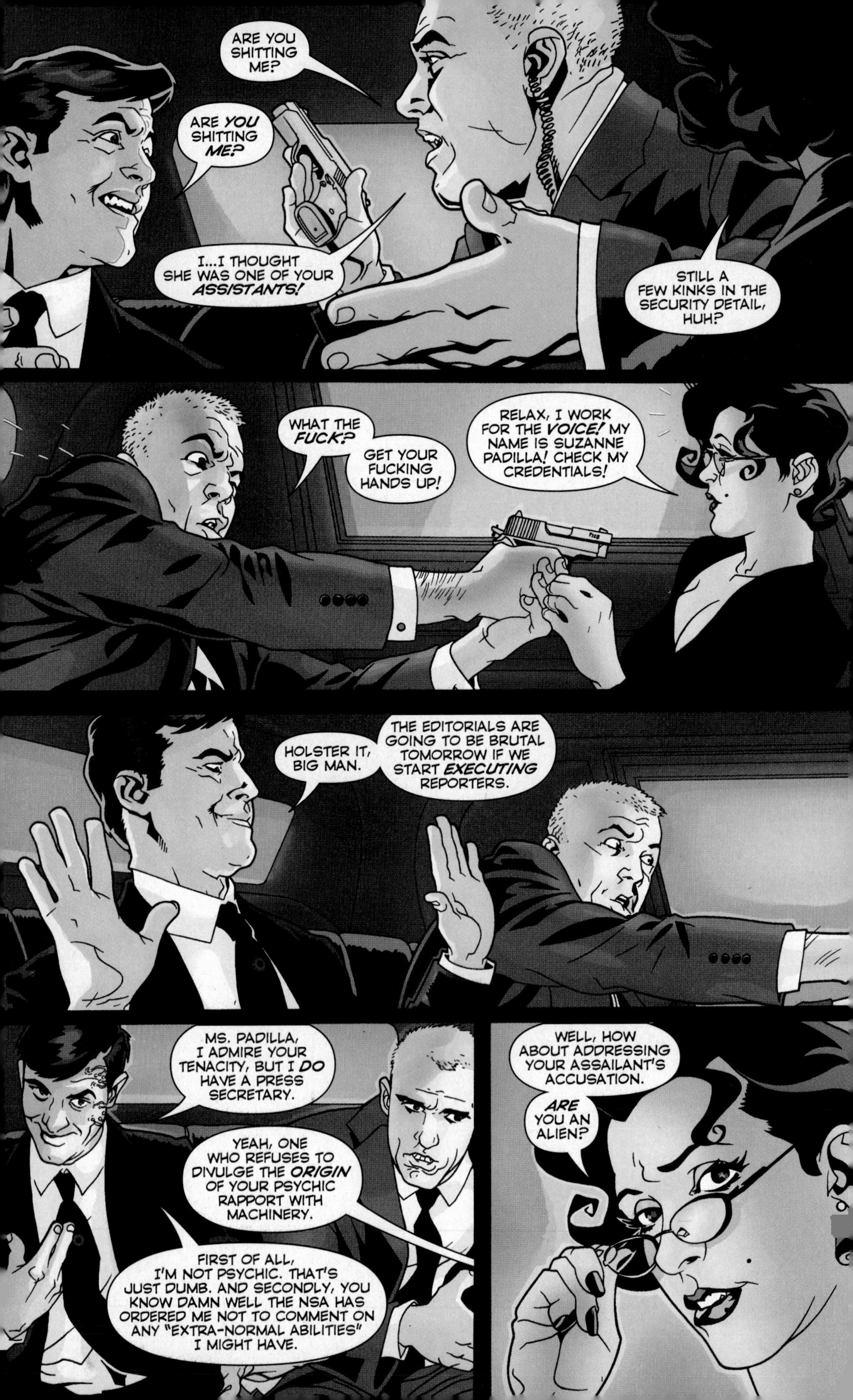
ARE YOU SHITTING ME?
ARE YOU SHITTING ME?
I...I THOUGHT SHE WAS ONE OF YOUR ASSISTANTS!
STILL A FEW KINKS IN THE SECURITY DETAIL, HUH?
WHAT THE FUCK?
GET YOUR FUCKING HANDS UP!
RELAX, I WORK FOR THE VOICE! MY NAME IS SUZANNE PADILLA! CHECK MY CREDENTIALS!
HOLSTER IT, BIG MAN.
THE EDITORIALS ARE GOING TO BE BRUTAL TOMORROW IF WE START EXECUTING REPORTERS.
MS. PADILLA, I ADMIRE YOUR TENACITY, BUT I DO HAVE A PRESS SECRETARY.
YEAH, ONE WHO REFUSES TO DIVULGE THE ORIGIN OF YOUR PSYCHIC RAPPORT WITH MACHINERY.
FIRST OF ALL, I'M NOT PSYCHIC. THAT'S JUST DUMB. AND SECONDLY, YOU KNOW DAMN WELL THE NSA HAS ORDERED ME NOT TO COMMENT ON ANY "EXTRA-NORMAL ABILITIES" I MIGHT HAVE.
WELL, HOW ABOUT ADDRESSING YOUR ASSAILANT'S ACCUSATION.
ARE YOU AN ALIEN?

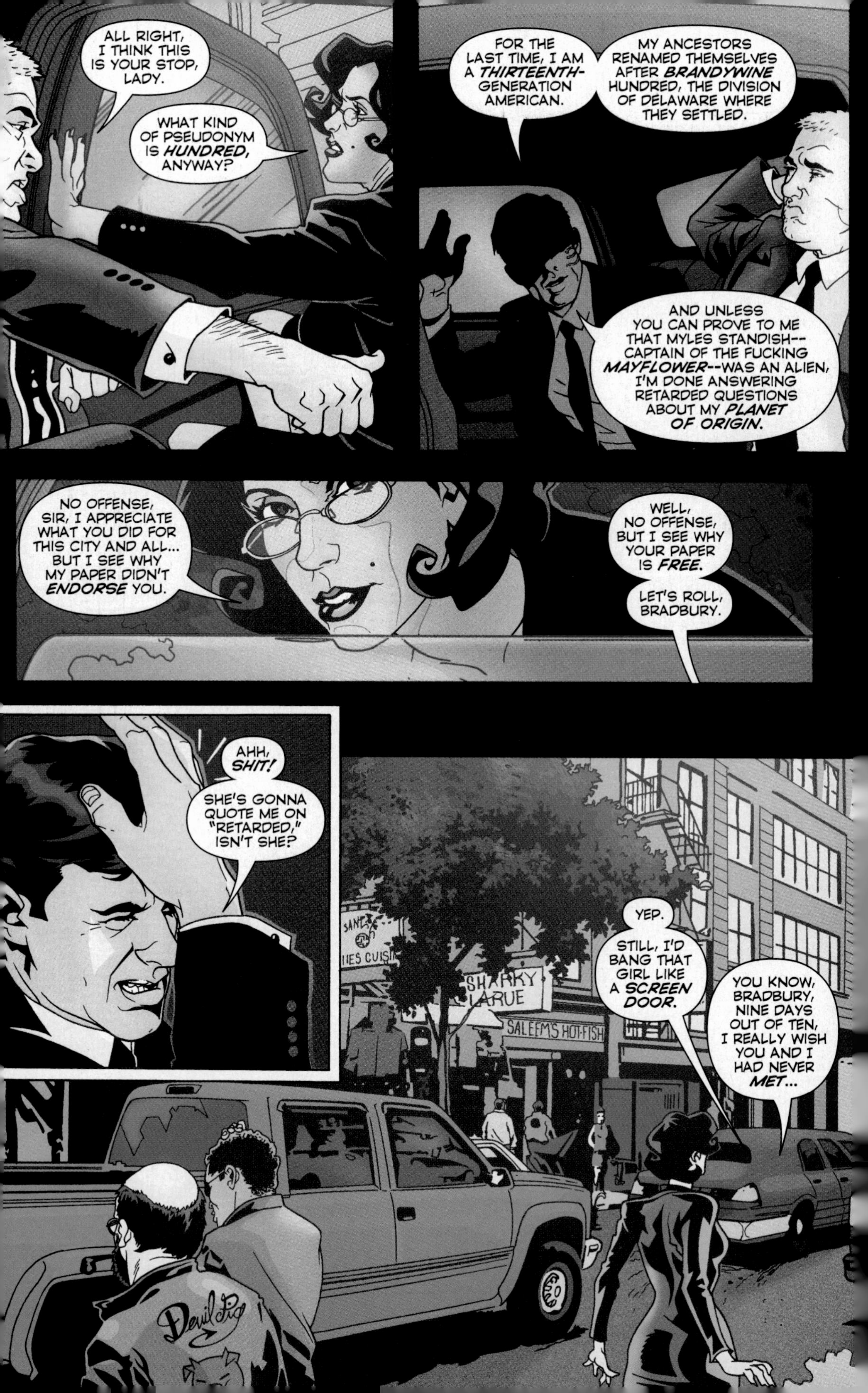
ALL RIGHT, I THINK THIS IS YOUR STOP, LADY.
WHAT KIND OF PSEUDONYM IS HUNDRED, ANYWAY?
FOR THE LAST TIME, I AM A THIRTEENTH-GENERATION AMERICAN.
MY ANCESTORS RENAMED THEMSELVES AFTER BRANDYWINE HUNDRED, THE DIVISION OF DELAWARE WHERE THEY SETTLED.
AND UNLESS YOU CAN PROVE TO ME THAT MYLES STANDISH--CAPTAIN OF THE FUCKING MAYFLOWER--WAS AN ALIEN, I'M DONE ANSWERING RETARDED QUESTIONS ABOUT MY PLANET OF ORIGIN.
NO OFFENSE, SIR, I APPRECIATE WHAT YOU DID FOR THIS CITY AND ALL... BUT I SEE WHY MY PAPER DIDN'T ENDORSE YOU.
WELL, NO OFFENSE, BUT I SEE WHY YOUR PAPER IS FREE.
LET'S ROLL, BRADBURY.
AHH, SHIT!
SHE'S GONNA QUOTE ME ON "RETARDED," ISN'T SHE?
YEP.
STILL, I'D BANG THAT GIRL LIKE A SCREEN DOOR.
YOU KNOW, BRADBURY, NINE DAYS OUT OF TEN, I REALLY WISH YOU AND I HAD NEVER MET...
SHARKY LARUE
SALEEM'S HOT-FISH
Devil Pig

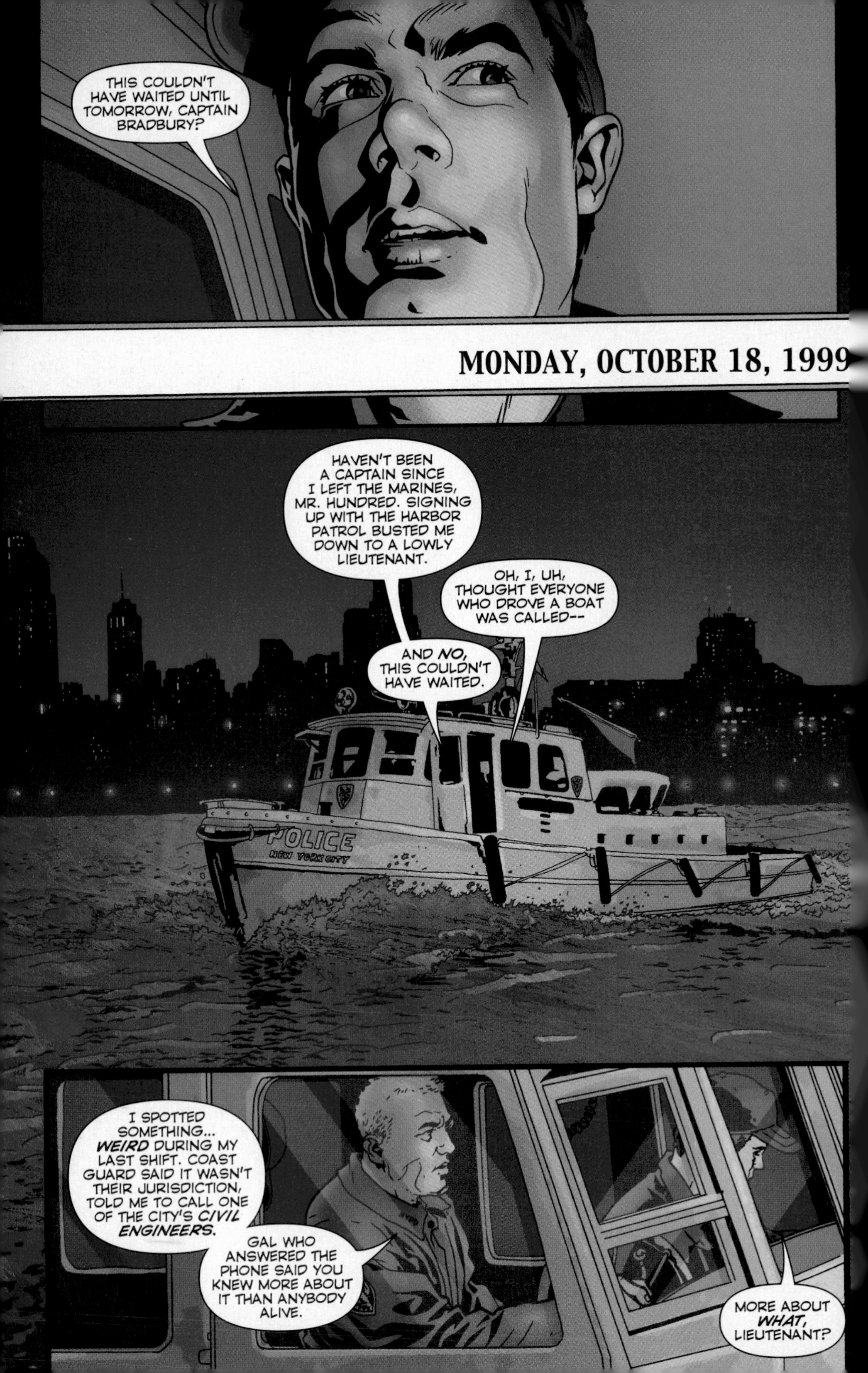
THIS COULDN'T HAVE WAITED UNTIL TOMORROW, CAPTAIN BRADBURY?
MONDAY, OCTOBER 18, 1999
HAVEN'T BEEN A CAPTAIN SINCE I LEFT THE MARINES, MR. HUNDRED. SIGNING UP WITH THE HARBOR PATROL BUSTED ME DOWN TO A LOWLY LIEUTENANT.
OH, I, UH, THOUGHT EVERYONE WHO DROVE A BOAT WAS CALLED--
AND NO, THIS COULDN'T HAVE WAITED.
POLICE
NEW YORK CITY
I SPOTTED SOMETHING... WEIRD DURING MY LAST SHIFT. COAST GUARD SAID IT WASN'T THEIR JURISDICTION, TOLD ME TO CALL ONE OF THE CITY'S CIVIL ENGINEERS.
GAL WHO ANSWERED THE PHONE SAID YOU KNEW MORE ABOUT IT THAN ANYBODY ALIVE.
MORE ABOUT WHAT, LIEUTENANT?

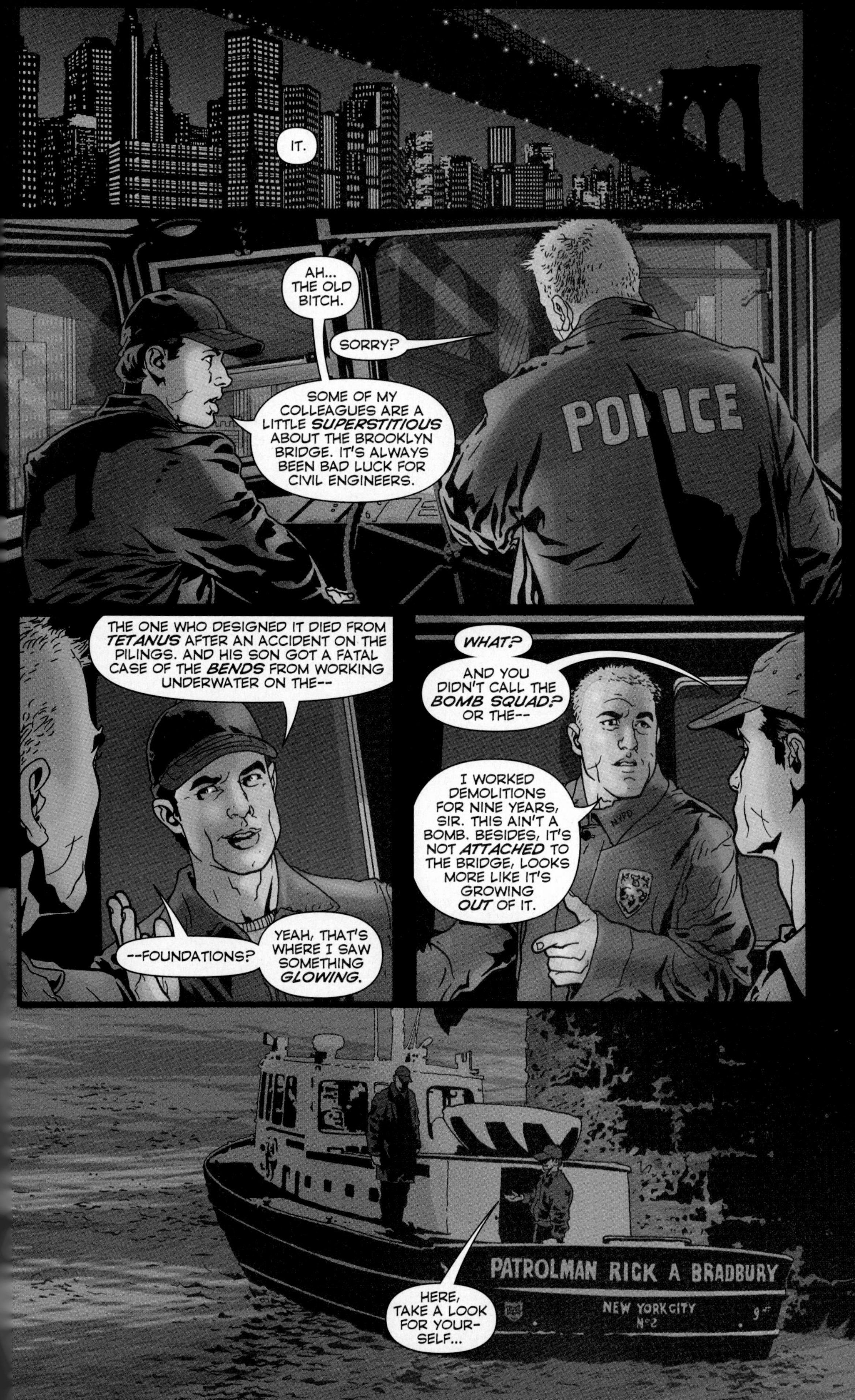
IT.
AH... THE OLD BITCH.
SORRY?
SOME OF MY COLLEAGUES ARE A LITTLE SUPERSTITIOUS ABOUT THE BROOKLYN BRIDGE. IT'S ALWAYS BEEN BAD LUCK FOR CIVIL ENGINEERS.
POLICE
THE ONE WHO DESIGNED IT DIED FROM TETANUS AFTER AN ACCIDENT ON THE PILINGS. AND HIS SON GOT A FATAL CASE OF THE BENDS FROM WORKING UNDERWATER ON THE--
--FOUNDATIONS?
YEAH, THAT'S WHERE I SAW SOMETHING GLOWING.
WHAT?
AND YOU DIDN'T CALL THE BOMB SQUAD? OR THE--
I WORKED DEMOLITIONS FOR NINE YEARS, SIR. THIS AIN'T A BOMB. BESIDES, IT'S NOT ATTACHED TO THE BRIDGE, LOOKS MORE LIKE IT'S GROWING OUT OF IT.
PATROLMAN RICK A BRADBURY
NEW YORK CITY
HERE, TAKE A LOOK FOR YOUR-SELF...

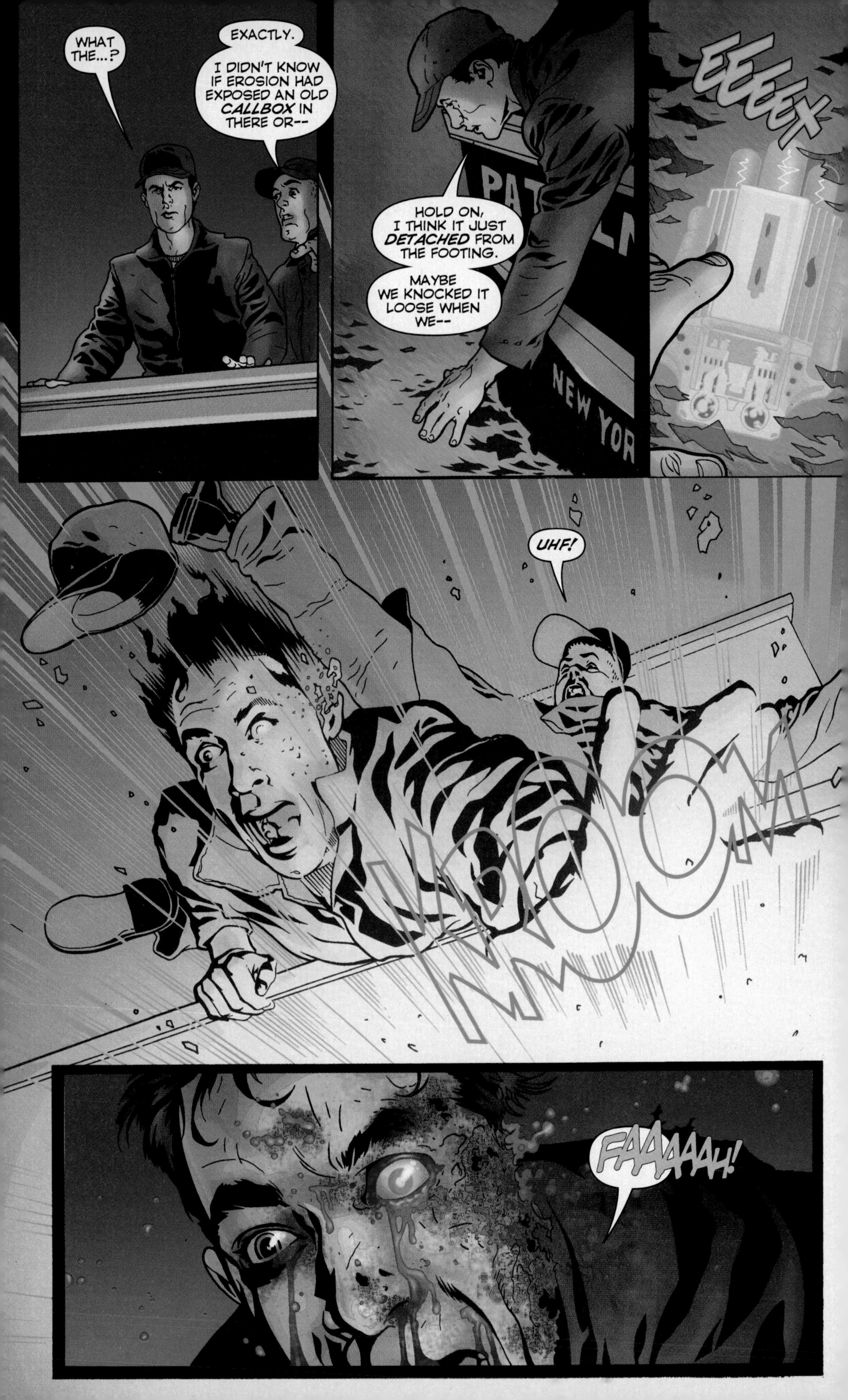
WHAT THE...?
EXACTLY.
I DIDN'T KNOW IF EROSION HAD EXPOSED AN OLD *CALLBOX* IN THERE OR--
HOLD ON, I THINK IT JUST *DETACHED* FROM THE FOOTING.
MAYBE WE KNOCKED IT LOOSE WHEN WE--
EEEEEX
UHF!
WHOOM
FAAAAAH!

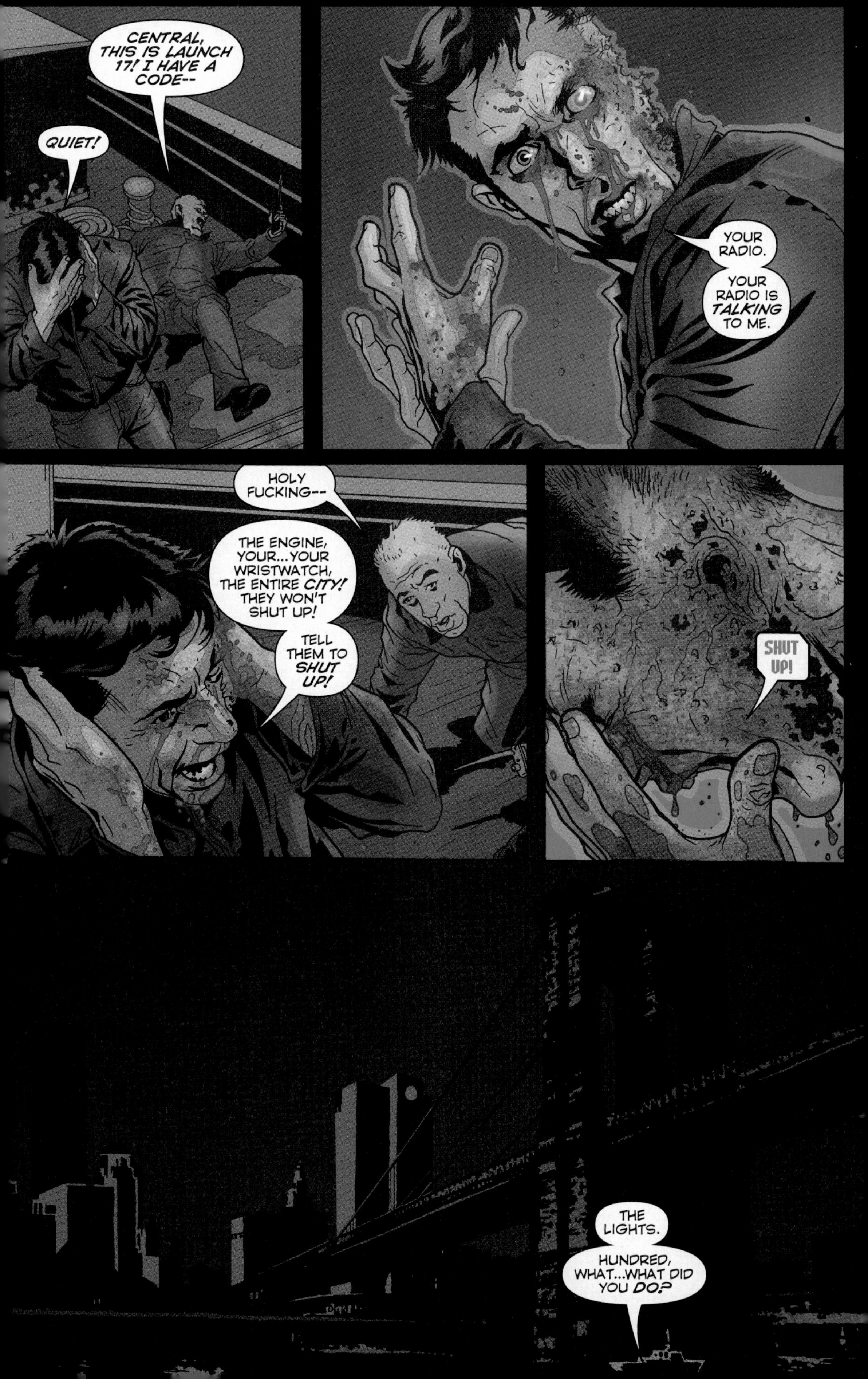
CENTRAL, THIS IS LAUNCH 17! I HAVE A CODE--
QUIET!
YOUR RADIO.
YOUR RADIO IS TALKING TO ME.
HOLY FUCKING--
THE ENGINE, YOUR...YOUR WRISTWATCH, THE ENTIRE CITY! THEY WON'T SHUT UP!
TELL THEM TO SHUT UP!
SHUT UP!
THE LIGHTS.
HUNDRED, WHAT...WHAT DID YOU DO?

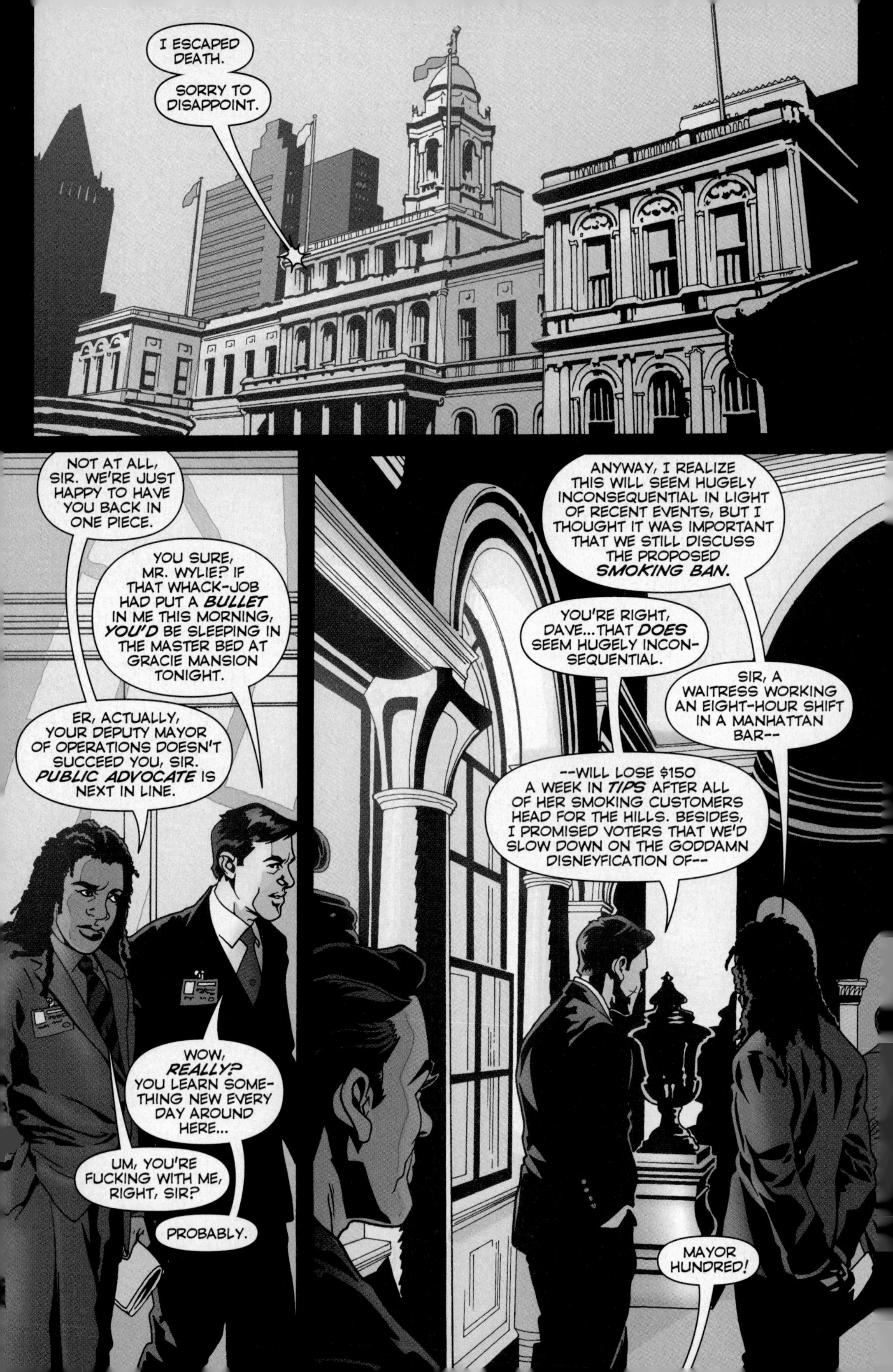

I ESCAPED DEATH.
SORRY TO DISAPPOINT.
NOT AT ALL, SIR. WE'RE JUST HAPPY TO HAVE YOU BACK IN ONE PIECE.
YOU SURE, MR. WYLIE? IF THAT WHACK-JOB HAD PUT A *BULLET* IN ME THIS MORNING, *YOU'D* BE SLEEPING IN THE MASTER BED AT GRACIE MANSION TONIGHT.
ER, ACTUALLY, YOUR DEPUTY MAYOR OF OPERATIONS DOESN'T SUCCEED YOU, SIR. *PUBLIC ADVOCATE* IS NEXT IN LINE.
WOW, *REALLY?* YOU LEARN SOMETHING NEW EVERY DAY AROUND HERE...
UM, YOU'RE FUCKING WITH ME, RIGHT, SIR?
PROBABLY.
ANYWAY, I REALIZE THIS WILL SEEM HUGELY INCONSEQUENTIAL IN LIGHT OF RECENT EVENTS, BUT I THOUGHT IT WAS IMPORTANT THAT WE STILL DISCUSS THE PROPOSED *SMOKING BAN.*
YOU'RE RIGHT, DAVE...THAT *DOES* SEEM HUGELY INCONSEQUENTIAL.
SIR, A WAITRESS WORKING AN EIGHT-HOUR SHIFT IN A MANHATTAN BAR--
--WILL LOSE $150 A WEEK IN *TIPS* AFTER ALL OF HER SMOKING CUSTOMERS HEAD FOR THE HILLS. BESIDES, I PROMISED VOTERS THAT WE'D SLOW DOWN ON THE GODDAMN DISNEYFICATION OF--
MAYOR HUNDRED!

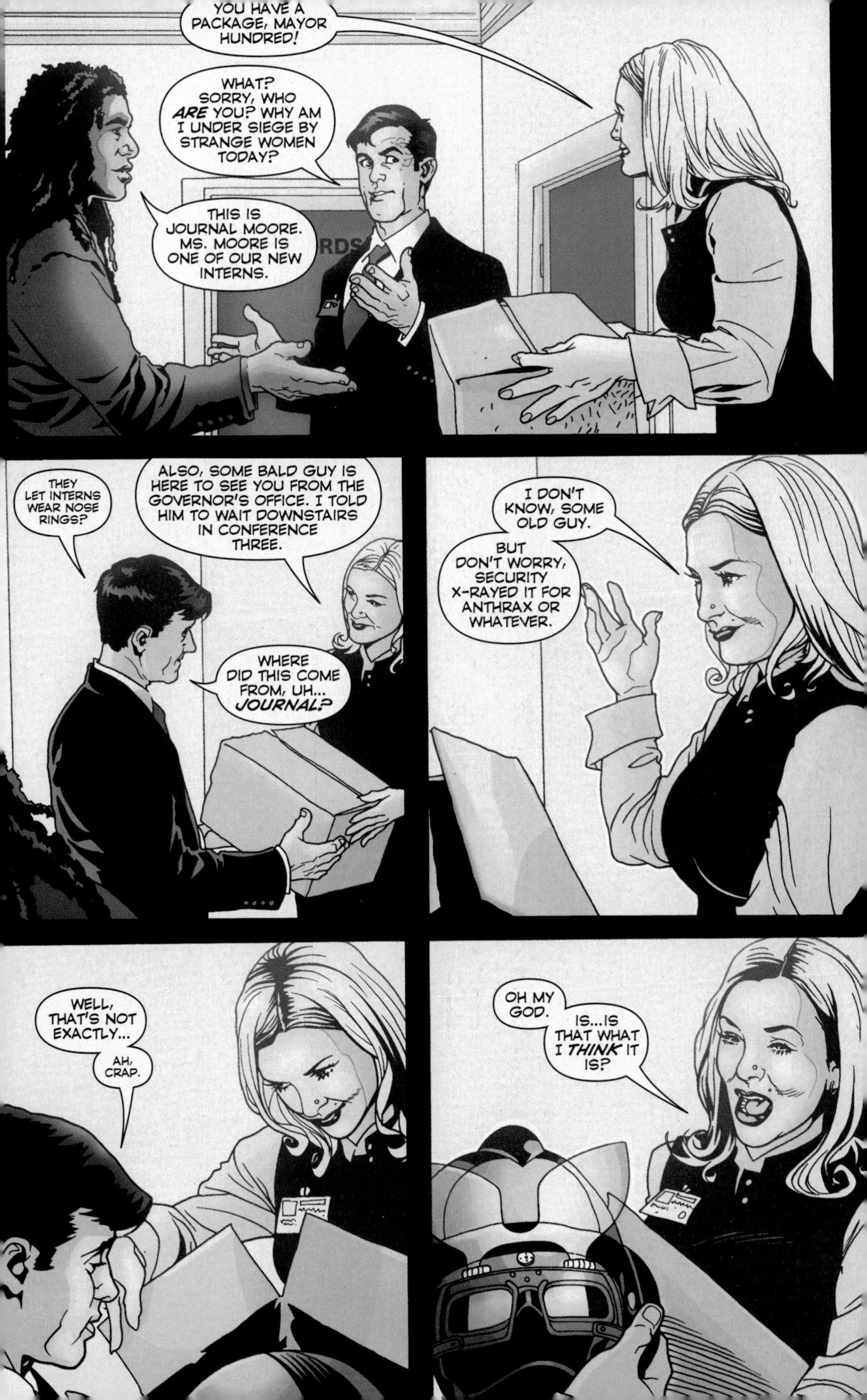
YOU HAVE A PACKAGE, MAYOR HUNDRED!
WHAT? SORRY, WHO ARE YOU? WHY AM I UNDER SIEGE BY STRANGE WOMEN TODAY?
THIS IS JOURNAL MOORE. MS. MOORE IS ONE OF OUR NEW INTERNS.
THEY LET INTERNS WEAR NOSE RINGS?
ALSO, SOME BALD GUY IS HERE TO SEE YOU FROM THE GOVERNOR'S OFFICE. I TOLD HIM TO WAIT DOWNSTAIRS IN CONFERENCE THREE.
WHERE DID THIS COME FROM, UH... JOURNAL?
I DON'T KNOW, SOME OLD GUY.
BUT DON'T WORRY, SECURITY X-RAYED IT FOR ANTHRAX OR WHATEVER.
WELL, THAT'S NOT EXACTLY...
AH, CRAP.
OH MY GOD.
IS...IS THAT WHAT I THINK IT IS?

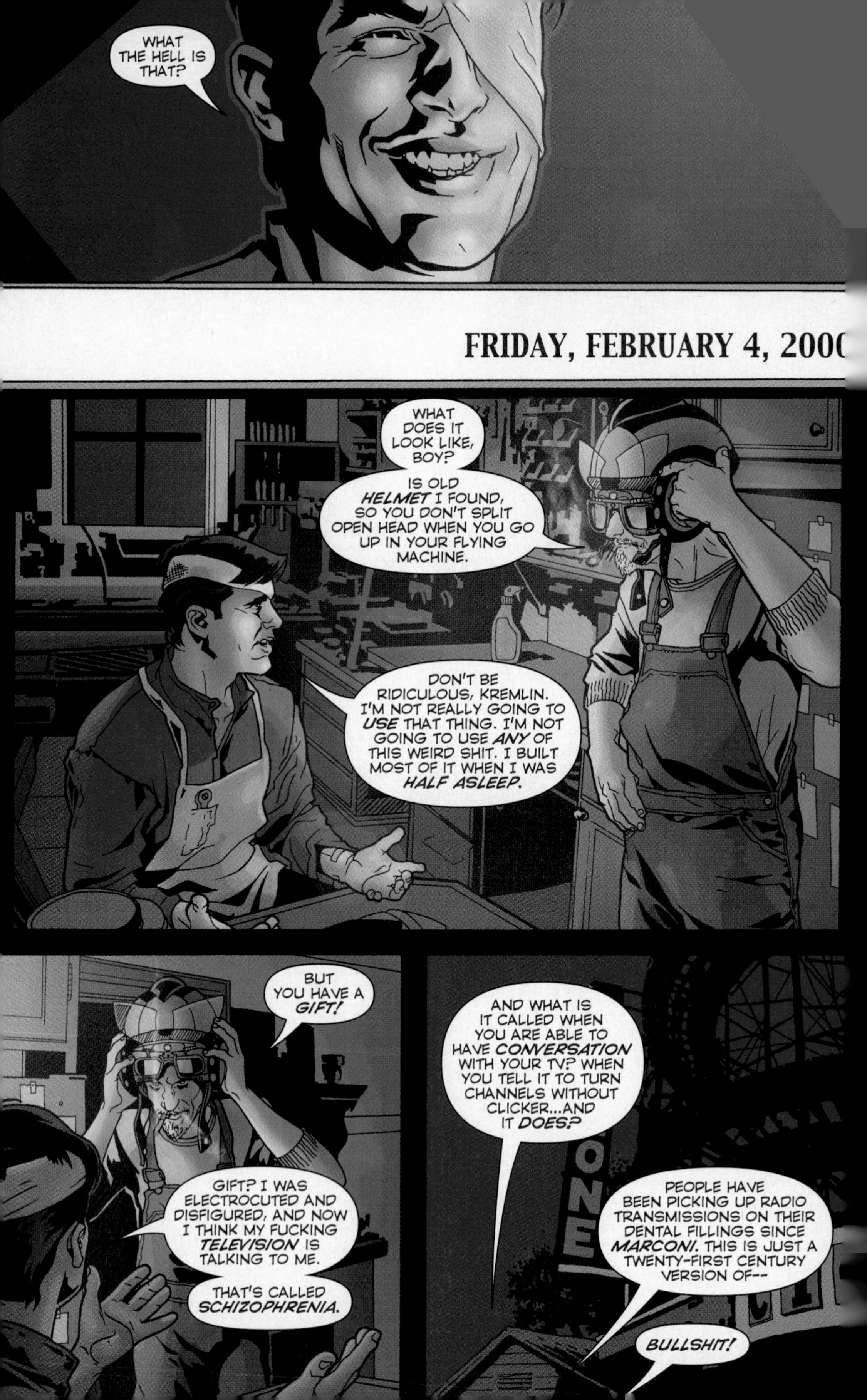
WHAT THE HELL IS THAT?
FRIDAY, FEBRUARY 4, 2000
WHAT DOES IT LOOK LIKE, BOY?
IS OLD HELMET I FOUND, SO YOU DON'T SPLIT OPEN HEAD WHEN YOU GO UP IN YOUR FLYING MACHINE.
DON'T BE RIDICULOUS, KREMLIN. I'M NOT REALLY GOING TO USE THAT THING. I'M NOT GOING TO USE ANY OF THIS WEIRD SHIT. I BUILT MOST OF IT WHEN I WAS HALF ASLEEP.
BUT YOU HAVE A GIFT!
GIFT? I WAS ELECTROCUTED AND DISFIGURED, AND NOW I THINK MY FUCKING TELEVISION IS TALKING TO ME.
THAT'S CALLED SCHIZOPHRENIA.
AND WHAT IS IT CALLED WHEN YOU ARE ABLE TO HAVE CONVERSATION WITH YOUR TV? WHEN YOU TELL IT TO TURN CHANNELS WITHOUT CLICKER...AND IT DOES?
PEOPLE HAVE BEEN PICKING UP RADIO TRANSMISSIONS ON THEIR DENTAL FILLINGS SINCE MARCONI. THIS IS JUST A TWENTY-FIRST CENTURY VERSION OF--
BULLSHIT!

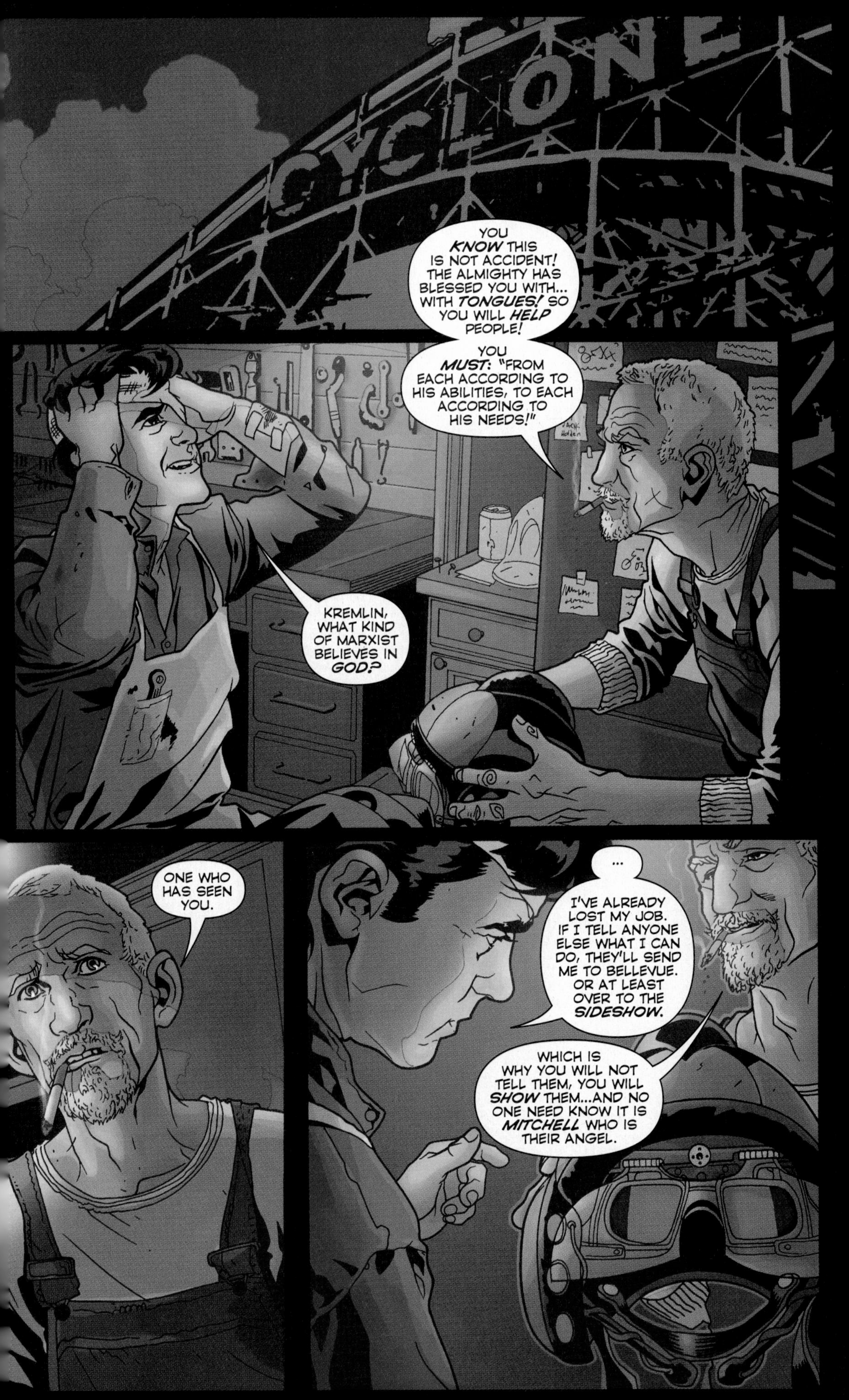
CYCLONE
YOU KNOW THIS IS NOT ACCIDENT! THE ALMIGHTY HAS BLESSED YOU WITH... WITH TONGUES! SO YOU WILL HELP PEOPLE!
YOU MUST: "FROM EACH ACCORDING TO HIS ABILITIES, TO EACH ACCORDING TO HIS NEEDS!"
KREMLIN, WHAT KIND OF MARXIST BELIEVES IN GOD?
ONE WHO HAS SEEN YOU.
...
I'VE ALREADY LOST MY JOB. IF I TELL ANYONE ELSE WHAT I CAN DO, THEY'LL SEND ME TO BELLEVUE. OR AT LEAST OVER TO THE SIDESHOW.
WHICH IS WHY YOU WILL NOT TELL THEM, YOU WILL SHOW THEM...AND NO ONE NEED KNOW IT IS MITCHELL WHO IS THEIR ANGEL.

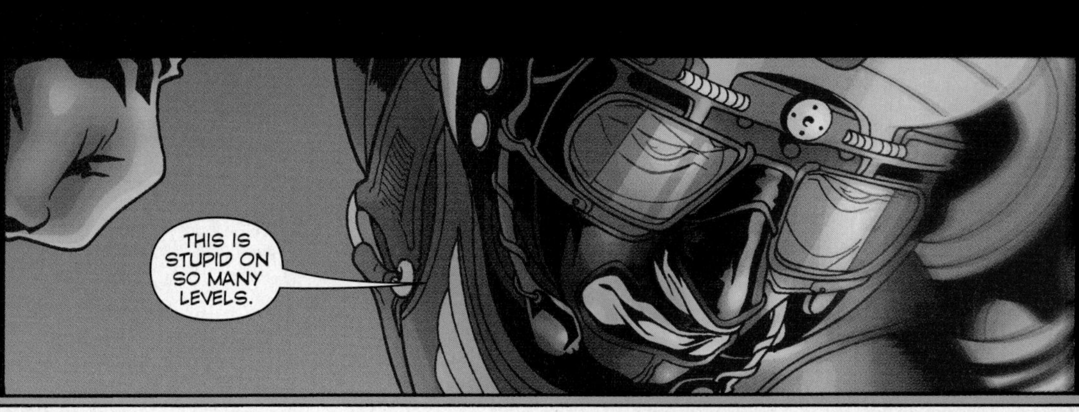
THIS IS STUPID ON SO MANY LEVELS.

MONDAY, APRIL 10, 2000

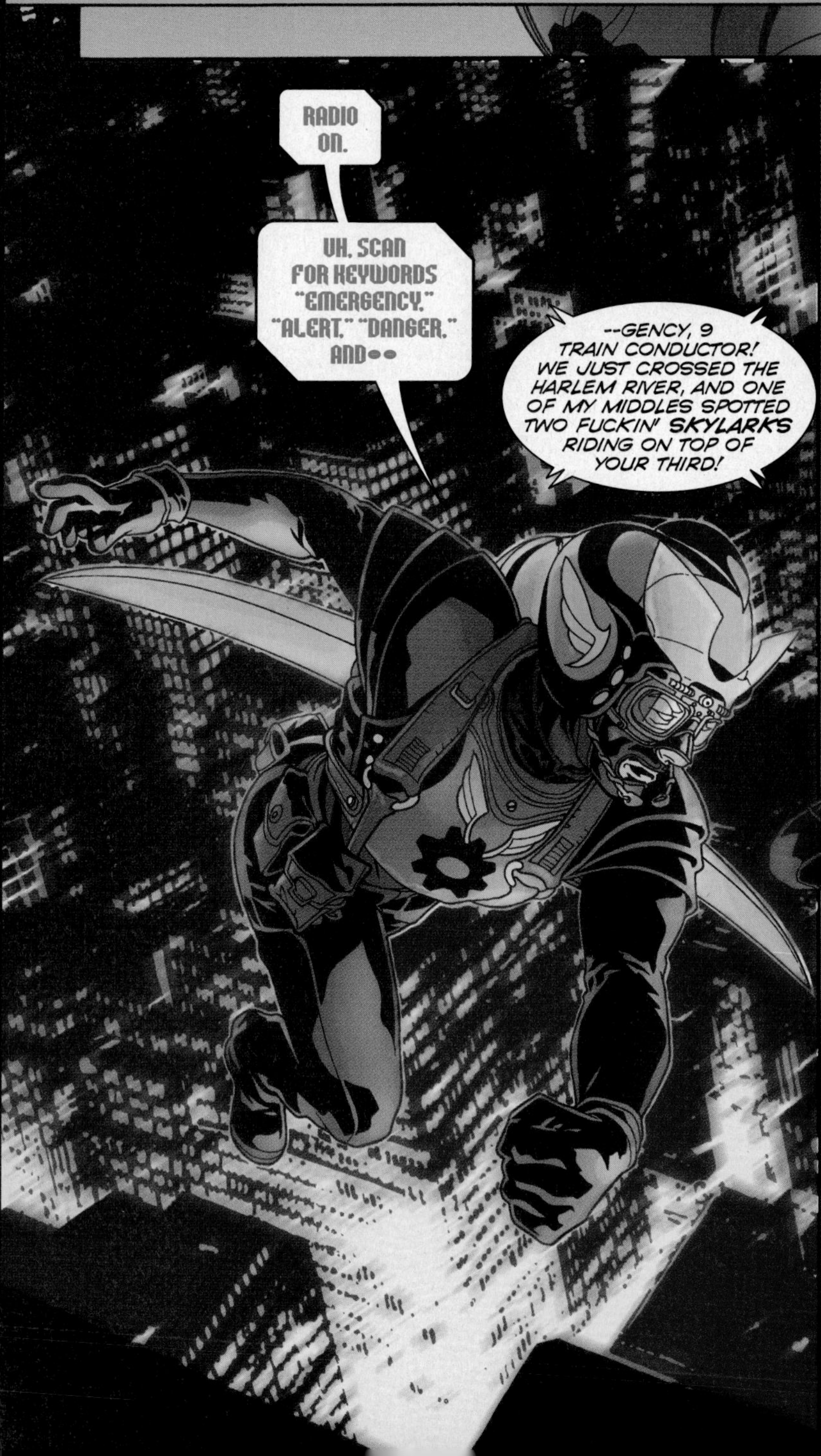
RADIO ON.
UH. SCAN FOR KEYWORDS "EMERGENCY," "ALERT," "DANGER," AND••
--GENCY, 9 TRAIN CONDUCTOR! WE JUST CROSSED THE HARLEM RIVER, AND ONE OF MY MIDDLES SPOTTED TWO FUCKIN' SKYLARKS RIDING ON TOP OF YOUR THIRD!

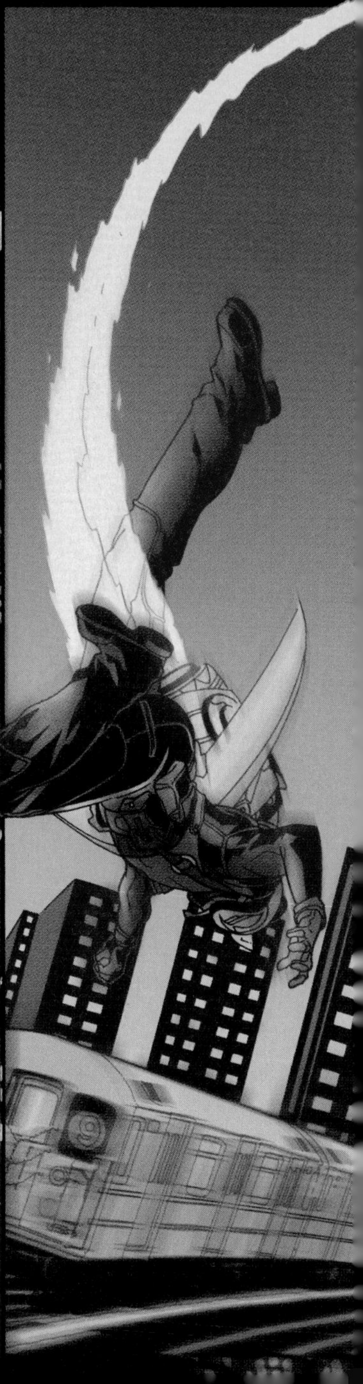

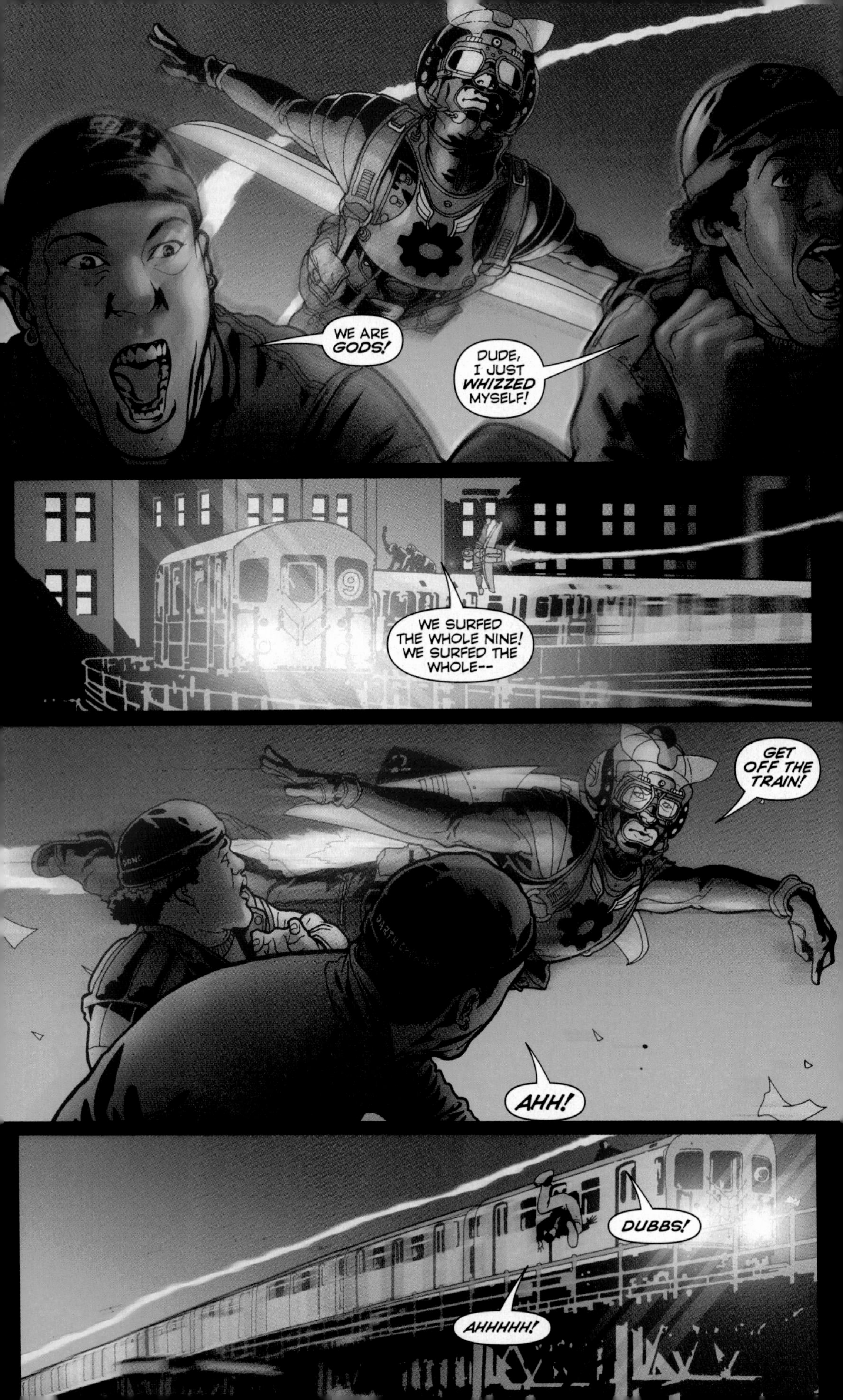
WE ARE GODS!
DUDE, I JUST WHIZZED MYSELF!
WE SURFED THE WHOLE NINE! WE SURFED THE WHOLE--
GET OFF THE TRAIN!
AHH!
DUBBS!
AHHHHH!

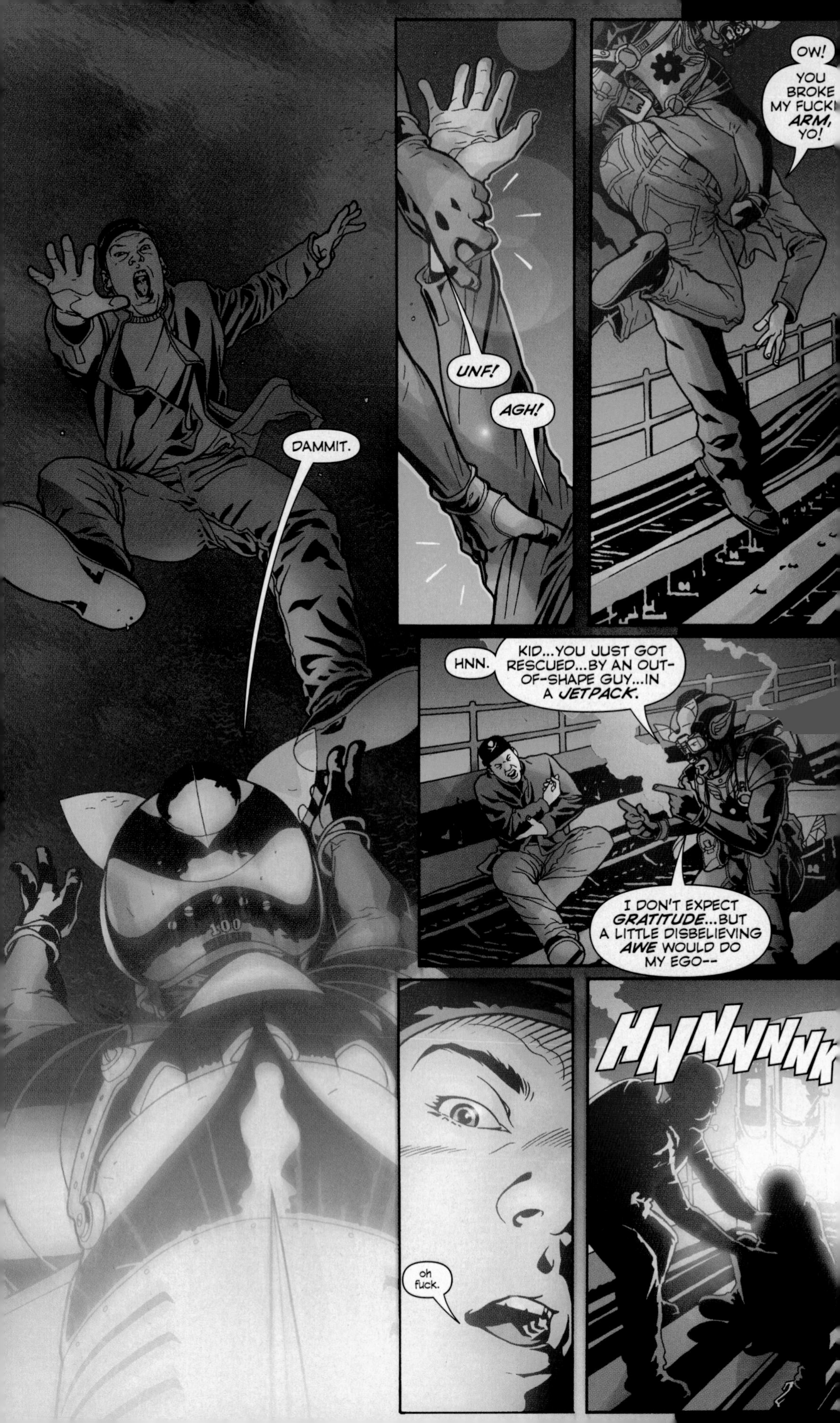
DAMMIT.
UNF!
AGH!
OW!
YOU BROKE MY FUCKI ARM, YO!
HNN.
KID...YOU JUST GOT RESCUED...BY AN OUT-OF-SHAPE GUY...IN A JETPACK.
I DON'T EXPECT GRATITUDE...BUT A LITTLE DISBELIEVING AWE WOULD DO MY EGO--
oh fuck.
HNNNNNNK

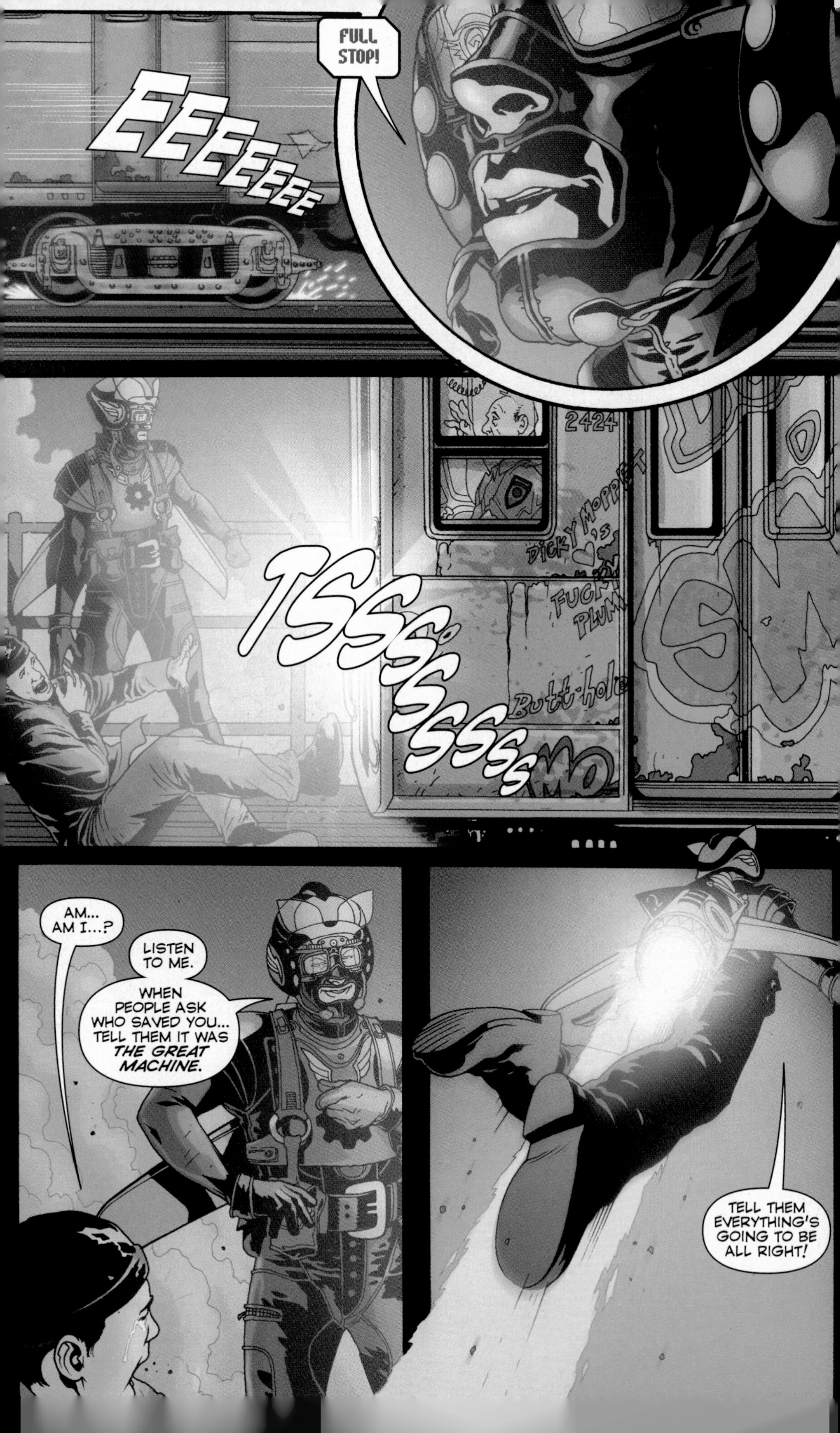
EEEEEEEE
FULL STOP!
TSSSSSSSS
2424
Butt-hole
AM... AM I...?
LISTEN TO ME.
WHEN PEOPLE ASK WHO SAVED YOU... TELL THEM IT WAS *THE GREAT MACHINE*.
TELL THEM EVERYTHING'S GOING TO BE ALL RIGHT!

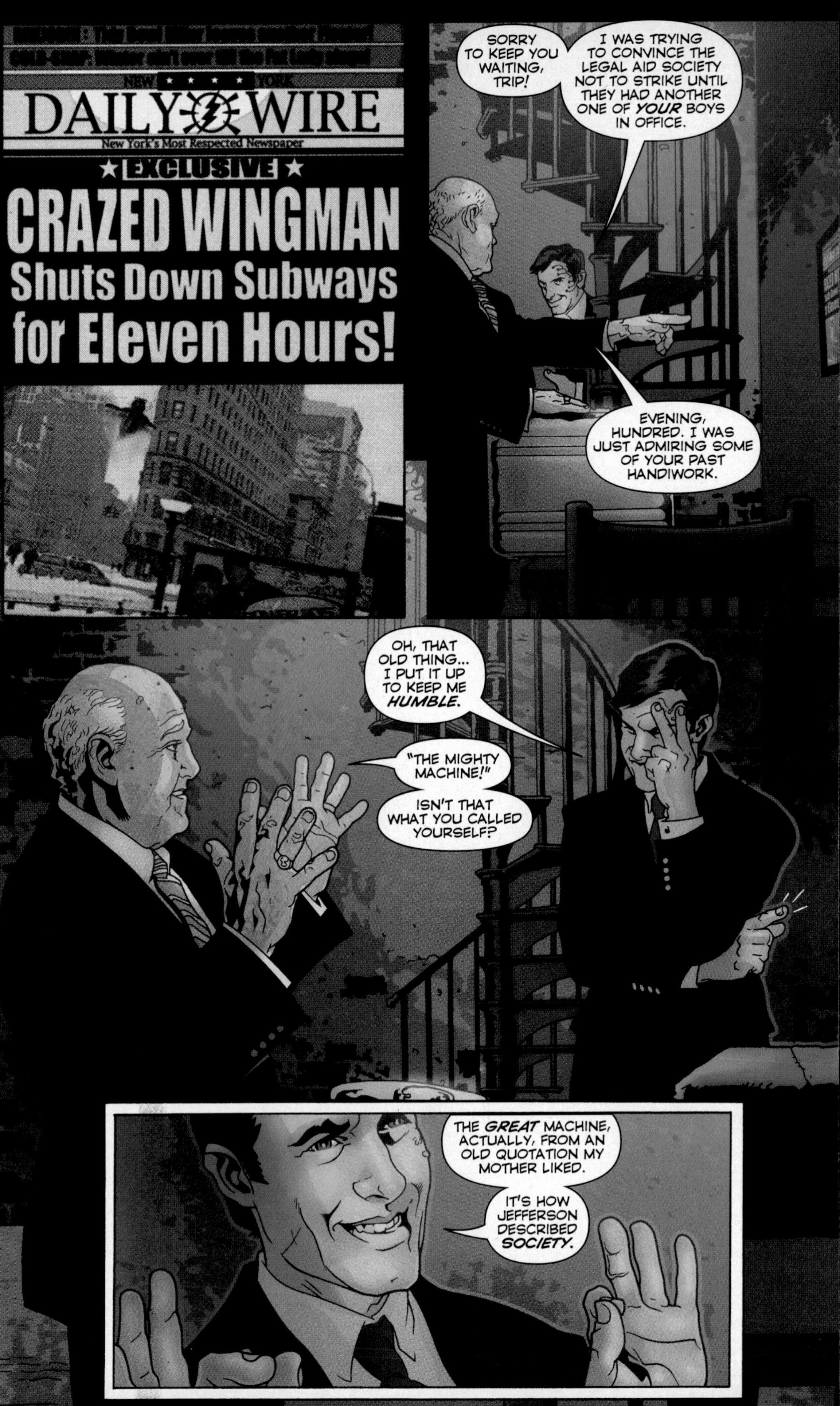
NEW YORK
DAILY WIRE
New York's Most Respected Newspaper
EXCLUSIVE
CRAZED WINGMAN Shuts Down Subways for Eleven Hours!
SORRY TO KEEP YOU WAITING, TRIP!
I WAS TRYING TO CONVINCE THE LEGAL AID SOCIETY NOT TO STRIKE UNTIL THEY HAD ANOTHER ONE OF YOUR BOYS IN OFFICE.
EVENING, HUNDRED. I WAS JUST ADMIRING SOME OF YOUR PAST HANDIWORK.
OH, THAT OLD THING... I PUT IT UP TO KEEP ME HUMBLE.
"THE MIGHTY MACHINE!"
ISN'T THAT WHAT YOU CALLED YOURSELF?
THE GREAT MACHINE, ACTUALLY, FROM AN OLD QUOTATION MY MOTHER LIKED.
IT'S HOW JEFFERSON DESCRIBED SOCIETY.

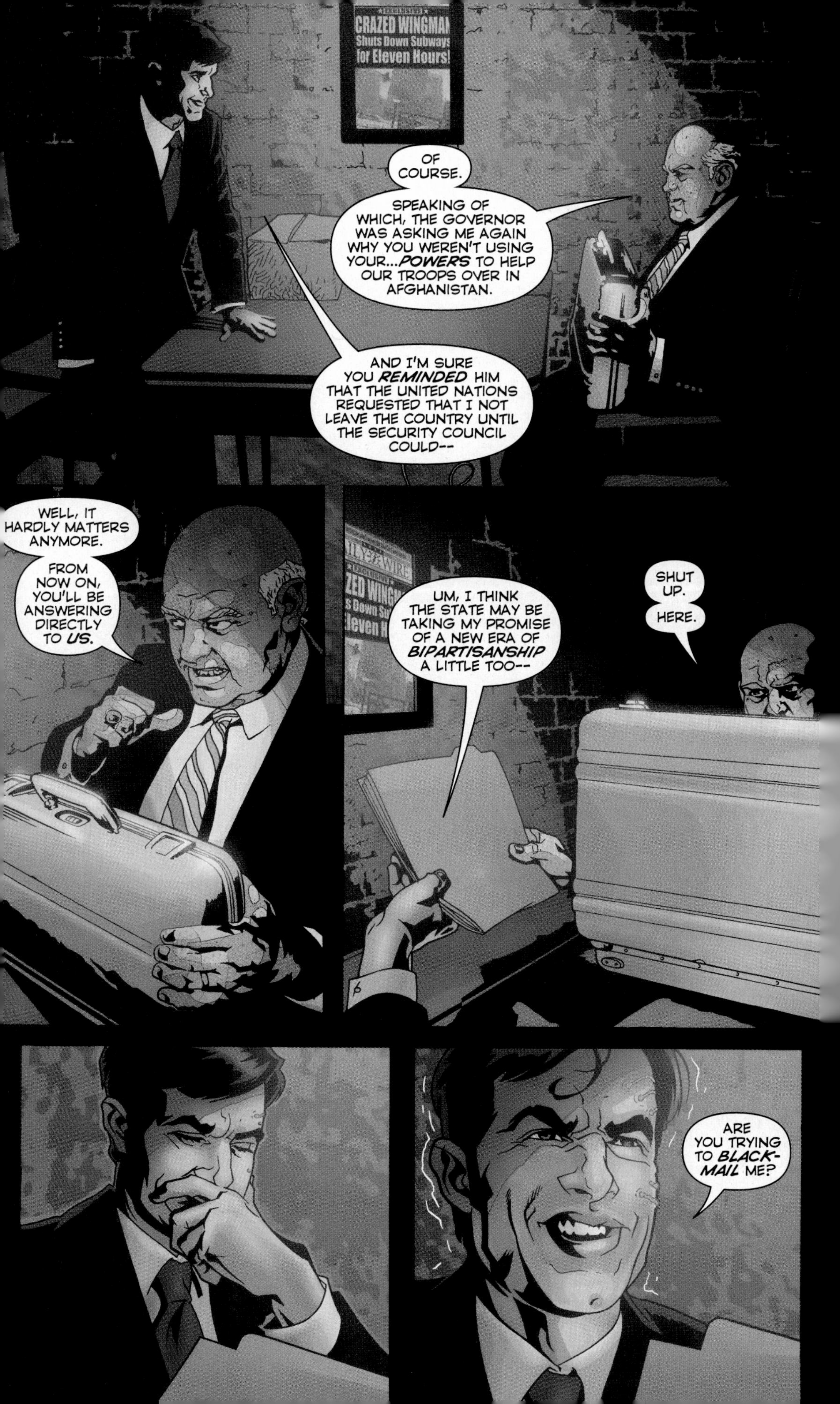
EXCLUSIVE
CRAZED WINGMAN
Shuts Down Subways for Eleven Hours!
OF COURSE.
SPEAKING OF WHICH, THE GOVERNOR WAS ASKING ME AGAIN WHY YOU WEREN'T USING YOUR...POWERS TO HELP OUR TROOPS OVER IN AFGHANISTAN.
AND I'M SURE YOU REMINDED HIM THAT THE UNITED NATIONS REQUESTED THAT I NOT LEAVE THE COUNTRY UNTIL THE SECURITY COUNCIL COULD--
WELL, IT HARDLY MATTERS ANYMORE.
FROM NOW ON, YOU'LL BE ANSWERING DIRECTLY TO US.
UM, I THINK THE STATE MAY BE TAKING MY PROMISE OF A NEW ERA OF BIPARTISANSHIP A LITTLE TOO--
SHUT UP.
HERE.
ARE YOU TRYING TO BLACK-MAIL ME?

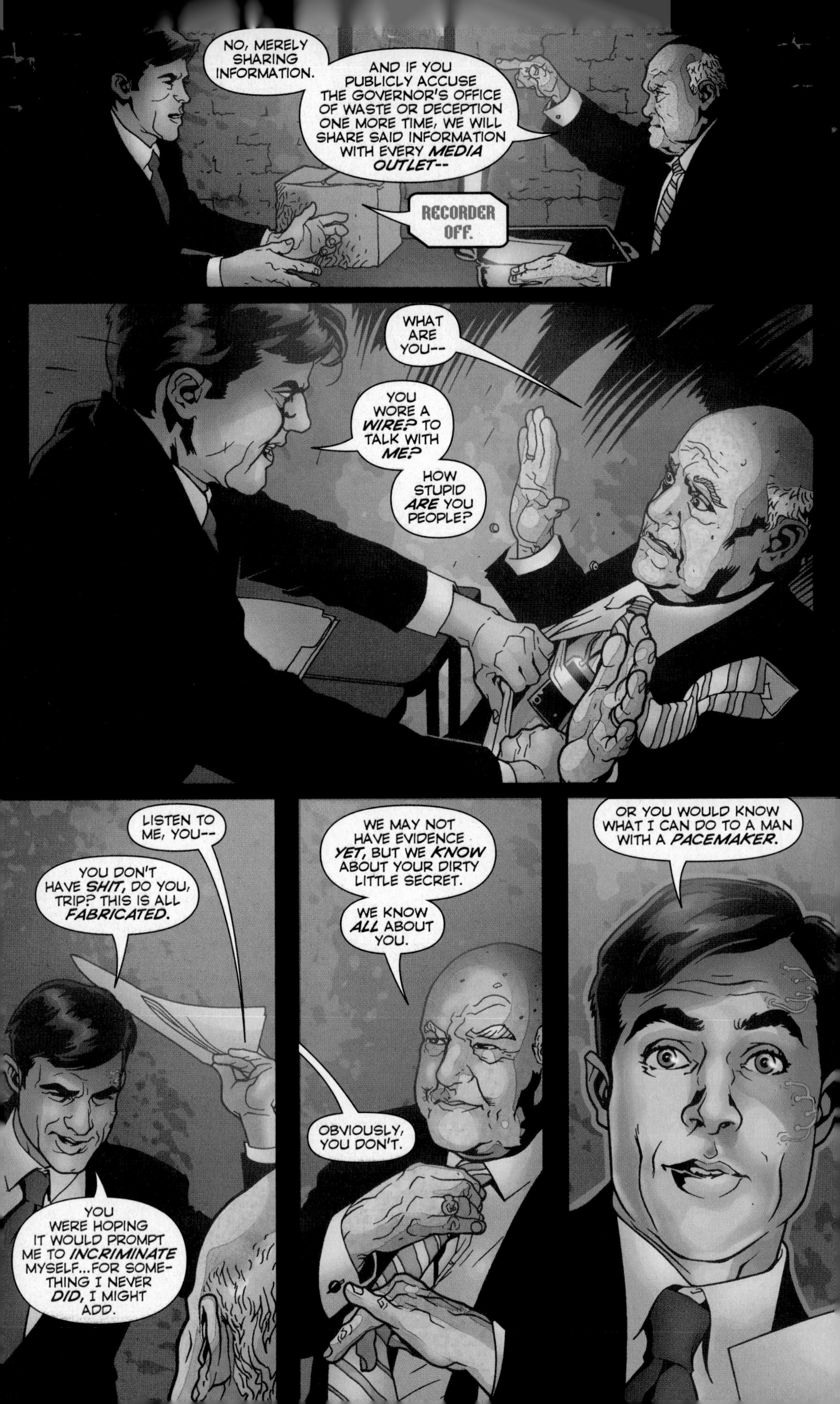
NO, MERELY SHARING INFORMATION.
AND IF YOU PUBLICLY ACCUSE THE GOVERNOR'S OFFICE OF WASTE OR DECEPTION ONE MORE TIME, WE WILL SHARE SAID INFORMATION WITH EVERY MEDIA OUTLET--
RECORDER OFF.
WHAT ARE YOU--
YOU WORE A WIRE? TO TALK WITH ME?
HOW STUPID ARE YOU PEOPLE?
LISTEN TO ME, YOU--
YOU DON'T HAVE SHIT, DO YOU, TRIP? THIS IS ALL FABRICATED.
YOU WERE HOPING IT WOULD PROMPT ME TO INCRIMINATE MYSELF...FOR SOMETHING I NEVER DID, I MIGHT ADD.
WE MAY NOT HAVE EVIDENCE YET, BUT WE KNOW ABOUT YOUR DIRTY LITTLE SECRET.
WE KNOW ALL ABOUT YOU.
OBVIOUSLY, YOU DON'T.
OR YOU WOULD KNOW WHAT I CAN DO TO A MAN WITH A PACEMAKER.

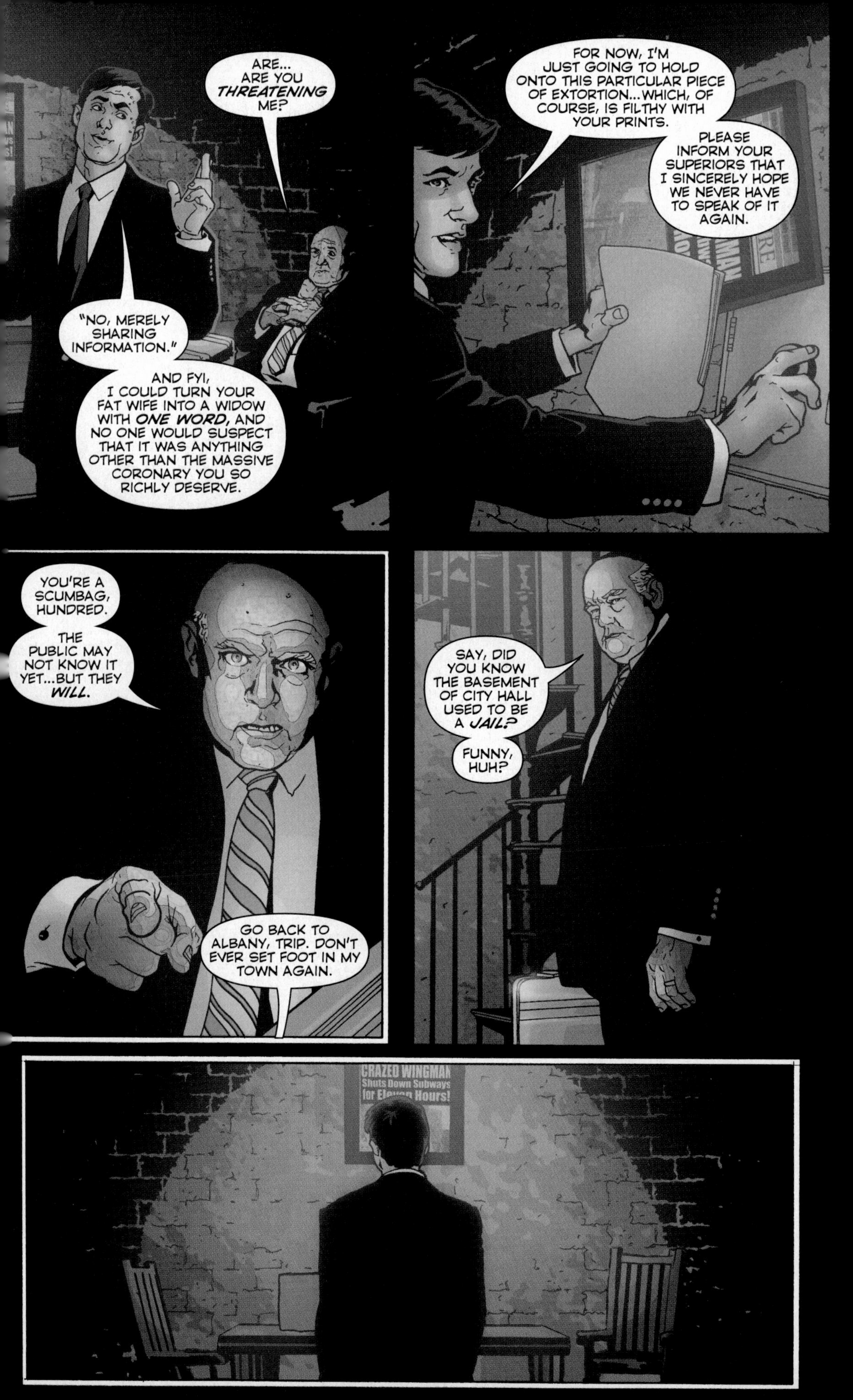
ARE... ARE YOU *THREATENING* ME?
"NO, MERELY SHARING INFORMATION."
AND FYI, I COULD TURN YOUR FAT WIFE INTO A WIDOW WITH *ONE WORD,* AND NO ONE WOULD SUSPECT THAT IT WAS ANYTHING OTHER THAN THE MASSIVE CORONARY YOU SO RICHLY DESERVE.
FOR NOW, I'M JUST GOING TO HOLD ONTO THIS PARTICULAR PIECE OF EXTORTION...WHICH, OF COURSE, IS FILTHY WITH YOUR PRINTS.
PLEASE INFORM YOUR SUPERIORS THAT I SINCERELY HOPE WE NEVER HAVE TO SPEAK OF IT AGAIN.
YOU'RE A SCUMBAG, HUNDRED.
THE PUBLIC MAY NOT KNOW IT YET...BUT THEY *WILL.*
GO BACK TO ALBANY, TRIP. DON'T EVER SET FOOT IN MY TOWN AGAIN.
SAY, DID YOU KNOW THE BASEMENT OF CITY HALL USED TO BE A *JAIL?*
FUNNY, HUH?
CRAZED WINGMAN
Shuts Down Subways

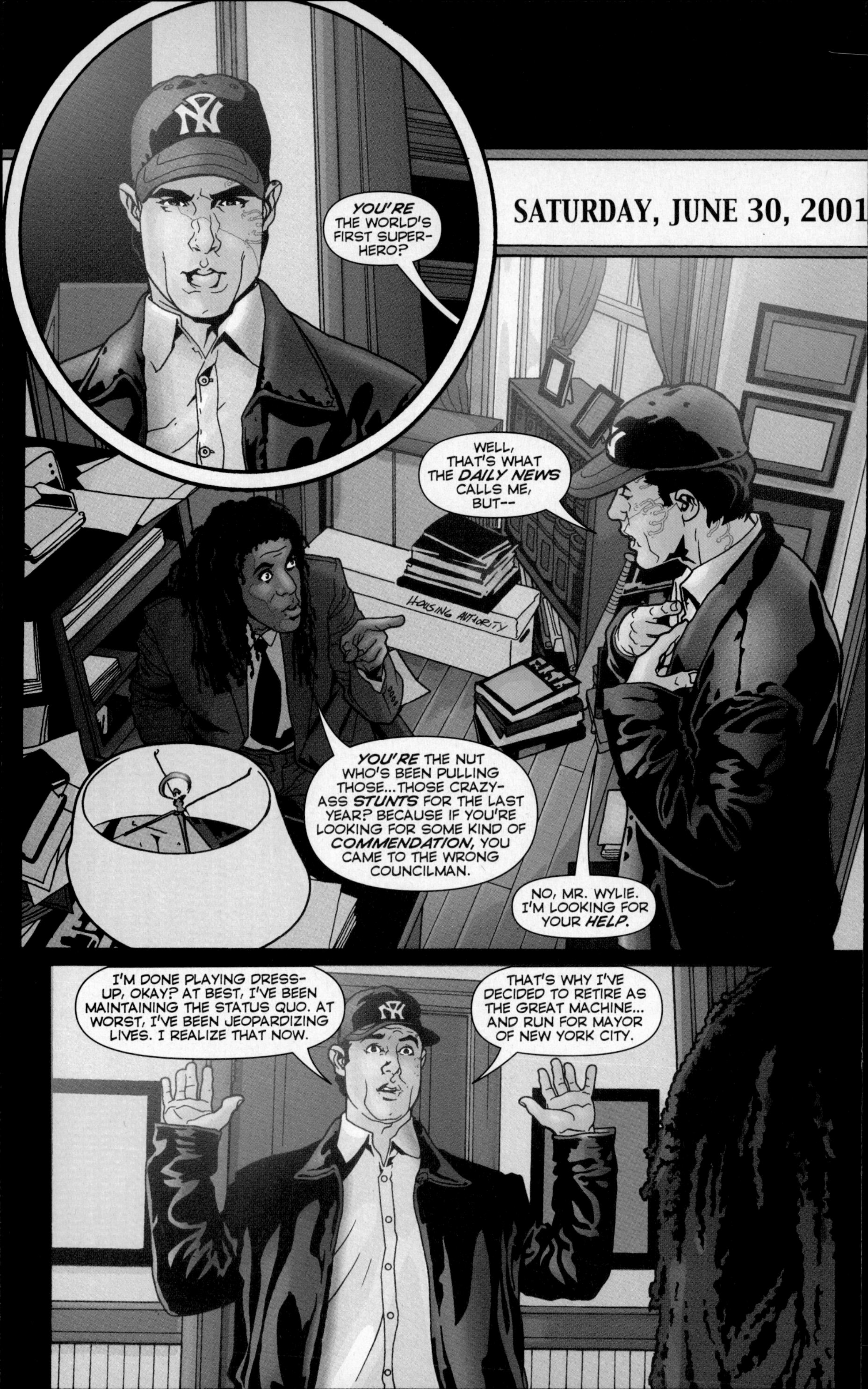
SATURDAY, JUNE 30, 2001
YOU'RE THE WORLD'S FIRST SUPER-HERO?
WELL, THAT'S WHAT THE DAILY NEWS CALLS ME, BUT--
HOUSING AUTHORITY
YOU'RE THE NUT WHO'S BEEN PULLING THOSE...THOSE CRAZY-ASS STUNTS FOR THE LAST YEAR? BECAUSE IF YOU'RE LOOKING FOR SOME KIND OF COMMENDATION, YOU CAME TO THE WRONG COUNCILMAN.
NO, MR. WYLIE. I'M LOOKING FOR YOUR HELP.
I'M DONE PLAYING DRESS-UP, OKAY? AT BEST, I'VE BEEN MAINTAINING THE STATUS QUO. AT WORST, I'VE BEEN JEOPARDIZING LIVES. I REALIZE THAT NOW.
THAT'S WHY I'VE DECIDED TO RETIRE AS THE GREAT MACHINE... AND RUN FOR MAYOR OF NEW YORK CITY.

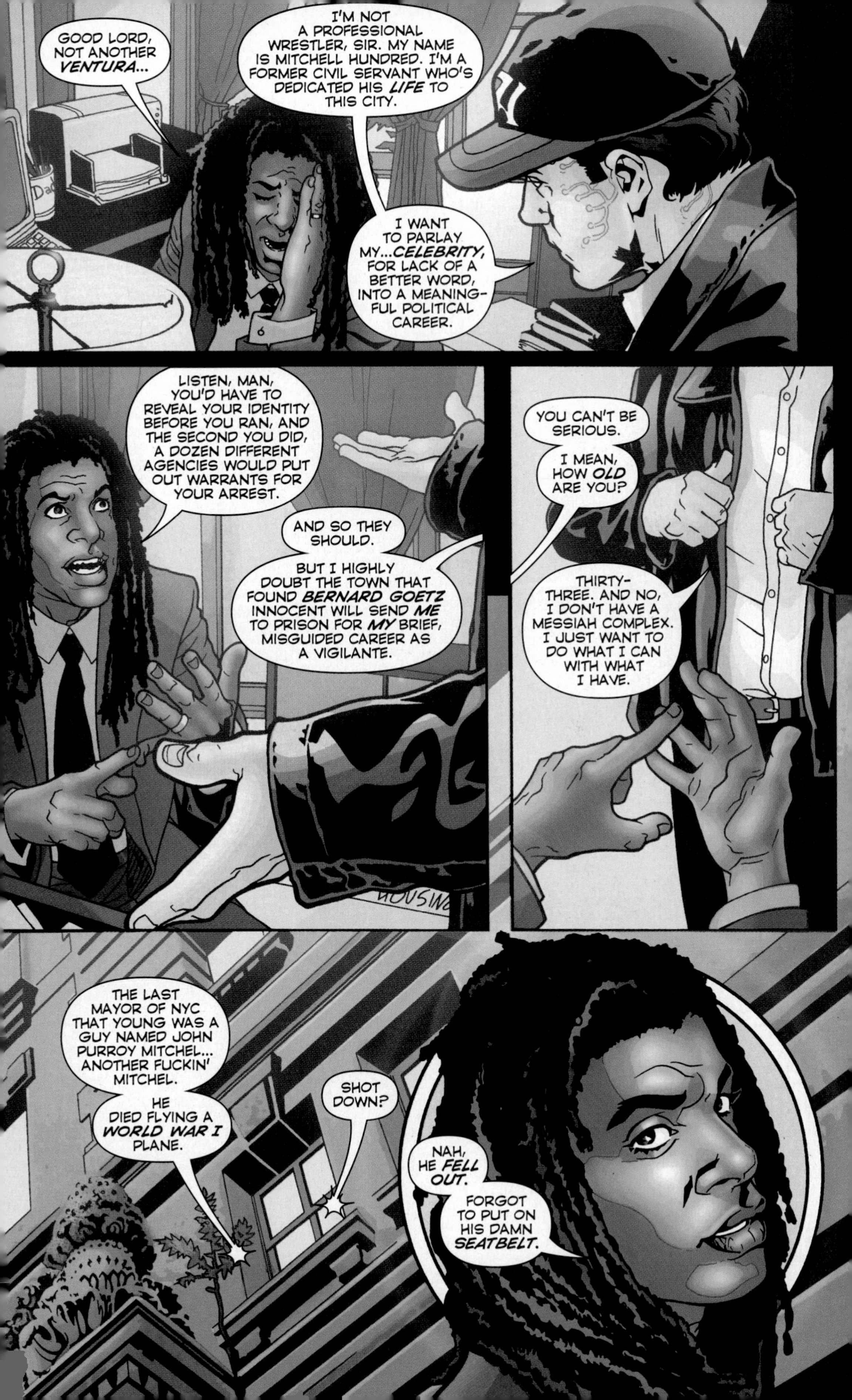
GOOD LORD, NOT ANOTHER VENTURA...
I'M NOT A PROFESSIONAL WRESTLER, SIR. MY NAME IS MITCHELL HUNDRED. I'M A FORMER CIVIL SERVANT WHO'S DEDICATED HIS LIFE TO THIS CITY.
I WANT TO PARLAY MY...CELEBRITY, FOR LACK OF A BETTER WORD, INTO A MEANINGFUL POLITICAL CAREER.
LISTEN, MAN, YOU'D HAVE TO REVEAL YOUR IDENTITY BEFORE YOU RAN, AND THE SECOND YOU DID, A DOZEN DIFFERENT AGENCIES WOULD PUT OUT WARRANTS FOR YOUR ARREST.
AND SO THEY SHOULD.
BUT I HIGHLY DOUBT THE TOWN THAT FOUND BERNARD GOETZ INNOCENT WILL SEND ME TO PRISON FOR MY BRIEF, MISGUIDED CAREER AS A VIGILANTE.
YOU CAN'T BE SERIOUS.
I MEAN, HOW OLD ARE YOU?
THIRTY-THREE. AND NO, I DON'T HAVE A MESSIAH COMPLEX. I JUST WANT TO DO WHAT I CAN WITH WHAT I HAVE.
THE LAST MAYOR OF NYC THAT YOUNG WAS A GUY NAMED JOHN PURROY MITCHEL... ANOTHER FUCKIN' MITCHEL.
HE DIED FLYING A WORLD WAR I PLANE.
SHOT DOWN?
NAH, HE FELL OUT.
FORGOT TO PUT ON HIS DAMN SEATBELT.

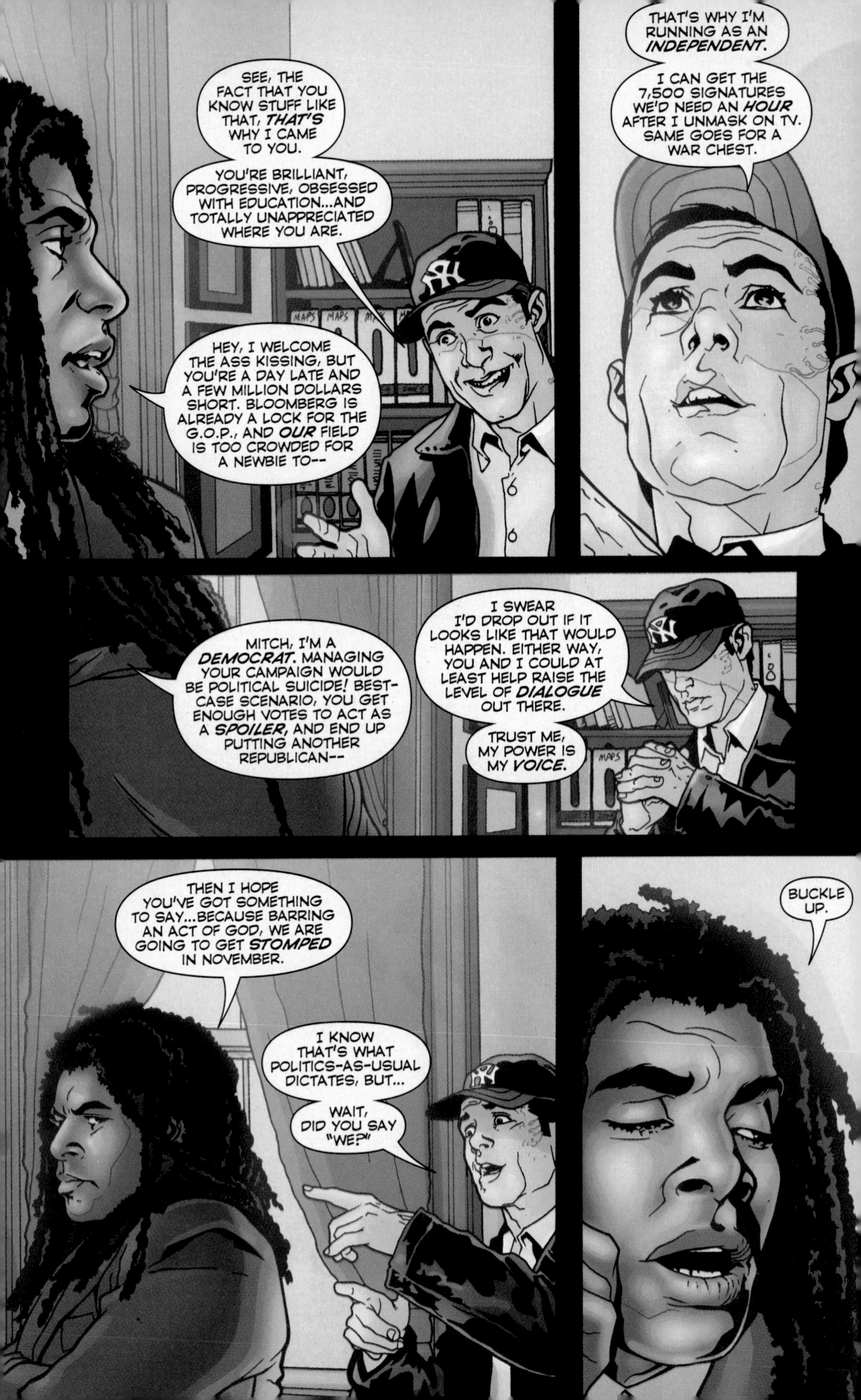
SEE, THE FACT THAT YOU KNOW STUFF LIKE THAT, *THAT'S* WHY I CAME TO YOU.
YOU'RE BRILLIANT, PROGRESSIVE, OBSESSED WITH EDUCATION...AND TOTALLY UNAPPRECIATED WHERE YOU ARE.
HEY, I WELCOME THE ASS KISSING, BUT YOU'RE A DAY LATE AND A FEW MILLION DOLLARS SHORT. BLOOMBERG IS ALREADY A LOCK FOR THE G.O.P., AND *OUR* FIELD IS TOO CROWDED FOR A NEWBIE TO--
THAT'S WHY I'M RUNNING AS AN *INDEPENDENT*.
I CAN GET THE 7,500 SIGNATURES WE'D NEED AN *HOUR* AFTER I UNMASK ON TV. SAME GOES FOR A WAR CHEST.
MITCH, I'M A *DEMOCRAT*. MANAGING YOUR CAMPAIGN WOULD BE POLITICAL SUICIDE! BEST-CASE SCENARIO, YOU GET ENOUGH VOTES TO ACT AS A *SPOILER*, AND END UP PUTTING ANOTHER REPUBLICAN--
I SWEAR I'D DROP OUT IF IT LOOKS LIKE THAT WOULD HAPPEN. EITHER WAY, YOU AND I COULD AT LEAST HELP RAISE THE LEVEL OF *DIALOGUE* OUT THERE.
TRUST ME, MY POWER IS MY *VOICE*.
THEN I HOPE YOU'VE GOT SOMETHING TO SAY...BECAUSE BARRING AN ACT OF GOD, WE ARE GOING TO GET *STOMPED* IN NOVEMBER.
I KNOW THAT'S WHAT POLITICS-AS-USUAL DICTATES, BUT...
WAIT, DID YOU SAY "WE?"
BUCKLE UP.

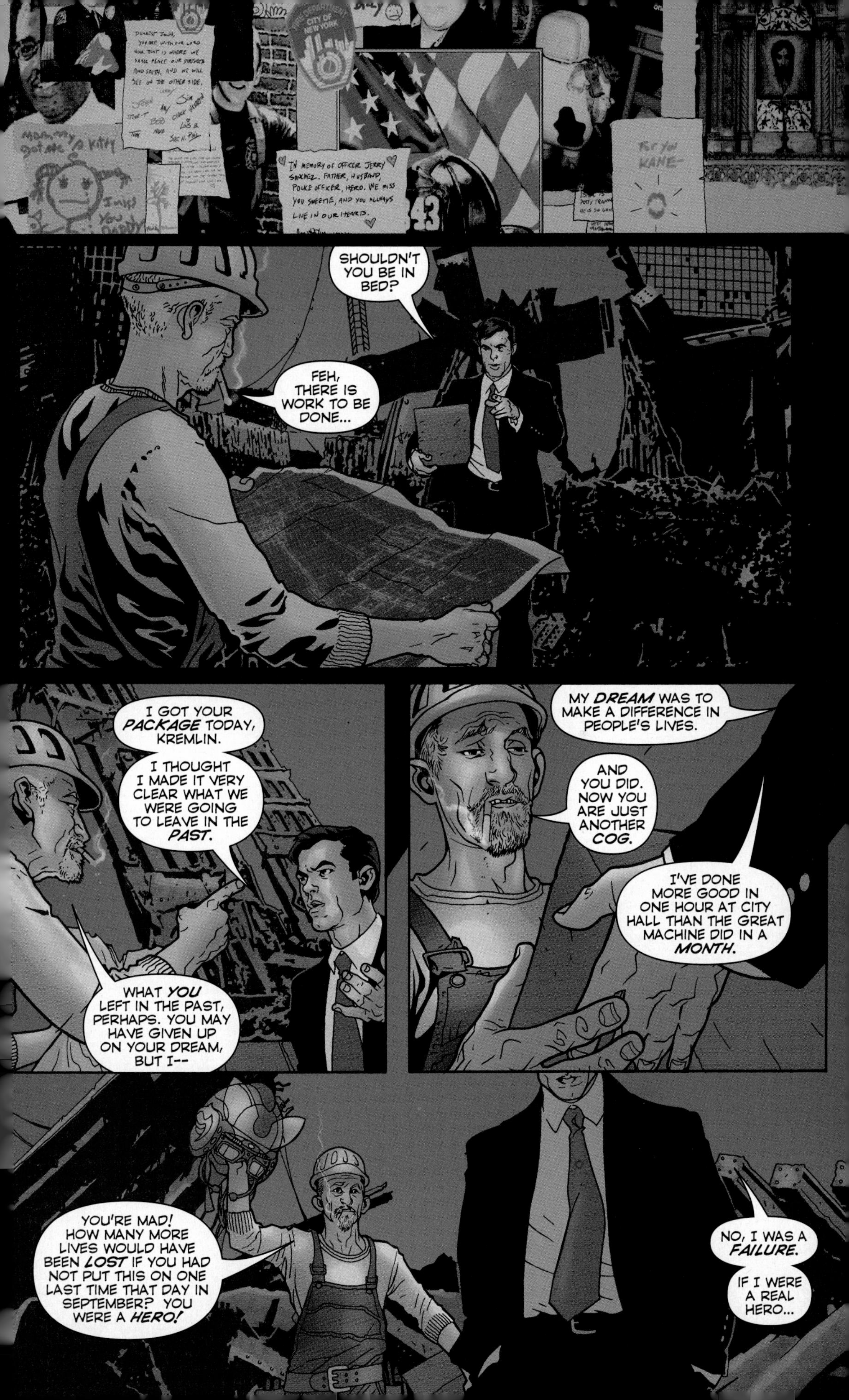

FIRE DEPARTMENT CITY OF NEW YORK
IN MEMORY OF OFFICER JERRY SANCHEZ. FATHER, HUSBAND, POLICE OFFICER, HERO. WE MISS YOU SWEETIE, AND YOU ALWAYS LIVE IN OUR HEARTS.
For you KANE
SHOULDN'T YOU BE IN BED?
FEH, THERE IS WORK TO BE DONE...
I GOT YOUR PACKAGE TODAY, KREMLIN.
I THOUGHT I MADE IT VERY CLEAR WHAT WE WERE GOING TO LEAVE IN THE PAST.
WHAT YOU LEFT IN THE PAST, PERHAPS. YOU MAY HAVE GIVEN UP ON YOUR DREAM, BUT I--
MY DREAM WAS TO MAKE A DIFFERENCE IN PEOPLE'S LIVES.
AND YOU DID. NOW YOU ARE JUST ANOTHER COG.
I'VE DONE MORE GOOD IN ONE HOUR AT CITY HALL THAN THE GREAT MACHINE DID IN A MONTH.
YOU'RE MAD! HOW MANY MORE LIVES WOULD HAVE BEEN LOST IF YOU HAD NOT PUT THIS ON ONE LAST TIME THAT DAY IN SEPTEMBER? YOU WERE A HERO!
NO, I WAS A FAILURE.
IF I WERE A REAL HERO...

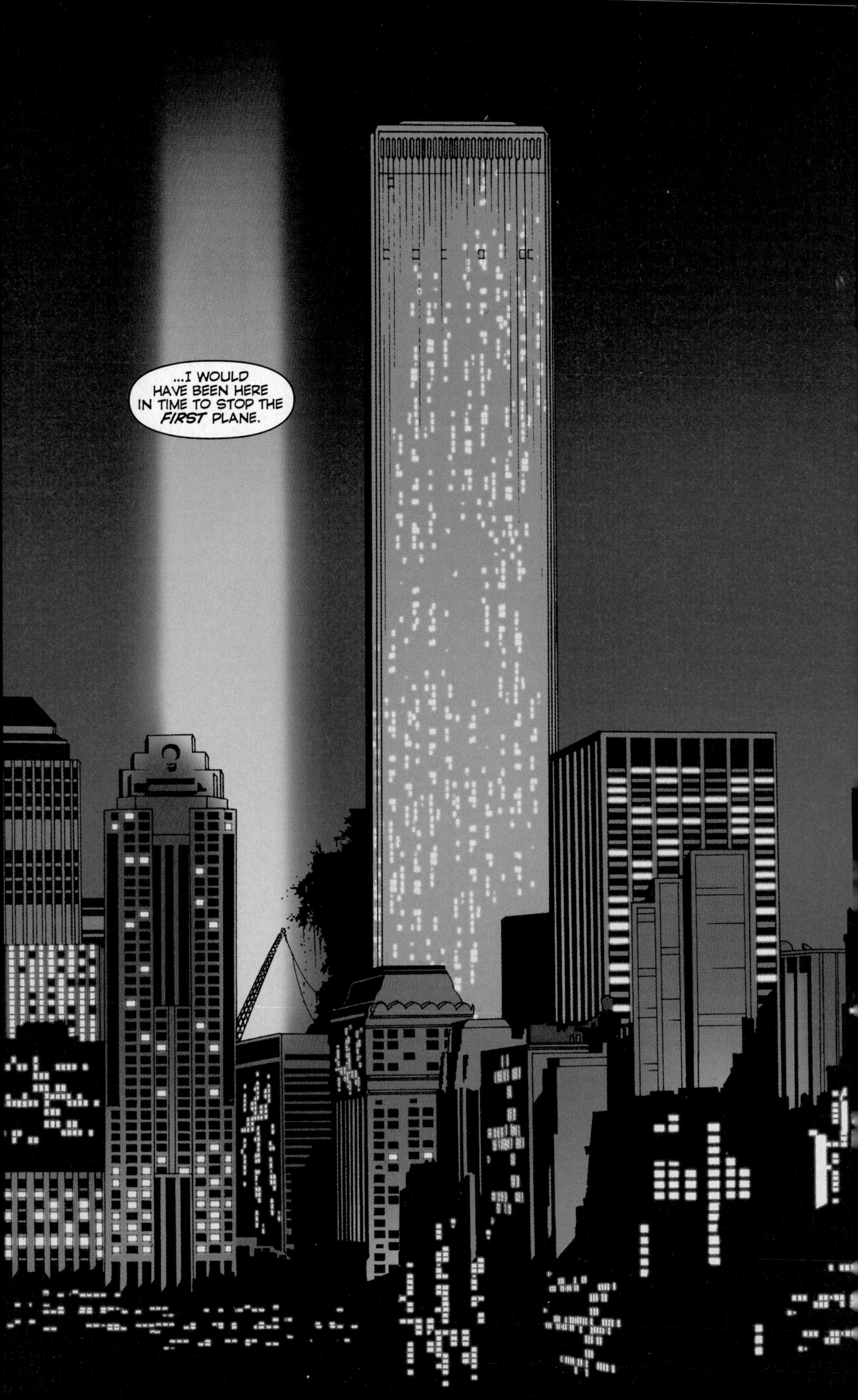
...I WOULD HAVE BEEN HERE IN TIME TO STOP THE *FIRST* PLANE.

CHAPTER 2

Part 1
State of Emergency

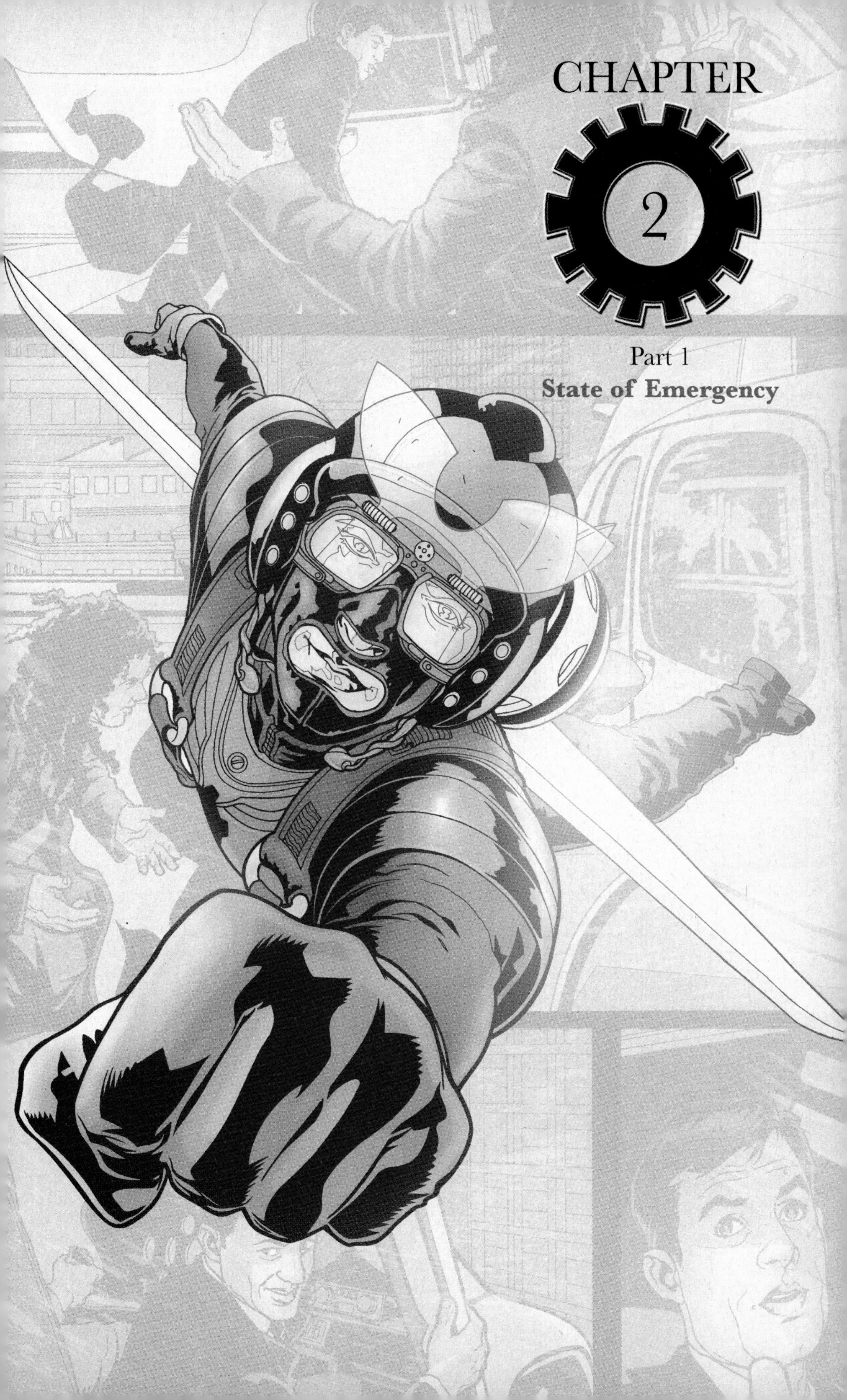

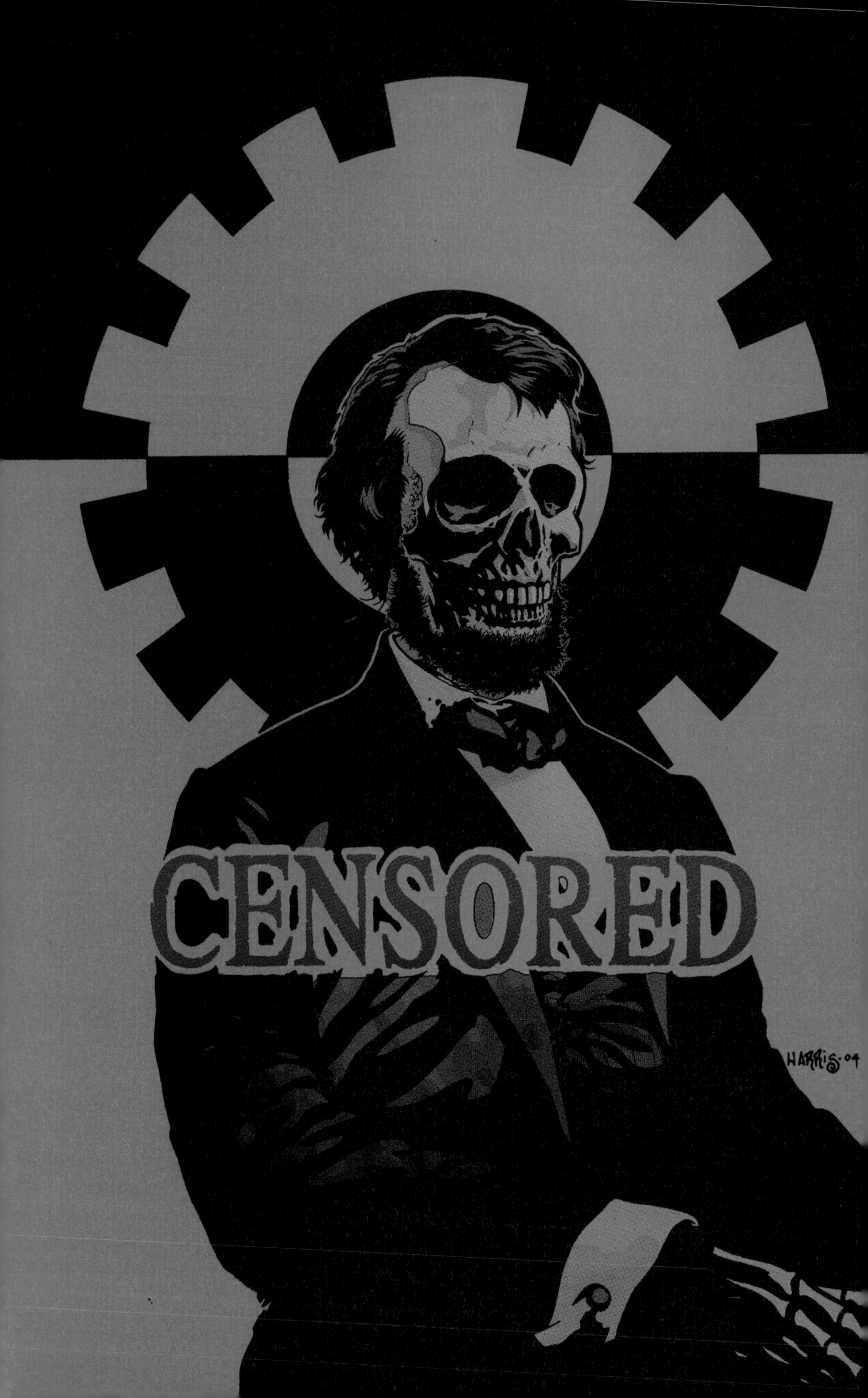
CENSORED
HARRIS 04

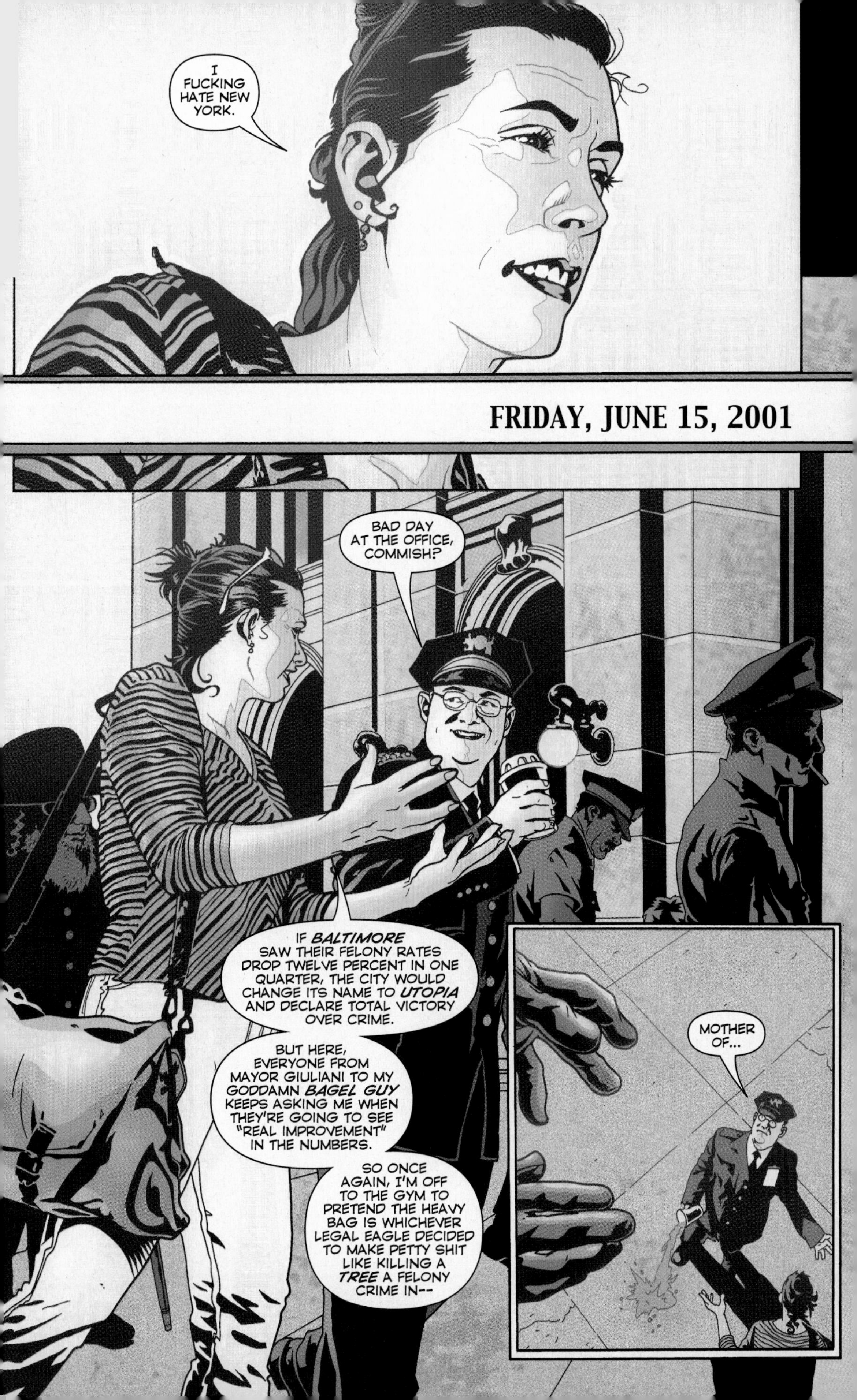
I FUCKING HATE NEW YORK.
FRIDAY, JUNE 15, 2001
BAD DAY AT THE OFFICE, COMMISH?
IF *BALTIMORE* SAW THEIR FELONY RATES DROP TWELVE PERCENT IN ONE QUARTER, THE CITY WOULD CHANGE ITS NAME TO *UTOPIA* AND DECLARE TOTAL VICTORY OVER CRIME.
BUT HERE, EVERYONE FROM MAYOR GIULIANI TO MY GODDAMN *BAGEL GUY* KEEPS ASKING ME WHEN THEY'RE GOING TO SEE "REAL IMPROVEMENT" IN THE NUMBERS.
SO ONCE AGAIN, I'M OFF TO THE GYM TO PRETEND THE HEAVY BAG IS WHICHEVER LEGAL EAGLE DECIDED TO MAKE PETTY SHIT LIKE KILLING A *TREE* A FELONY CRIME IN--
MOTHER OF...

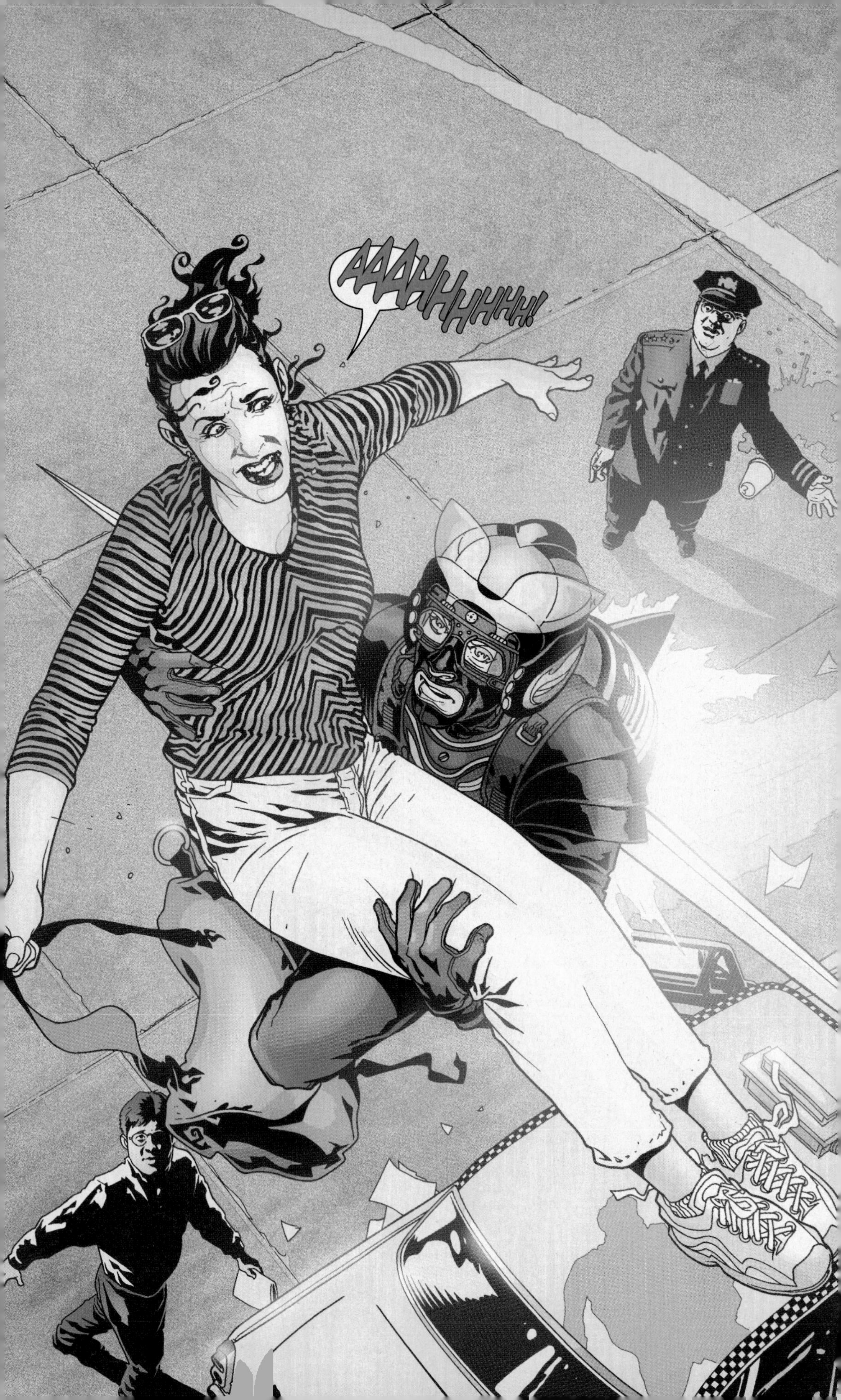
AAAHHHHHH!

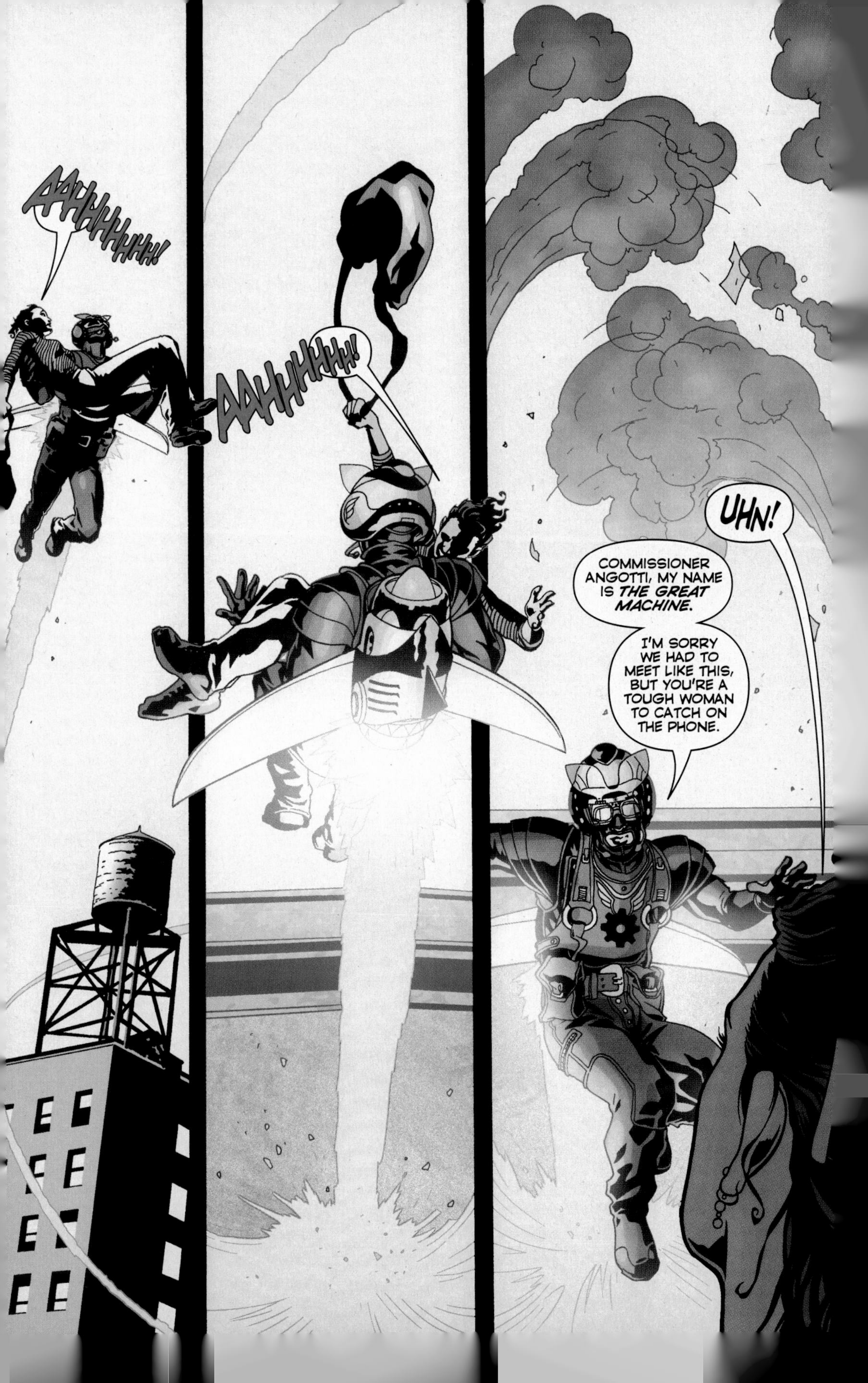
AAHHHHHHH!
AAHHHHHHH!
UHN!
COMMISSIONER ANGOTTI, MY NAME IS *THE GREAT MACHINE*.
I'M SORRY WE HAD TO MEET LIKE THIS, BUT YOU'RE A TOUGH WOMAN TO CATCH ON THE PHONE.

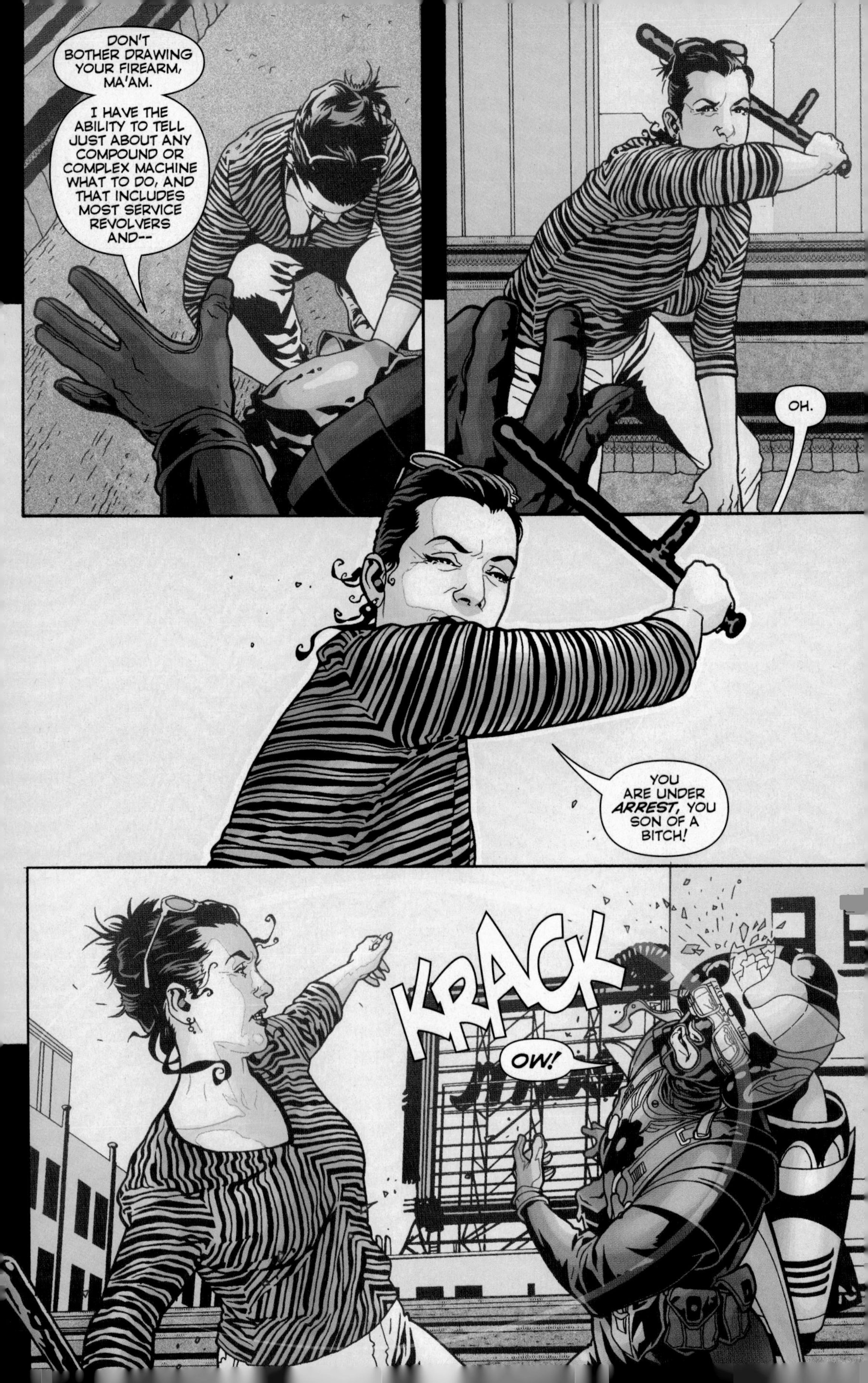
DON'T BOTHER DRAWING YOUR FIREARM, MA'AM.
I HAVE THE ABILITY TO TELL JUST ABOUT ANY COMPOUND OR COMPLEX MACHINE WHAT TO DO, AND THAT INCLUDES MOST SERVICE REVOLVERS AND--
OH.
YOU ARE UNDER *ARREST,* YOU SON OF A BITCH!
KRACK
OW!

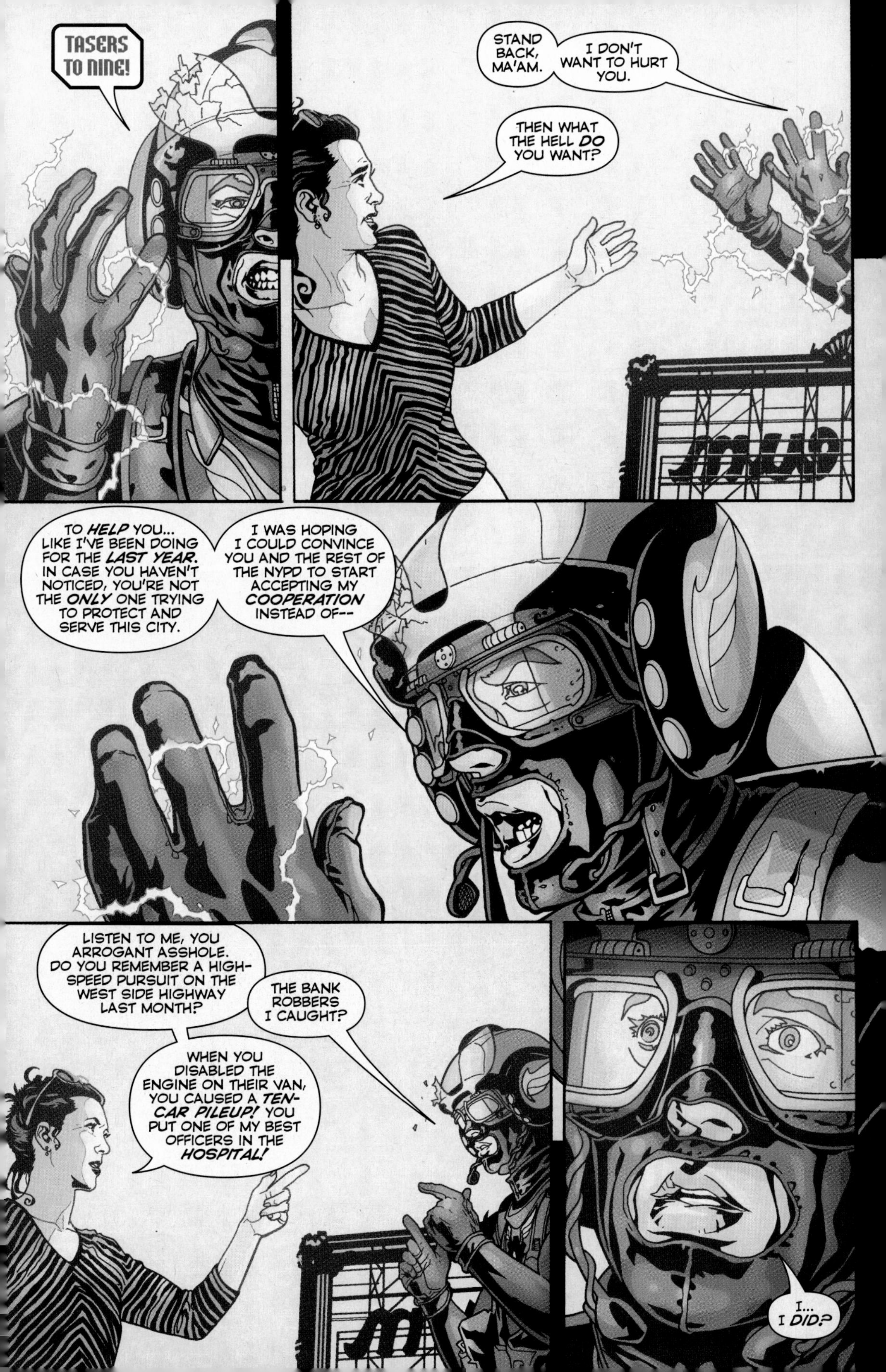
TASERS TO NINE!
STAND BACK, MA'AM.
I DON'T WANT TO HURT YOU.
THEN WHAT THE HELL DO YOU WANT?
TO HELP YOU... LIKE I'VE BEEN DOING FOR THE LAST YEAR. IN CASE YOU HAVEN'T NOTICED, YOU'RE NOT THE ONLY ONE TRYING TO PROTECT AND SERVE THIS CITY.
I WAS HOPING I COULD CONVINCE YOU AND THE REST OF THE NYPD TO START ACCEPTING MY COOPERATION INSTEAD OF--
LISTEN TO ME, YOU ARROGANT ASSHOLE. DO YOU REMEMBER A HIGH-SPEED PURSUIT ON THE WEST SIDE HIGHWAY LAST MONTH?
THE BANK ROBBERS I CAUGHT?
WHEN YOU DISABLED THE ENGINE ON THEIR VAN, YOU CAUSED A TEN-CAR PILEUP! YOU PUT ONE OF MY BEST OFFICERS IN THE HOSPITAL!
I... I DID?

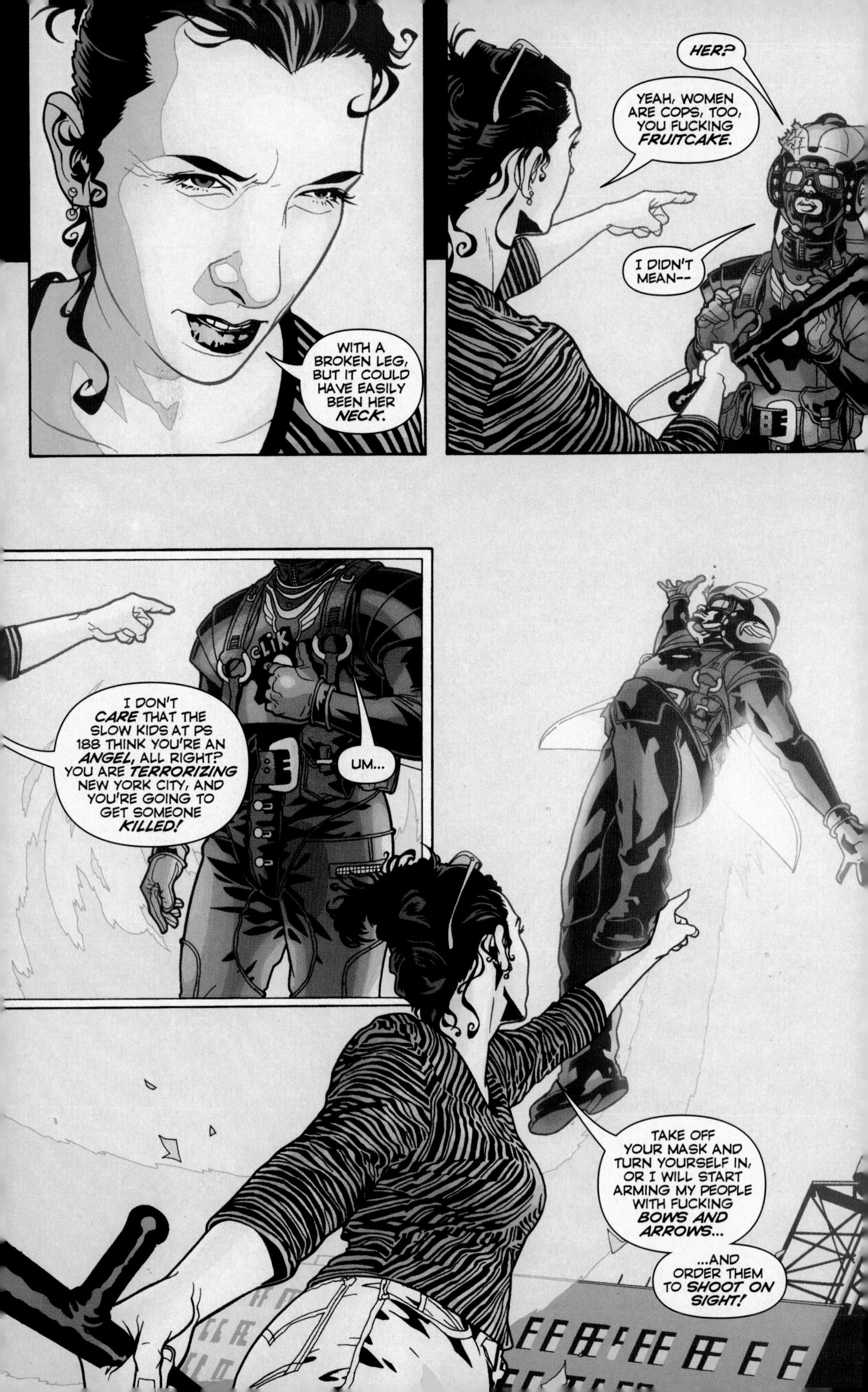

WITH A BROKEN LEG, BUT IT COULD HAVE EASILY BEEN HER NECK.
HER?
YEAH, WOMEN ARE COPS, TOO, YOU FUCKING FRUITCAKE.
I DIDN'T MEAN--
CLIK
I DON'T CARE THAT THE SLOW KIDS AT PS 188 THINK YOU'RE AN ANGEL, ALL RIGHT? YOU ARE TERRORIZING NEW YORK CITY, AND YOU'RE GOING TO GET SOMEONE KILLED!
UM...
TAKE OFF YOUR MASK AND TURN YOURSELF IN, OR I WILL START ARMING MY PEOPLE WITH FUCKING BOWS AND ARROWS...
...AND ORDER THEM TO SHOOT ON SIGHT!

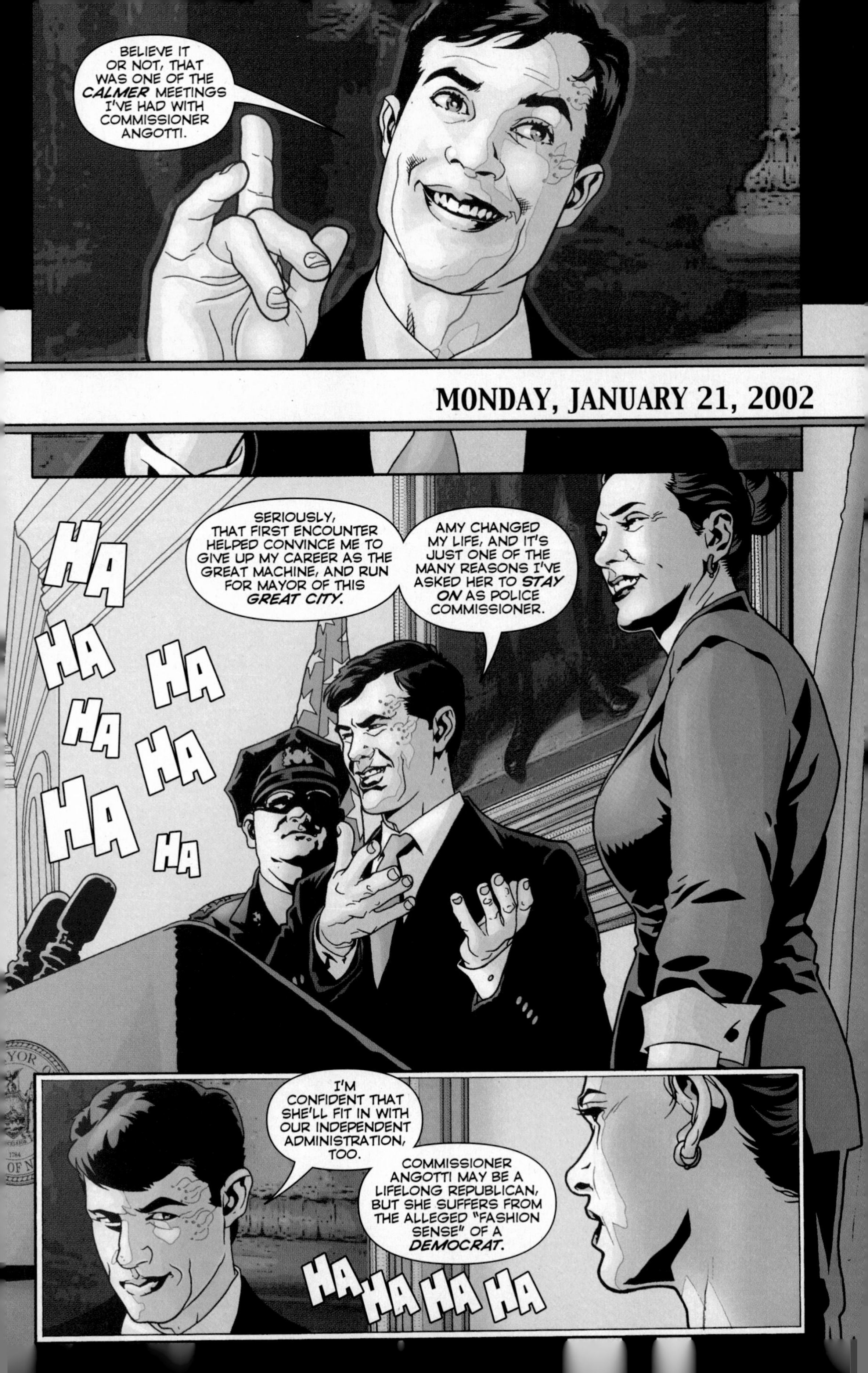

BELIEVE IT OR NOT, THAT WAS ONE OF THE CALMER MEETINGS I'VE HAD WITH COMMISSIONER ANGOTTI.
MONDAY, JANUARY 21, 2002
SERIOUSLY, THAT FIRST ENCOUNTER HELPED CONVINCE ME TO GIVE UP MY CAREER AS THE GREAT MACHINE, AND RUN FOR MAYOR OF THIS GREAT CITY.
AMY CHANGED MY LIFE, AND IT'S JUST ONE OF THE MANY REASONS I'VE ASKED HER TO STAY ON AS POLICE COMMISSIONER.
HA HA HA HA HA HA HA
I'M CONFIDENT THAT SHE'LL FIT IN WITH OUR INDEPENDENT ADMINISTRATION, TOO.
COMMISSIONER ANGOTTI MAY BE A LIFELONG REPUBLICAN, BUT SHE SUFFERS FROM THE ALLEGED "FASHION SENSE" OF A DEMOCRAT.
HA HA HA HA HA

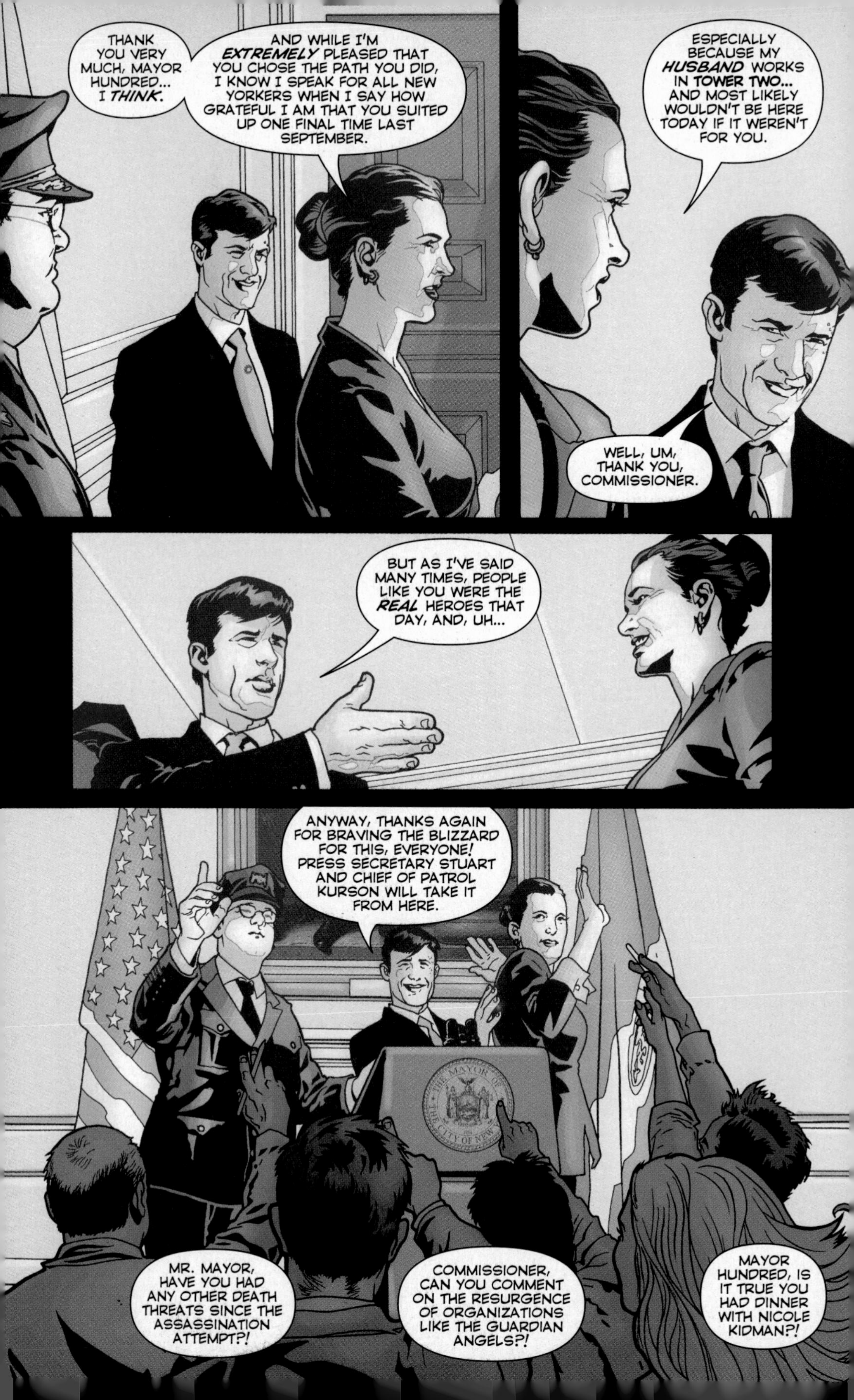
THANK YOU VERY MUCH, MAYOR HUNDRED... I THINK.
AND WHILE I'M EXTREMELY PLEASED THAT YOU CHOSE THE PATH YOU DID, I KNOW I SPEAK FOR ALL NEW YORKERS WHEN I SAY HOW GRATEFUL I AM THAT YOU SUITED UP ONE FINAL TIME LAST SEPTEMBER.
ESPECIALLY BECAUSE MY HUSBAND WORKS IN TOWER TWO... AND MOST LIKELY WOULDN'T BE HERE TODAY IF IT WEREN'T FOR YOU.
WELL, UM, THANK YOU, COMMISSIONER.
BUT AS I'VE SAID MANY TIMES, PEOPLE LIKE YOU WERE THE REAL HEROES THAT DAY, AND, UH...
ANYWAY, THANKS AGAIN FOR BRAVING THE BLIZZARD FOR THIS, EVERYONE! PRESS SECRETARY STUART AND CHIEF OF PATROL KURSON WILL TAKE IT FROM HERE.
THE MAYOR OF THE CITY OF NEW
MR. MAYOR, HAVE YOU HAD ANY OTHER DEATH THREATS SINCE THE ASSASSINATION ATTEMPT?!
COMMISSIONER, CAN YOU COMMENT ON THE RESURGENCE OF ORGANIZATIONS LIKE THE GUARDIAN ANGELS?!
MAYOR HUNDRED, IS IT TRUE YOU HAD DINNER WITH NICOLE KIDMAN?!

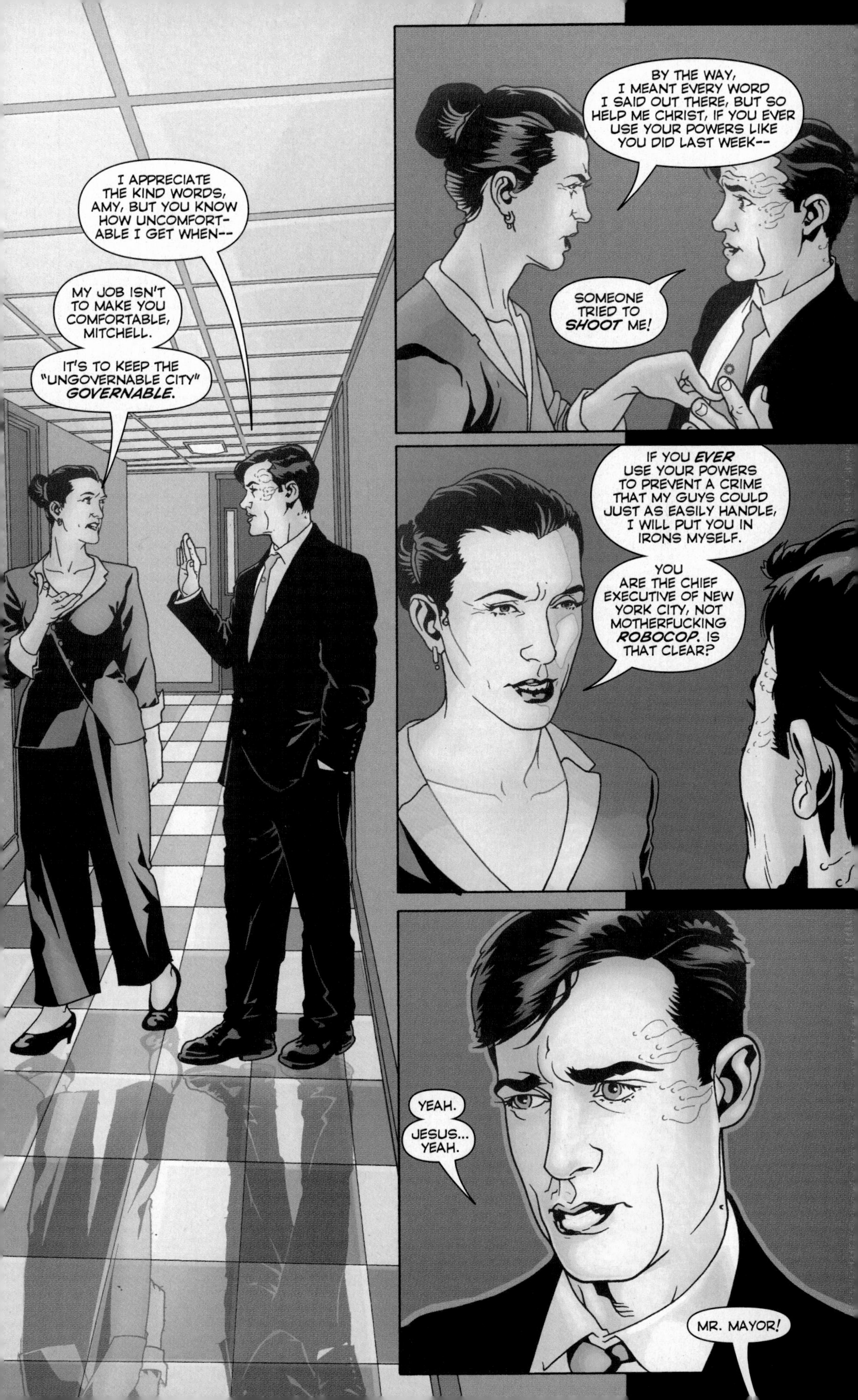
I APPRECIATE THE KIND WORDS, AMY, BUT YOU KNOW HOW UNCOMFORT-ABLE I GET WHEN--
MY JOB ISN'T TO MAKE YOU COMFORTABLE, MITCHELL.
IT'S TO KEEP THE "UNGOVERNABLE CITY" GOVERNABLE.
BY THE WAY, I MEANT EVERY WORD I SAID OUT THERE, BUT SO HELP ME CHRIST, IF YOU EVER USE YOUR POWERS LIKE YOU DID LAST WEEK--
SOMEONE TRIED TO SHOOT ME!
IF YOU EVER USE YOUR POWERS TO PREVENT A CRIME THAT MY GUYS COULD JUST AS EASILY HANDLE, I WILL PUT YOU IN IRONS MYSELF.
YOU ARE THE CHIEF EXECUTIVE OF NEW YORK CITY, NOT MOTHERFUCKING ROBOCOP. IS THAT CLEAR?
YEAH.
JESUS... YEAH.
MR. MAYOR!

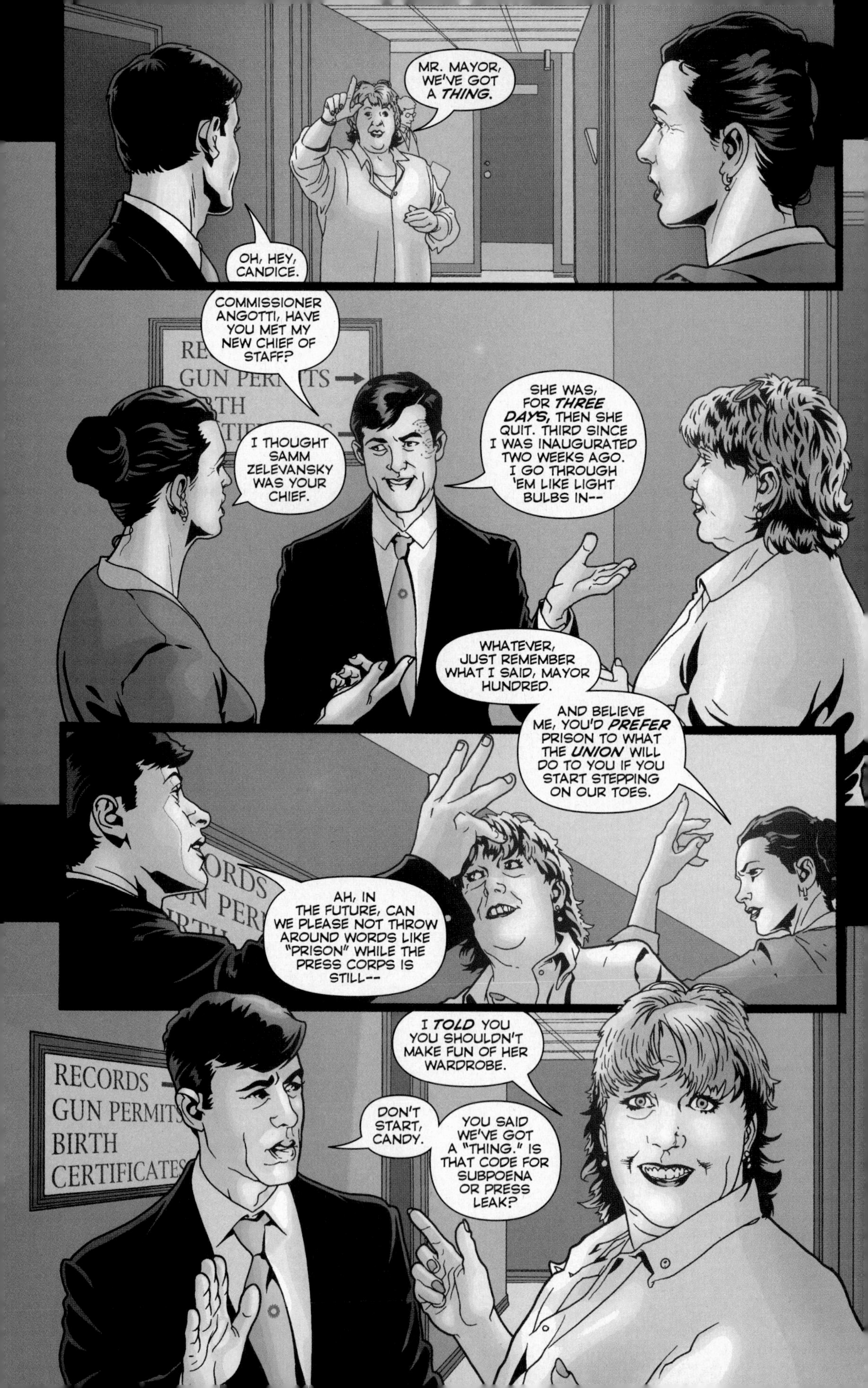
MR. MAYOR, WE'VE GOT A *THING*.
OH, HEY, CANDICE.
COMMISSIONER ANGOTTI, HAVE YOU MET MY NEW CHIEF OF STAFF?
I THOUGHT SAMM ZELEVANSKY WAS YOUR CHIEF.
SHE WAS, FOR *THREE DAYS,* THEN SHE QUIT. THIRD SINCE I WAS INAUGURATED TWO WEEKS AGO. I GO THROUGH 'EM LIKE LIGHT BULBS IN--
WHATEVER, JUST REMEMBER WHAT I SAID, MAYOR HUNDRED.
AND BELIEVE ME, YOU'D *PREFER* PRISON TO WHAT THE *UNION* WILL DO TO YOU IF YOU START STEPPING ON OUR TOES.
AH, IN THE FUTURE, CAN WE PLEASE NOT THROW AROUND WORDS LIKE "PRISON" WHILE THE PRESS CORPS IS STILL--
I *TOLD* YOU YOU SHOULDN'T MAKE FUN OF HER WARDROBE.
DON'T START, CANDY.
YOU SAID WE'VE GOT A "THING." IS THAT CODE FOR SUBPOENA OR PRESS LEAK?
RECORDS
GUN PERMITS
BIRTH
CERTIFICATES

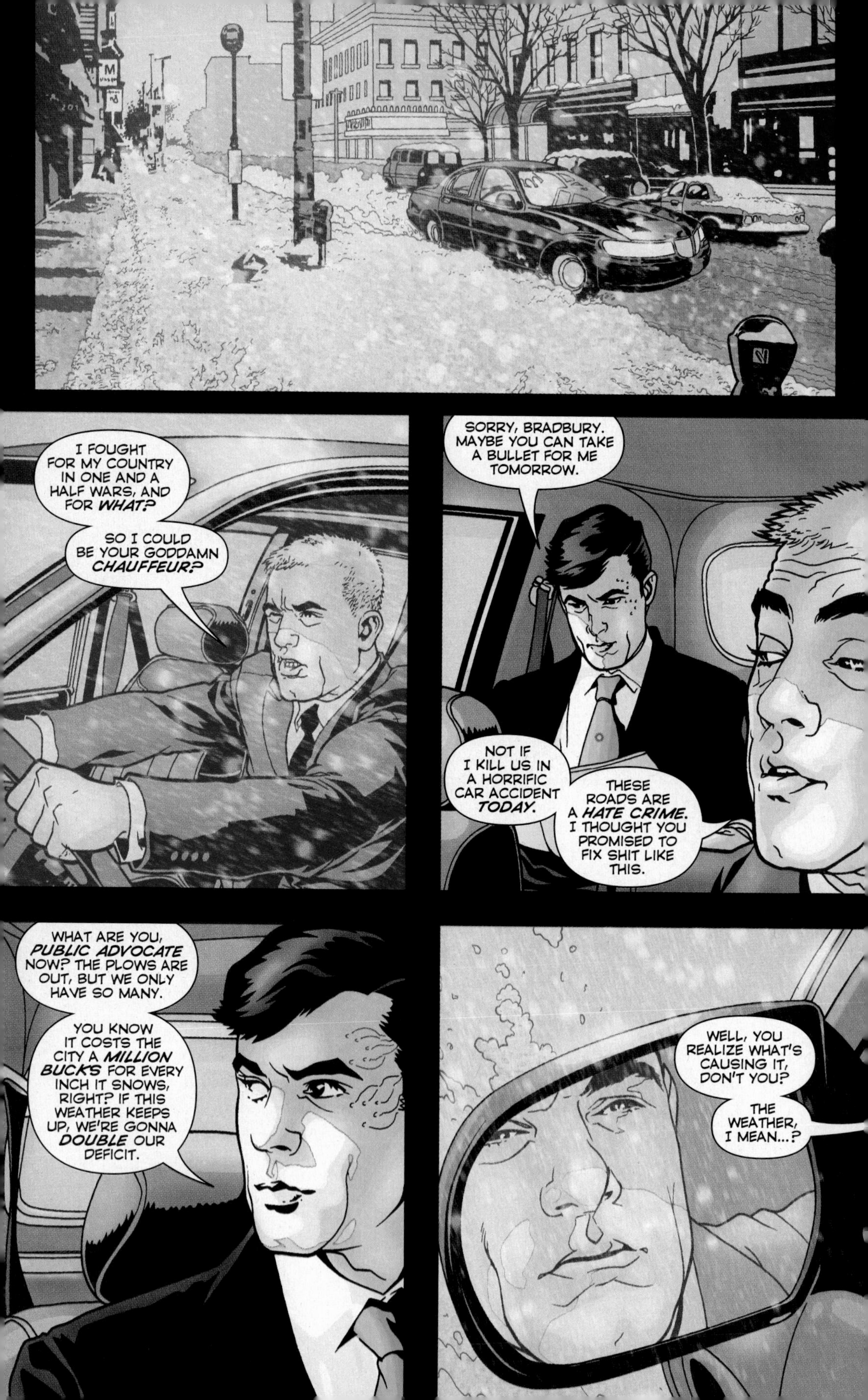
I FOUGHT FOR MY COUNTRY IN ONE AND A HALF WARS, AND FOR WHAT?
SO I COULD BE YOUR GODDAMN CHAUFFEUR?
SORRY, BRADBURY. MAYBE YOU CAN TAKE A BULLET FOR ME TOMORROW.
NOT IF I KILL US IN A HORRIFIC CAR ACCIDENT TODAY.
THESE ROADS ARE A HATE CRIME. I THOUGHT YOU PROMISED TO FIX SHIT LIKE THIS.
WHAT ARE YOU, PUBLIC ADVOCATE NOW? THE PLOWS ARE OUT, BUT WE ONLY HAVE SO MANY.
YOU KNOW IT COSTS THE CITY A MILLION BUCKS FOR EVERY INCH IT SNOWS, RIGHT? IF THIS WEATHER KEEPS UP, WE'RE GONNA DOUBLE OUR DEFICIT.
WELL, YOU REALIZE WHAT'S CAUSING IT, DON'T YOU?
THE WEATHER, I MEAN...?

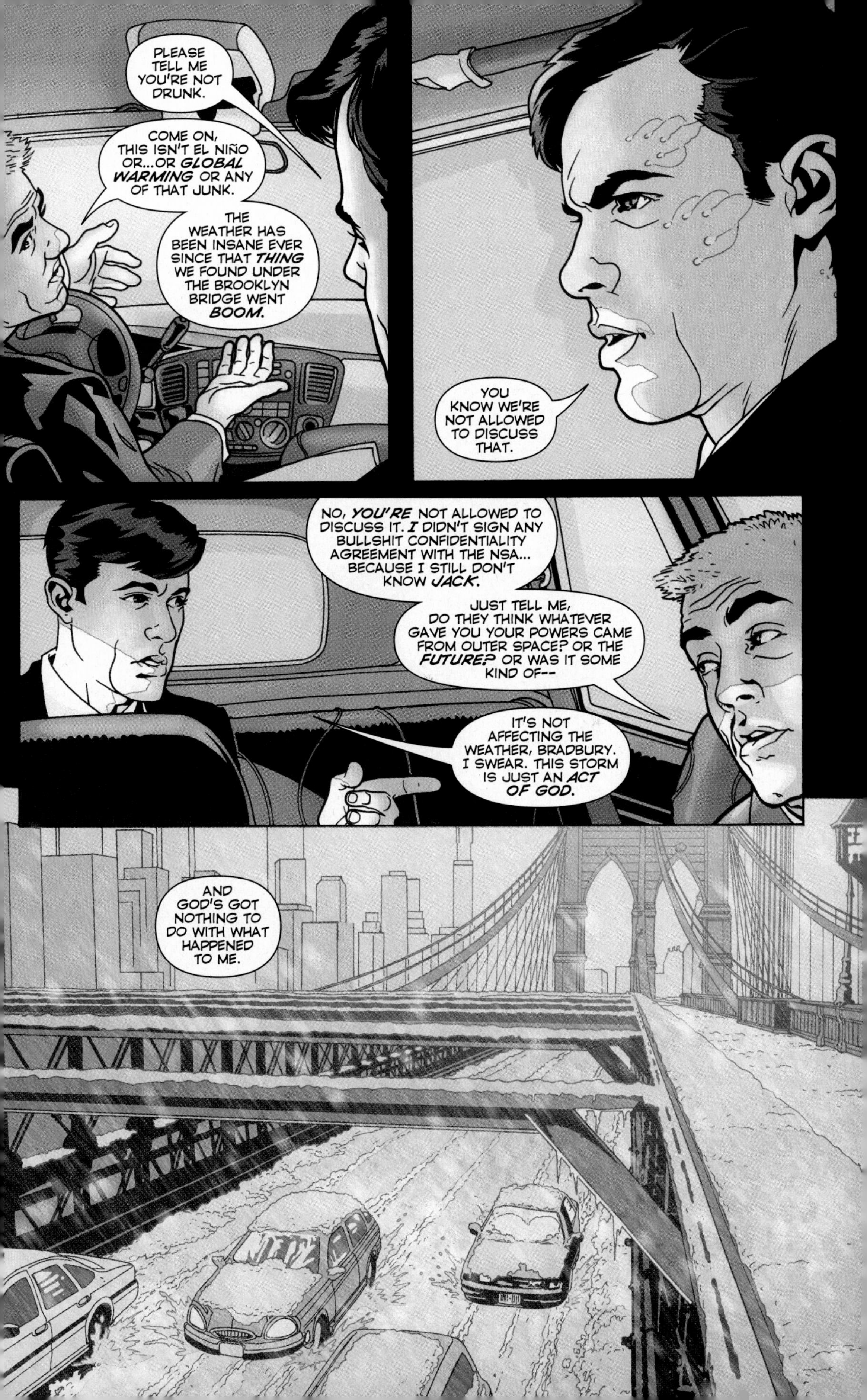
PLEASE TELL ME YOU'RE NOT DRUNK.
COME ON, THIS ISN'T EL NIÑO OR...OR *GLOBAL WARMING* OR ANY OF THAT JUNK.
THE WEATHER HAS BEEN INSANE EVER SINCE THAT *THING* WE FOUND UNDER THE BROOKLYN BRIDGE WENT *BOOM*.
YOU KNOW WE'RE NOT ALLOWED TO DISCUSS THAT.
NO, *YOU'RE* NOT ALLOWED TO DISCUSS IT. *I* DIDN'T SIGN ANY BULLSHIT CONFIDENTIALITY AGREEMENT WITH THE NSA... BECAUSE I STILL DON'T KNOW *JACK*.
JUST TELL ME, DO THEY THINK WHATEVER GAVE YOU YOUR POWERS CAME FROM OUTER SPACE? OR THE *FUTURE?* OR WAS IT SOME KIND OF--
IT'S NOT AFFECTING THE WEATHER, BRADBURY. I SWEAR. THIS STORM IS JUST AN *ACT OF GOD*.
AND GOD'S GOT NOTHING TO DO WITH WHAT HAPPENED TO ME.

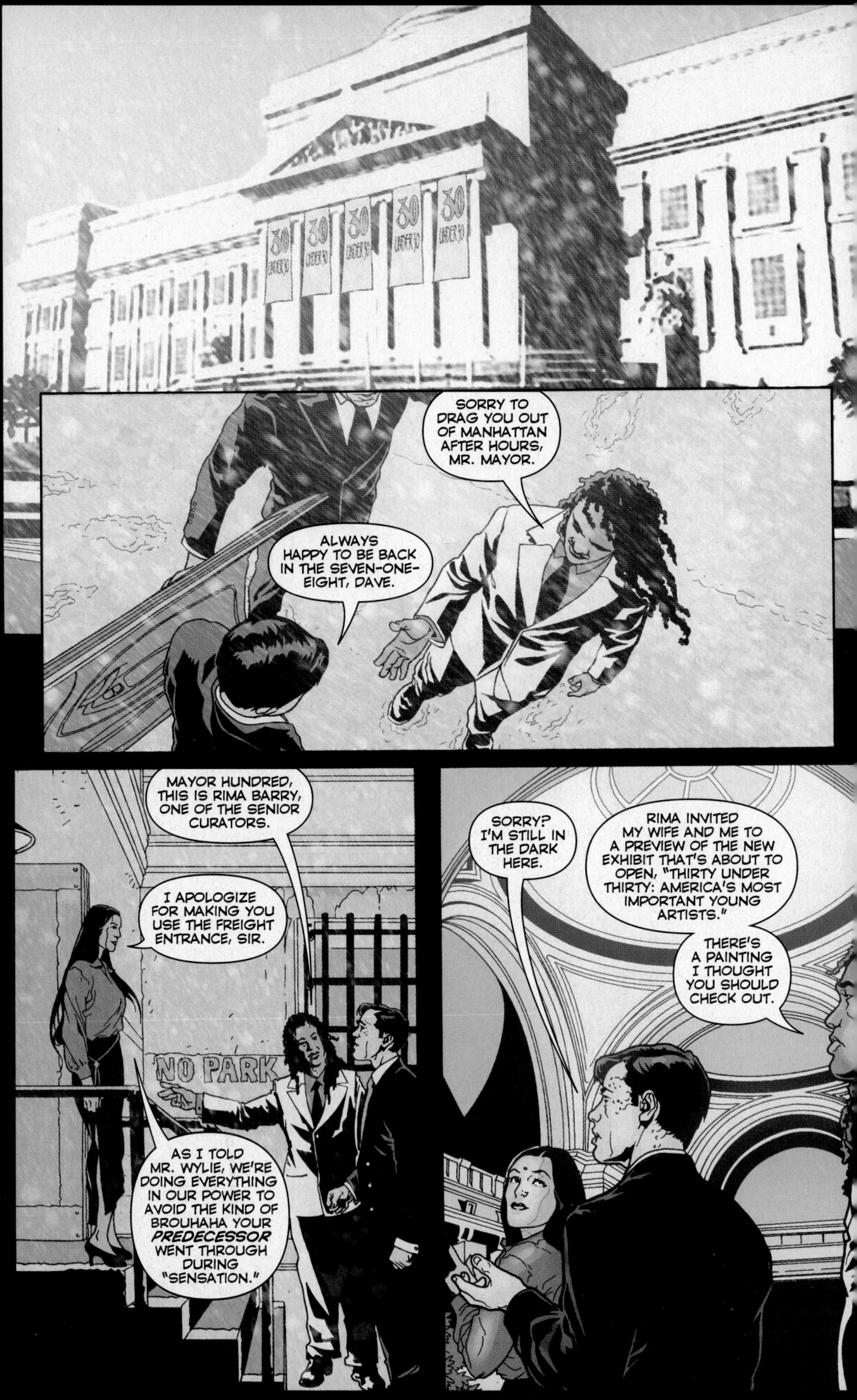
30 UNDER 30
SORRY TO DRAG YOU OUT OF MANHATTAN AFTER HOURS, MR. MAYOR.
ALWAYS HAPPY TO BE BACK IN THE SEVEN-ONE-EIGHT, DAVE.
MAYOR HUNDRED, THIS IS RIMA BARRY, ONE OF THE SENIOR CURATORS.
I APOLOGIZE FOR MAKING YOU USE THE FREIGHT ENTRANCE, SIR.
NO PARK
AS I TOLD MR. WYLIE, WE'RE DOING EVERYTHING IN OUR POWER TO AVOID THE KIND OF BROUHAHA YOUR *PREDECESSOR* WENT THROUGH DURING "SENSATION."
SORRY? I'M STILL IN THE DARK HERE.
RIMA INVITED MY WIFE AND ME TO A PREVIEW OF THE NEW EXHIBIT THAT'S ABOUT TO OPEN, "THIRTY UNDER THIRTY: AMERICA'S MOST IMPORTANT YOUNG ARTISTS."
THERE'S A PAINTING I THOUGHT YOU SHOULD CHECK OUT.

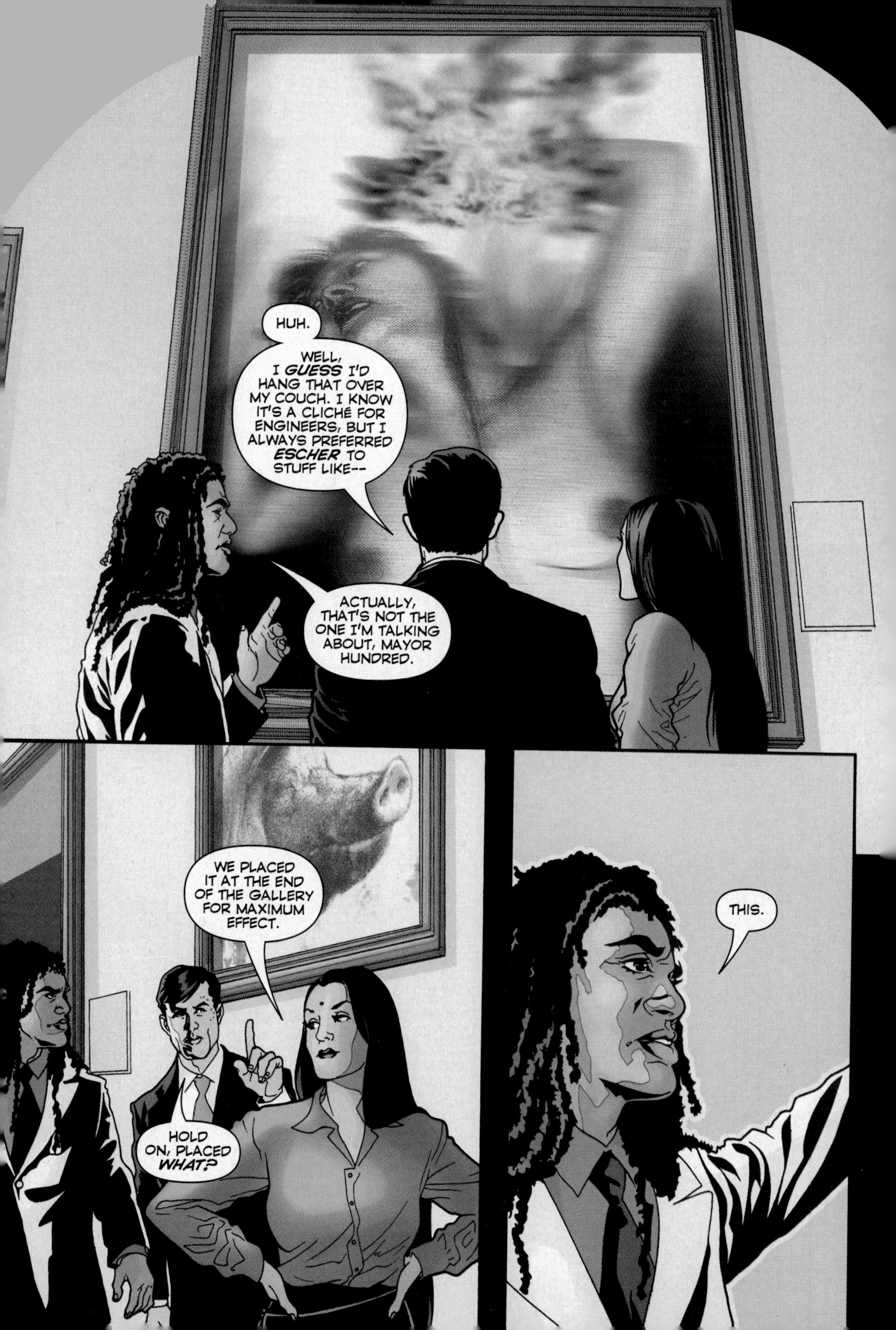
HUH.
WELL, I GUESS I'D HANG THAT OVER MY COUCH. I KNOW IT'S A CLICHÉ FOR ENGINEERS, BUT I ALWAYS PREFERRED ESCHER TO STUFF LIKE--
ACTUALLY, THAT'S NOT THE ONE I'M TALKING ABOUT, MAYOR HUNDRED.
WE PLACED IT AT THE END OF THE GALLERY FOR MAXIMUM EFFECT.
HOLD ON, PLACED WHAT?
THIS.

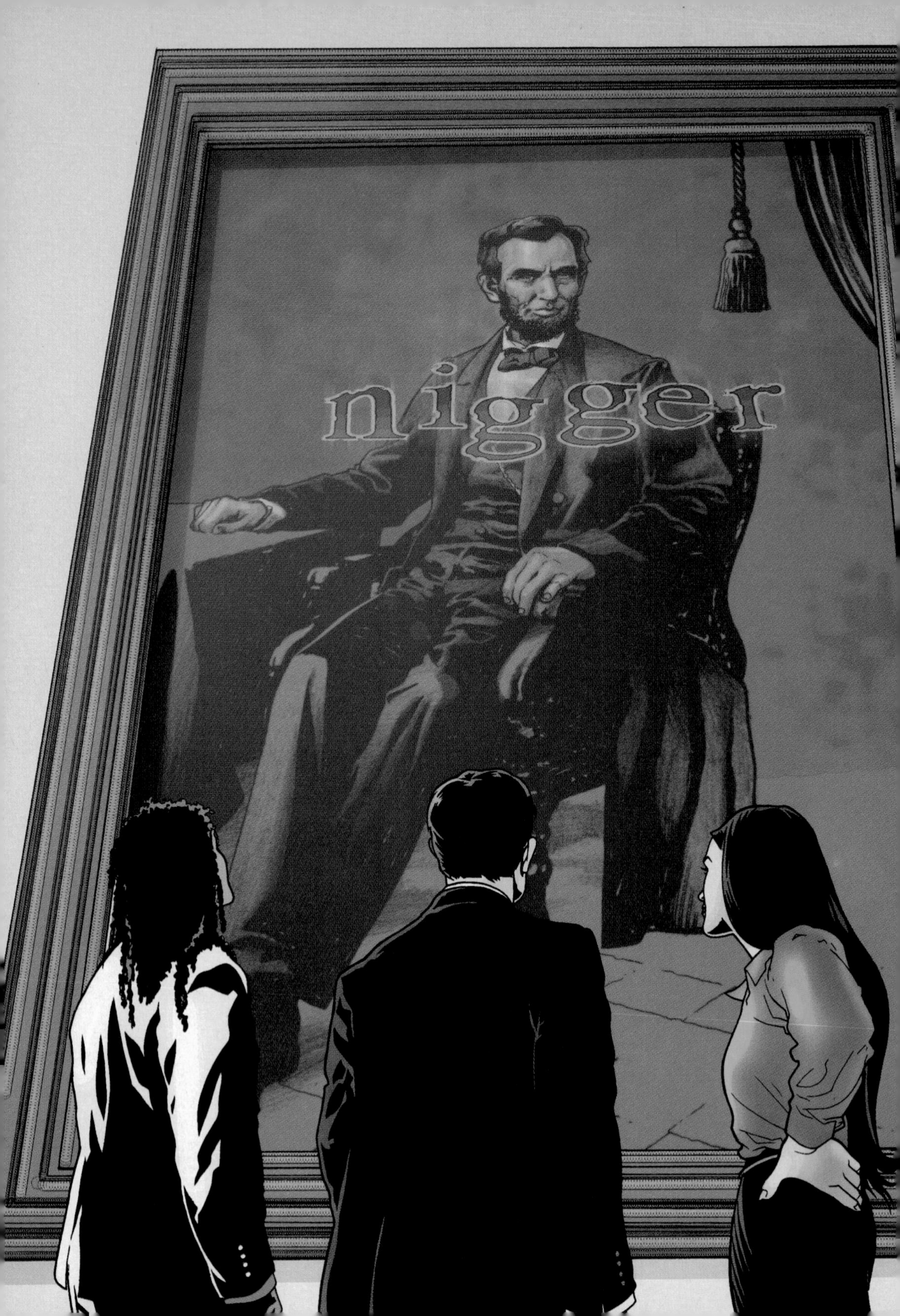
nigger

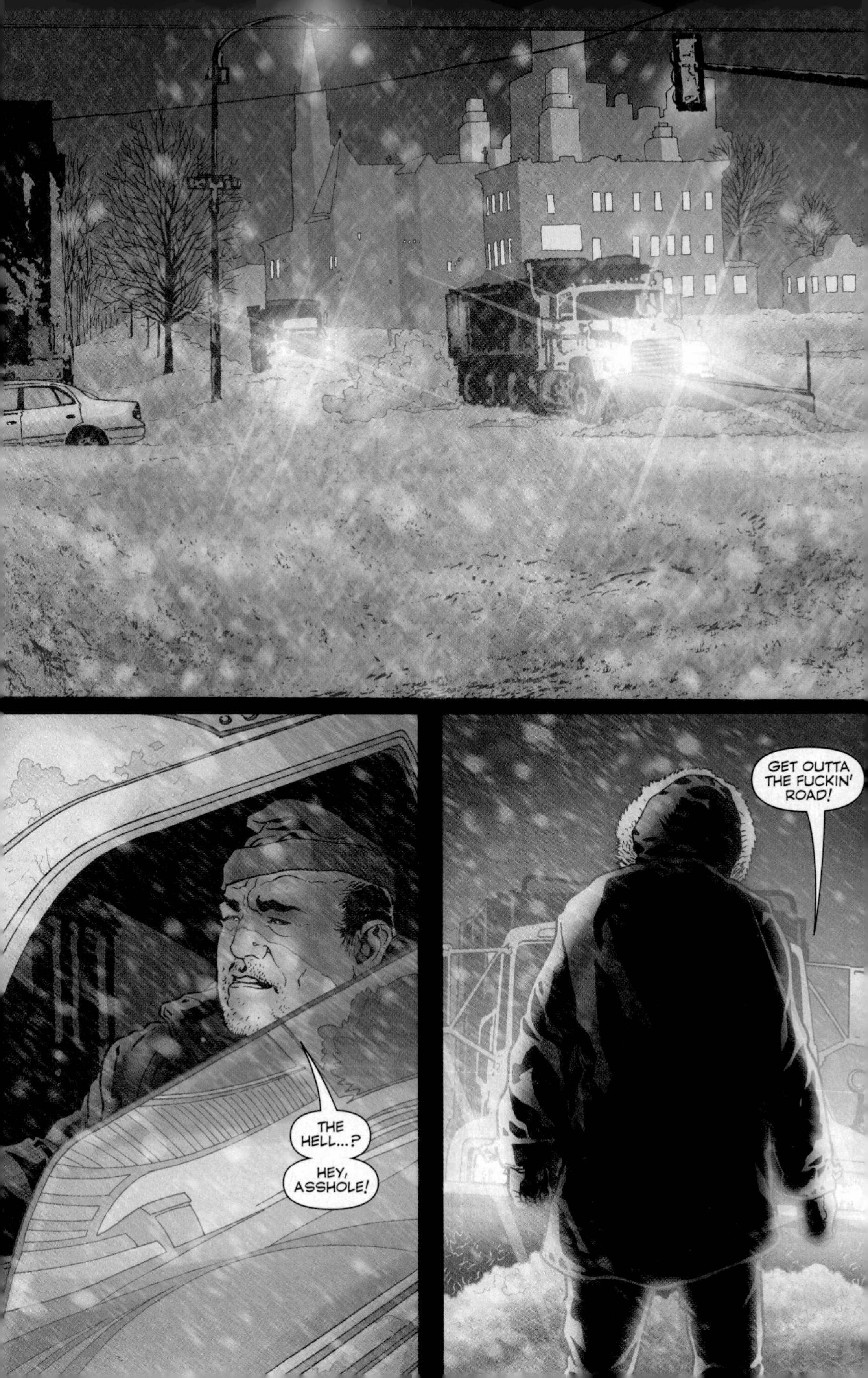
THE HELL...?
HEY, ASSHOLE!
GET OUTTA THE FUCKIN' ROAD!

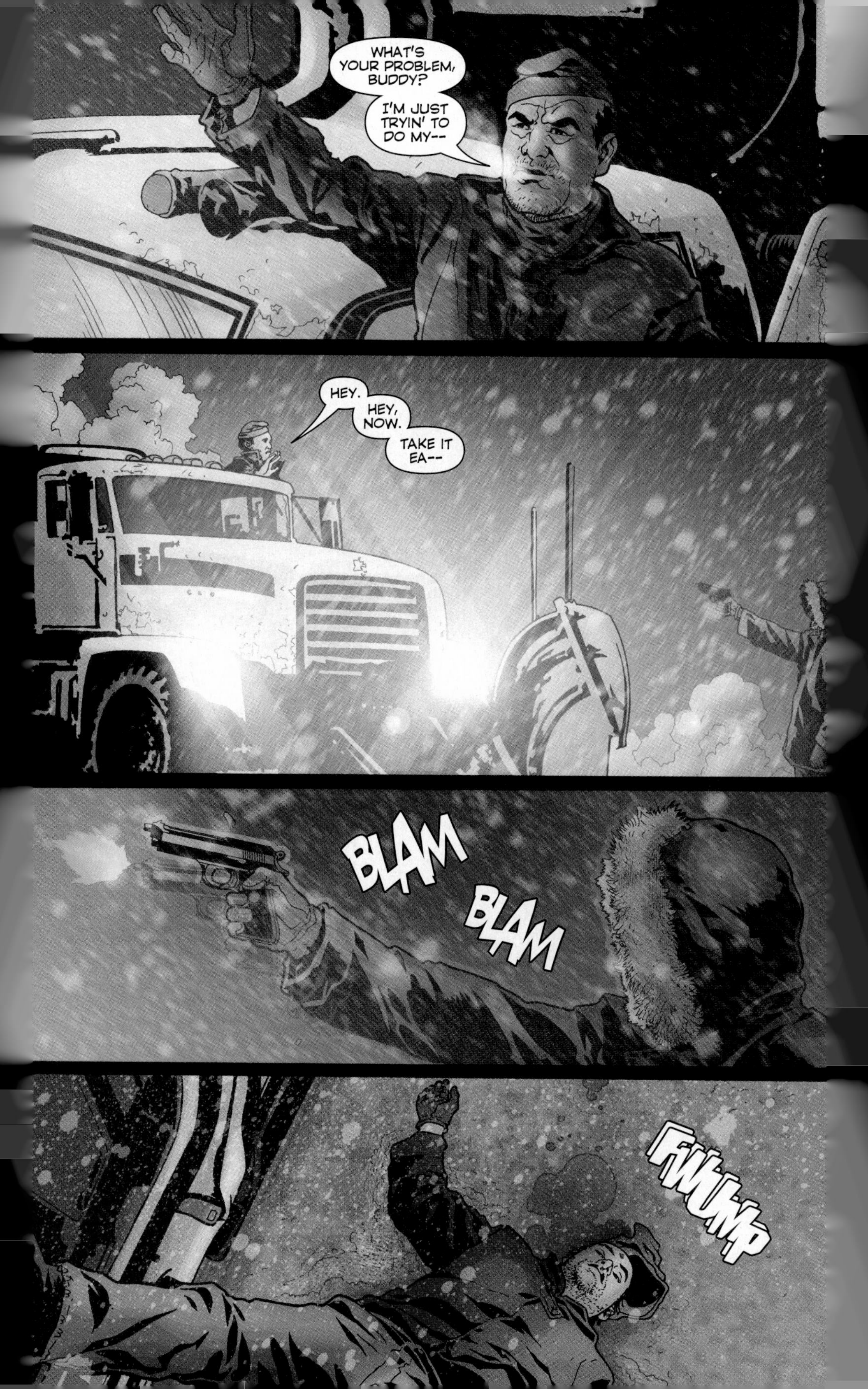
WHAT'S YOUR PROBLEM, BUDDY?
I'M JUST TRYIN' TO DO MY--
HEY.
HEY, NOW.
TAKE IT EA--
BLAM
BLAM
FWUMP

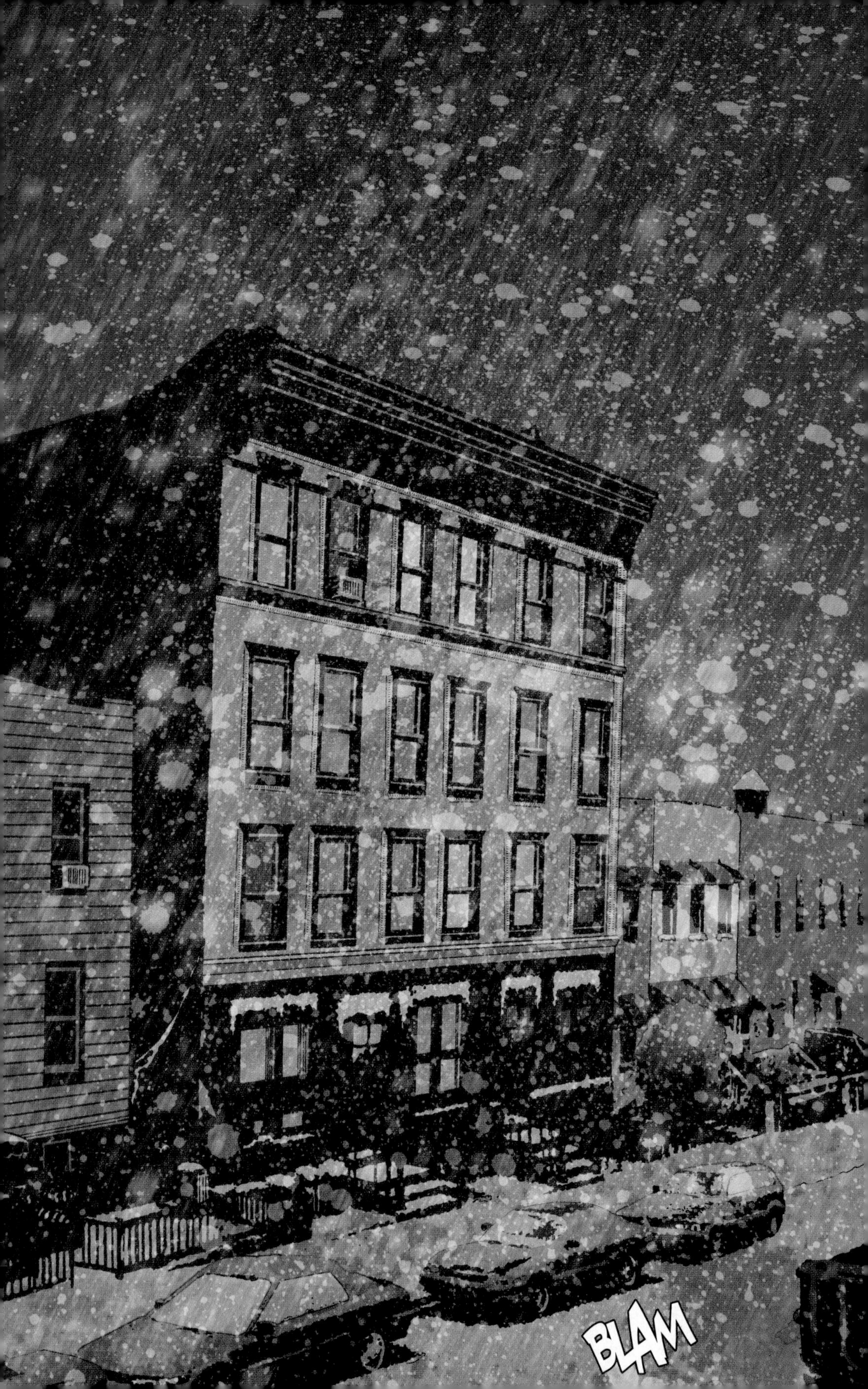
BLAM

CHAPTER 3

Part 2
State of Emergency

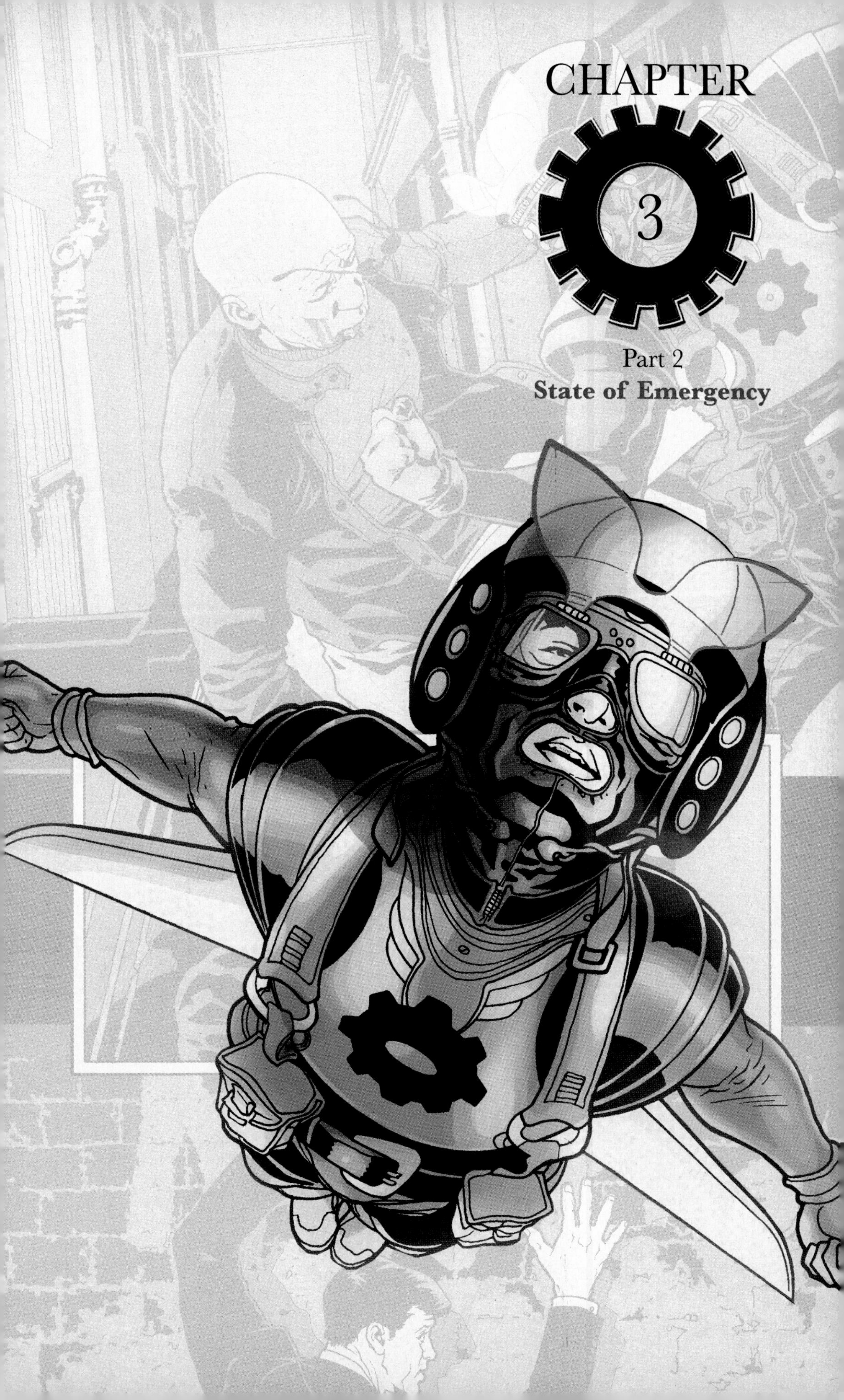

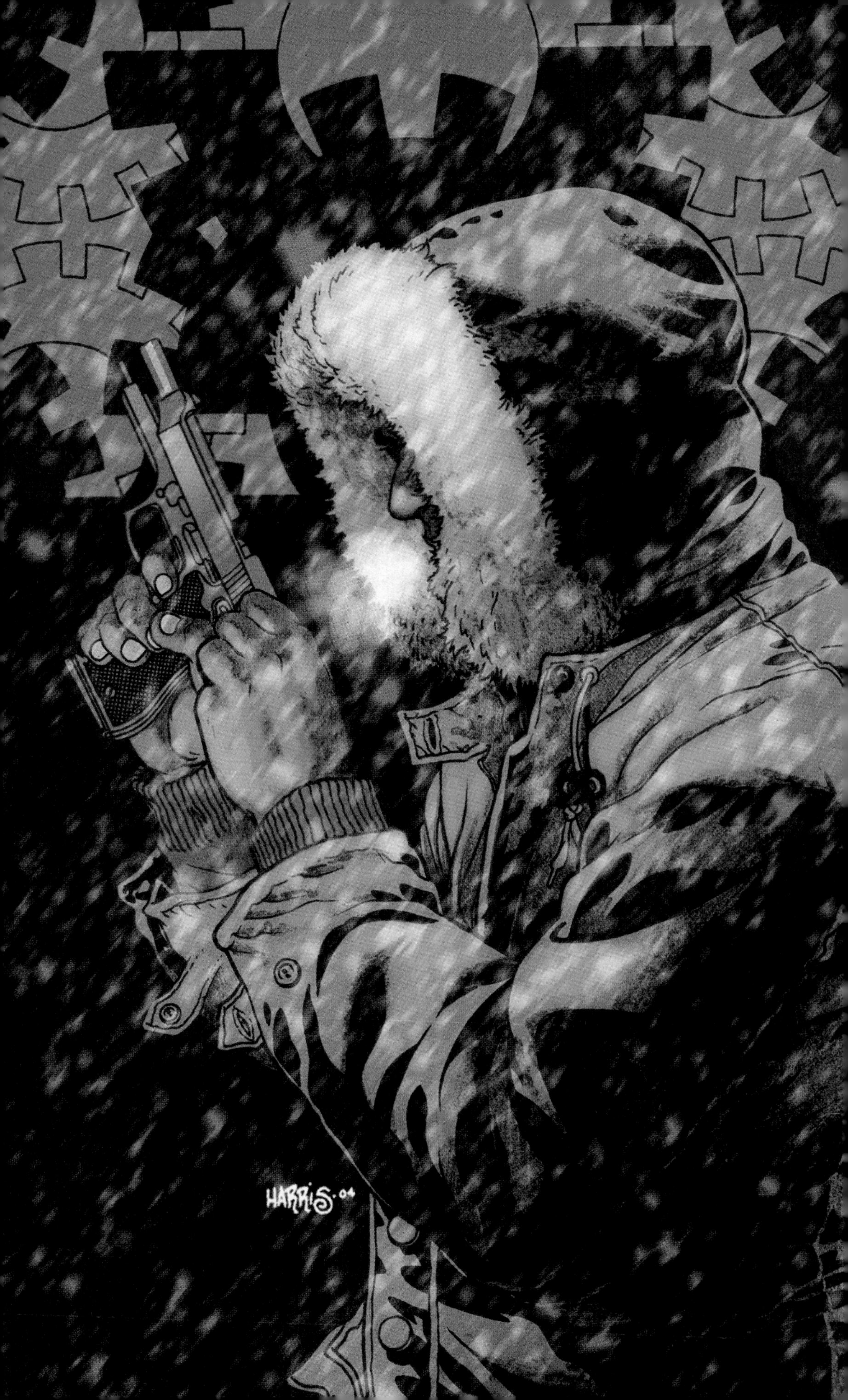
HARRIS·04

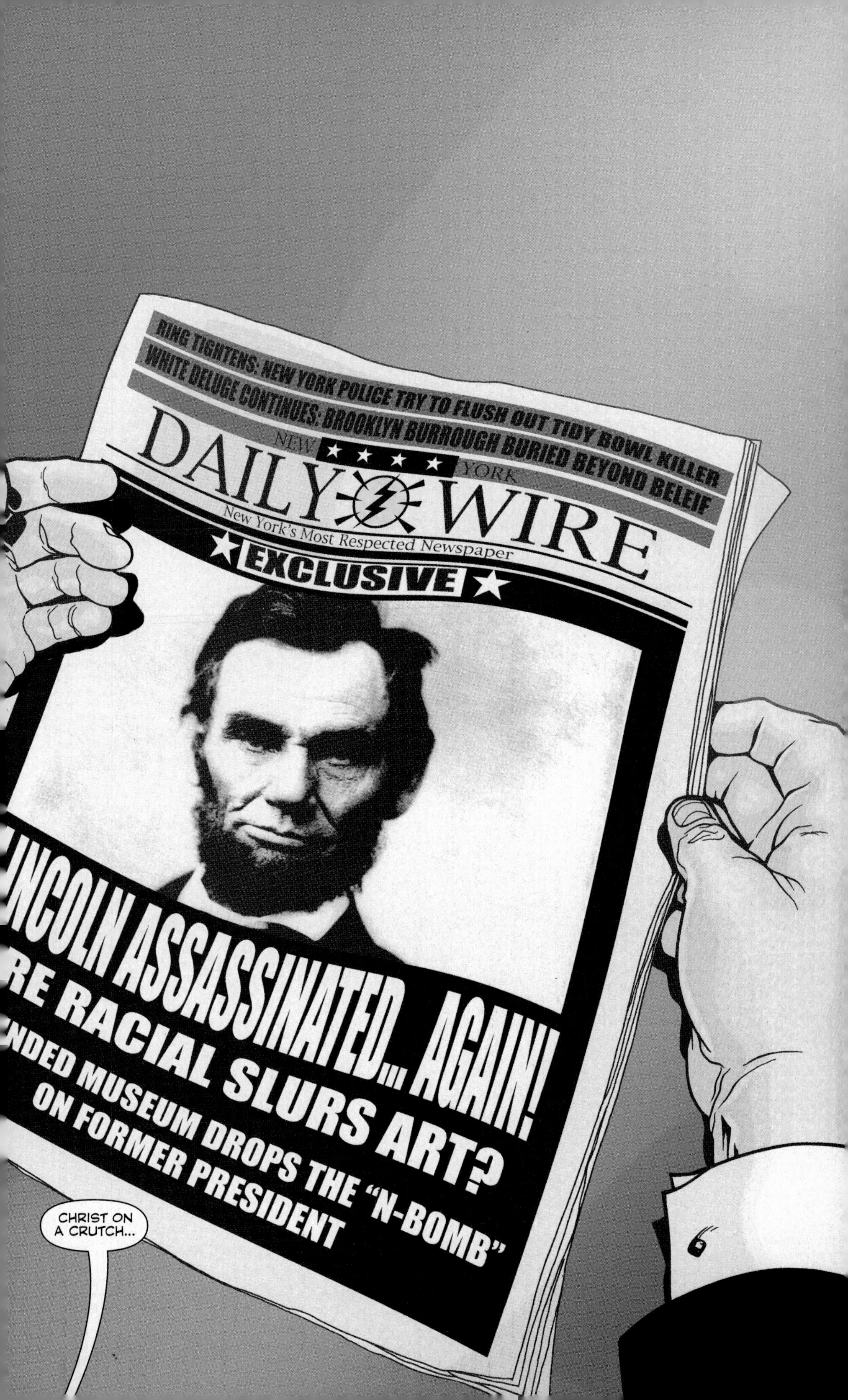
RING TIGHTENS: NEW YORK POLICE TRY TO FLUSH OUT TIDY BOWL KILLER
WHITE DELUGE CONTINUES: BROOKLYN BURROUGH BURIED BEYOND BELEIF
NEW YORK DAILY WIRE
New York's Most Respected Newspaper
EXCLUSIVE
INCOLN ASSASSINATED... AGAIN!
RE RACIAL SLURS ART?
NDED MUSEUM DROPS THE "N-BOMB"
ON FORMER PRESIDENT
CHRIST ON A CRUTCH...

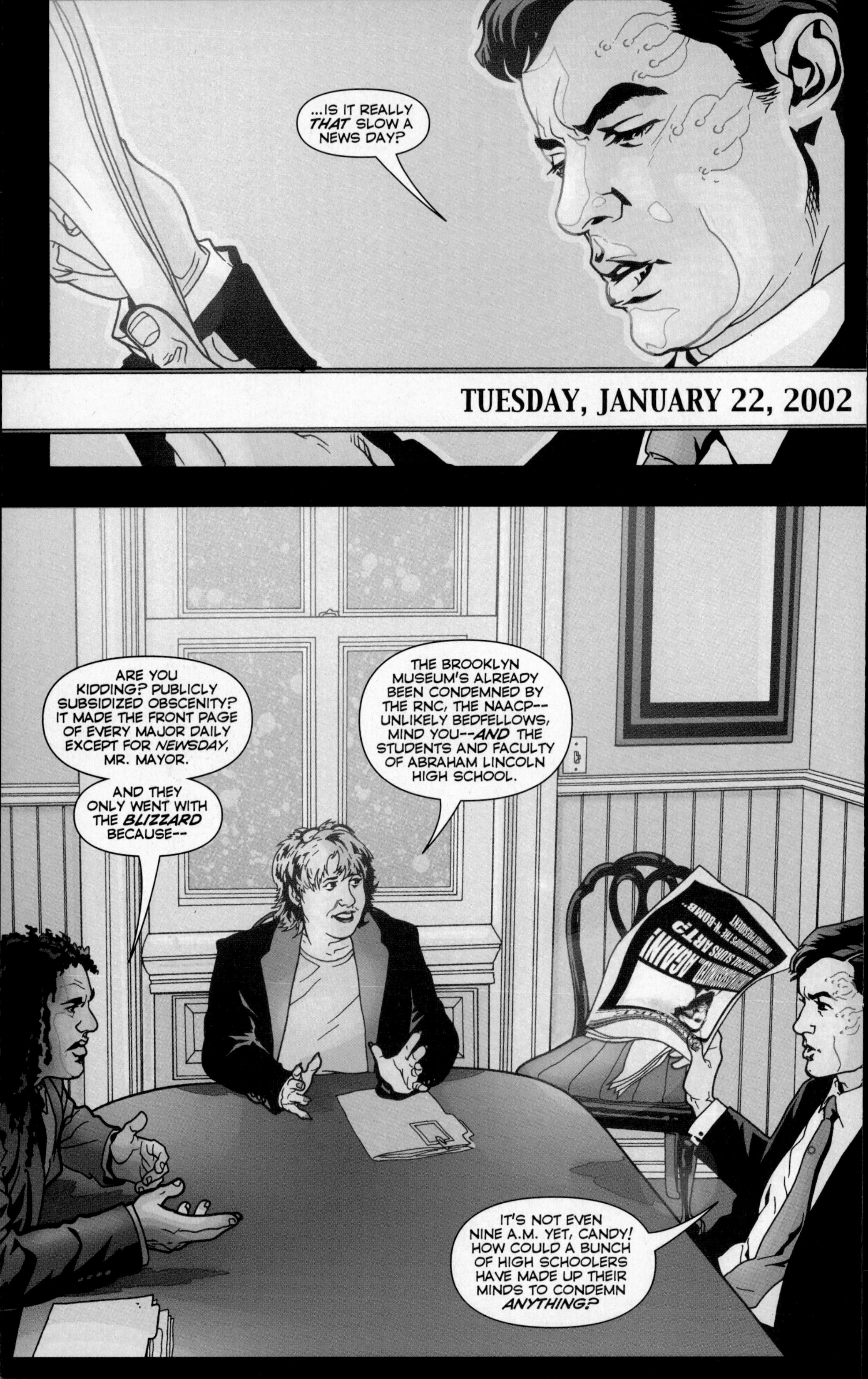
...IS IT REALLY *THAT* SLOW A NEWS DAY?
TUESDAY, JANUARY 22, 2002
ARE YOU KIDDING? PUBLICLY SUBSIDIZED OBSCENITY? IT MADE THE FRONT PAGE OF EVERY MAJOR DAILY EXCEPT FOR *NEWSDAY*, MR. MAYOR.
AND THEY ONLY WENT WITH THE *BLIZZARD* BECAUSE--
THE BROOKLYN MUSEUM'S ALREADY BEEN CONDEMNED BY THE RNC, THE NAACP-- UNLIKELY BEDFELLOWS, MIND YOU--*AND* THE STUDENTS AND FACULTY OF ABRAHAM LINCOLN HIGH SCHOOL.
IT'S NOT EVEN NINE A.M. YET, CANDY! HOW COULD A BUNCH OF HIGH SCHOOLERS HAVE MADE UP THEIR MINDS TO CONDEMN *ANYTHING?*

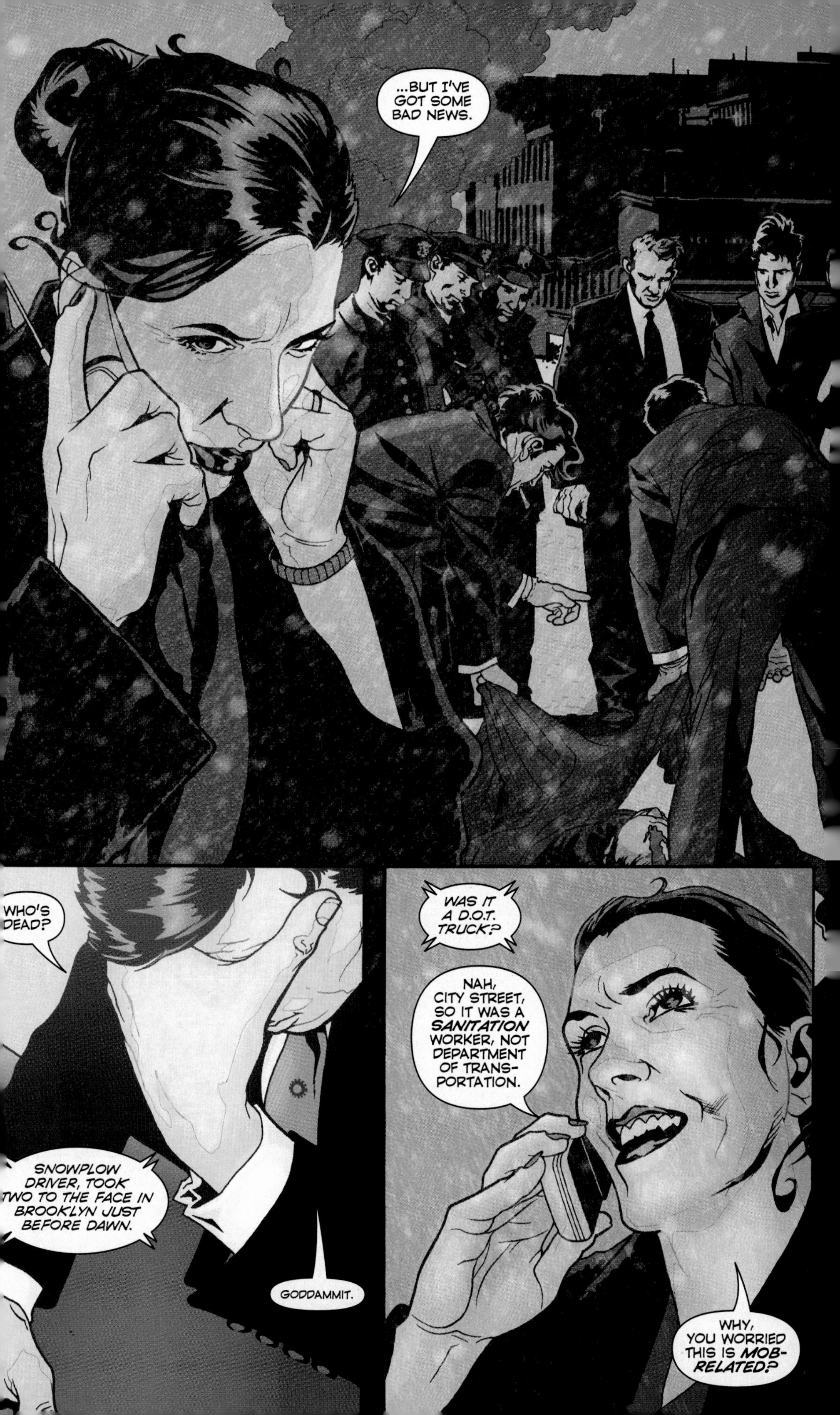

...BUT I'VE GOT SOME BAD NEWS.
WHO'S DEAD?
SNOWPLOW DRIVER, TOOK TWO TO THE FACE IN BROOKLYN JUST BEFORE DAWN.
GODDAMMIT.
WAS IT A D.O.T. TRUCK?
NAH, CITY STREET, SO IT WAS A SANITATION WORKER, NOT DEPARTMENT OF TRANS-PORTATION.
WHY, YOU WORRIED THIS IS MOB-RELATED?

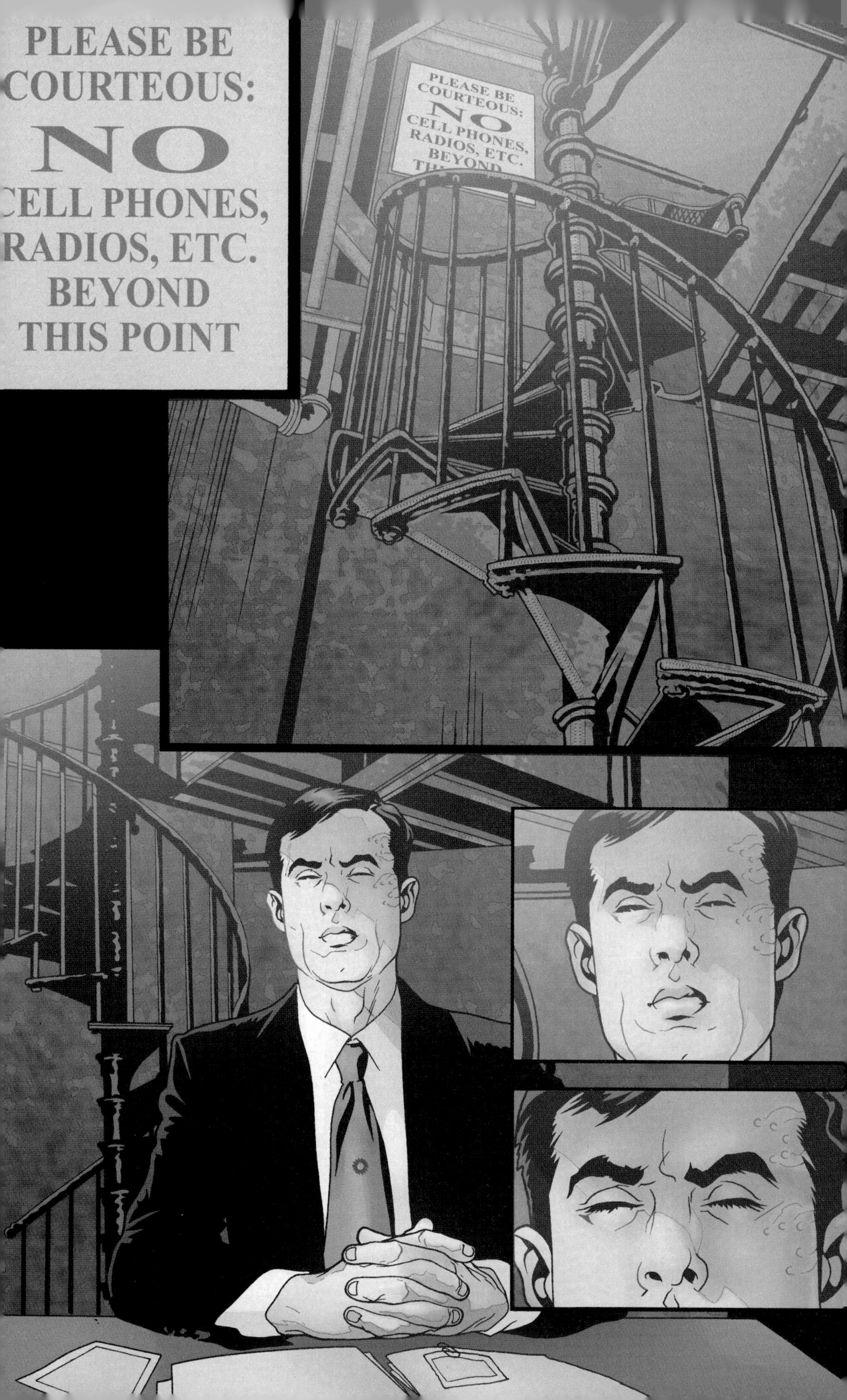
PLEASE BE COURTEOUS: NO CELL PHONES, RADIOS, ETC. BEYOND THIS POINT

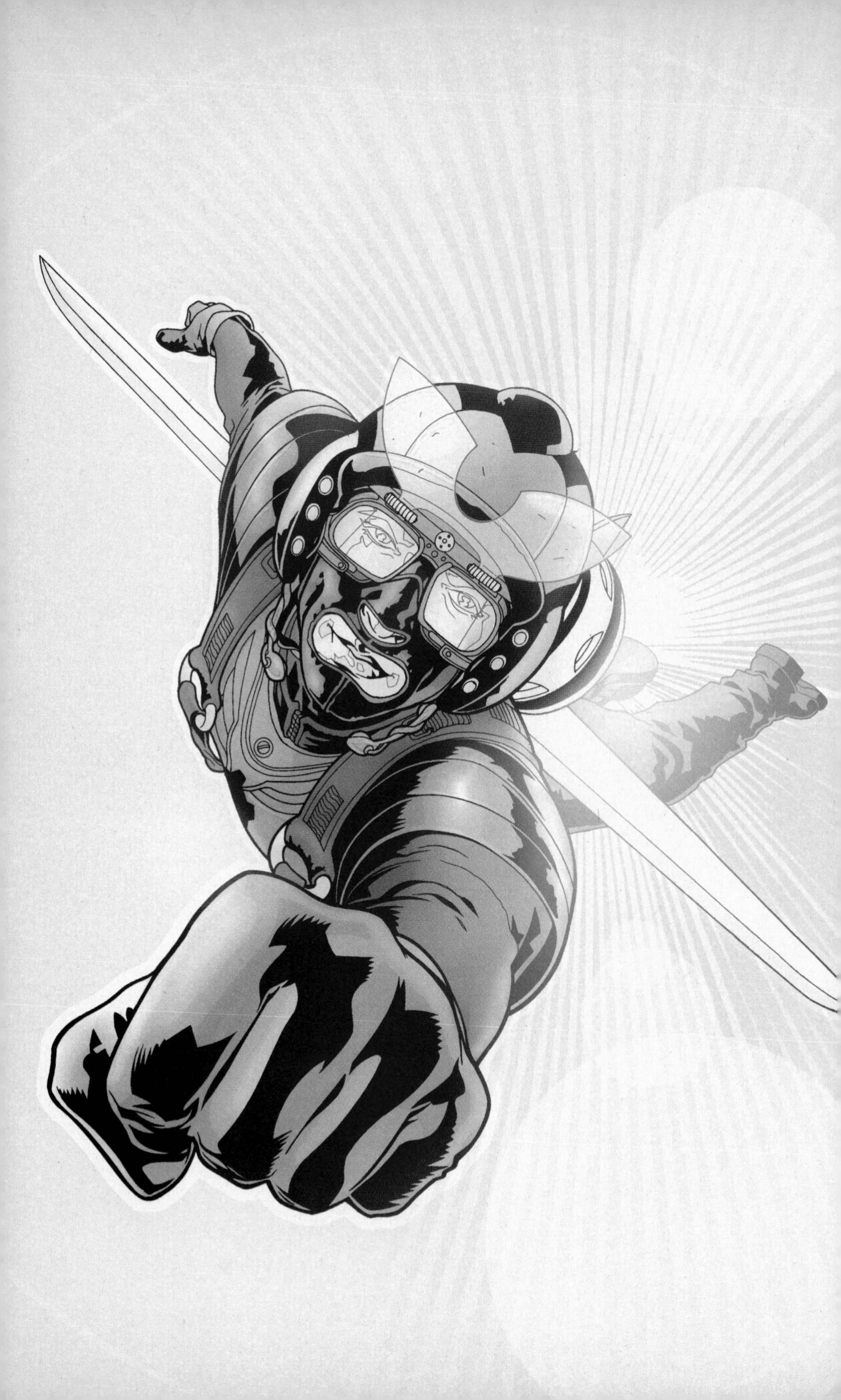

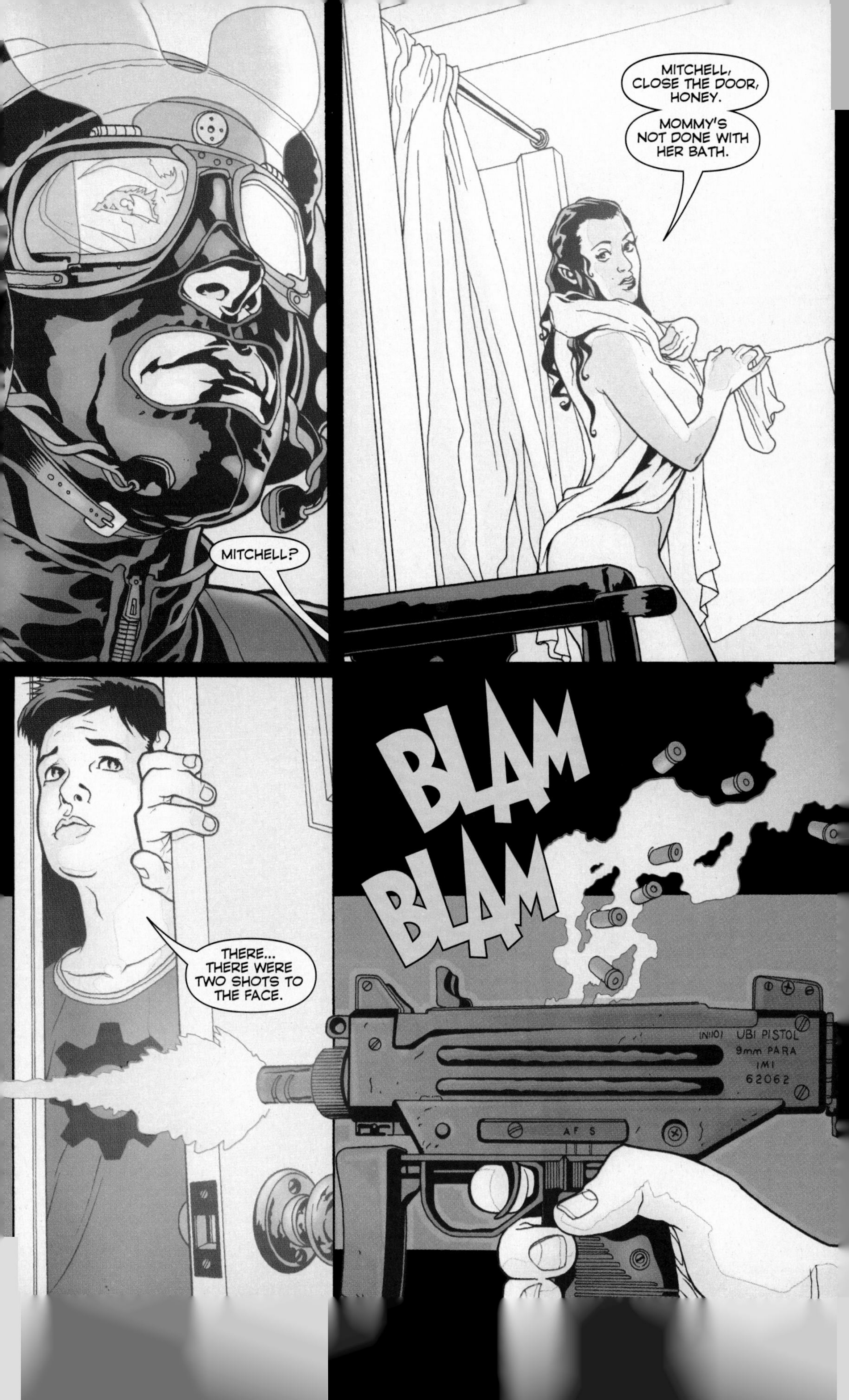
MITCHELL?
MITCHELL, CLOSE THE DOOR, HONEY.
MOMMY'S NOT DONE WITH HER BATH.
THERE... THERE WERE TWO SHOTS TO THE FACE.
BLAM
BLAM
UBI PISTOL
9mm PARA
IMI
62062
AF S

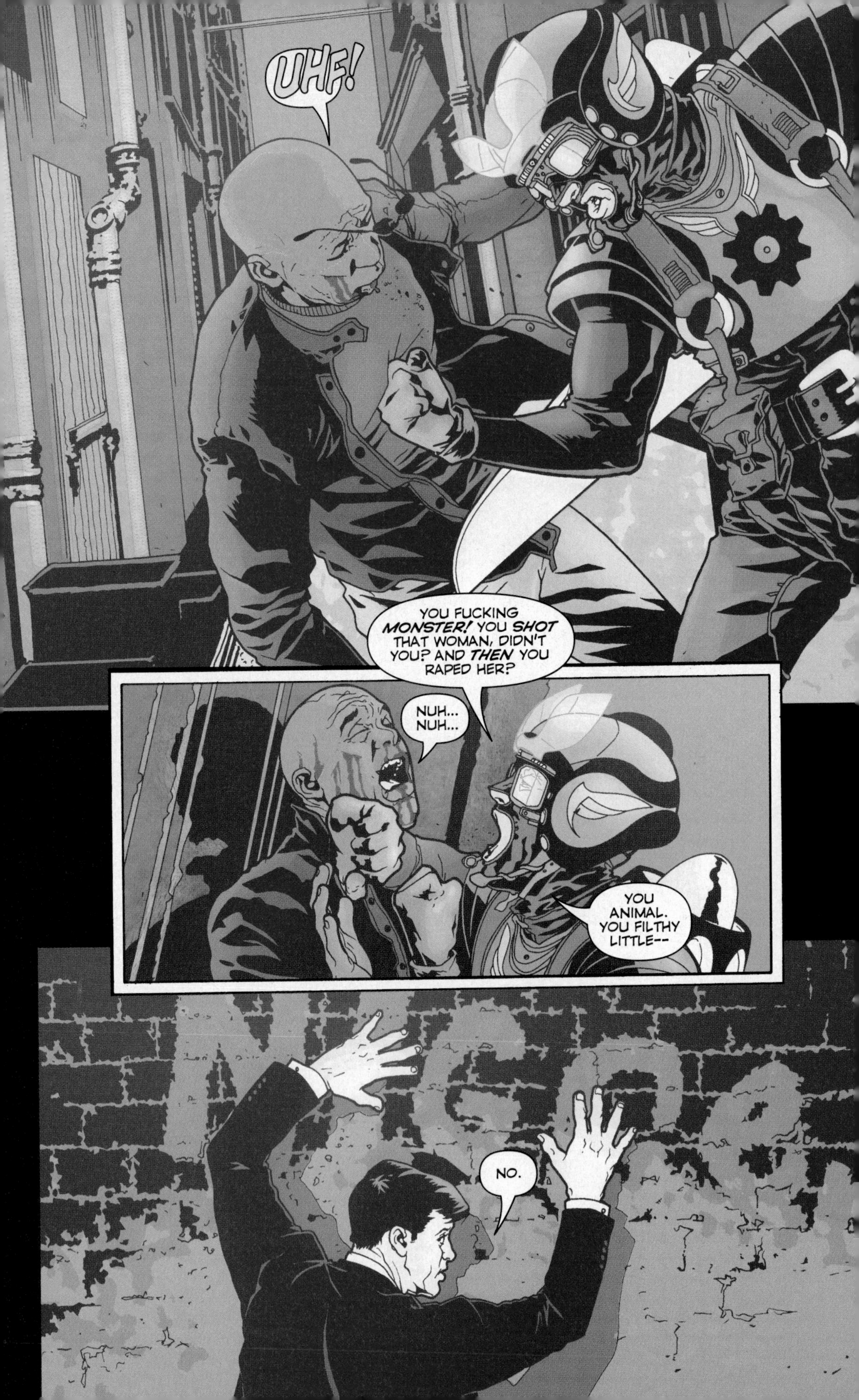
UHF!
YOU FUCKING MONSTER! YOU SHOT THAT WOMAN, DIDN'T YOU? AND THEN YOU RAPED HER?
NUH... NUH...
YOU ANIMAL. YOU FILTHY LITTLE--
NO.

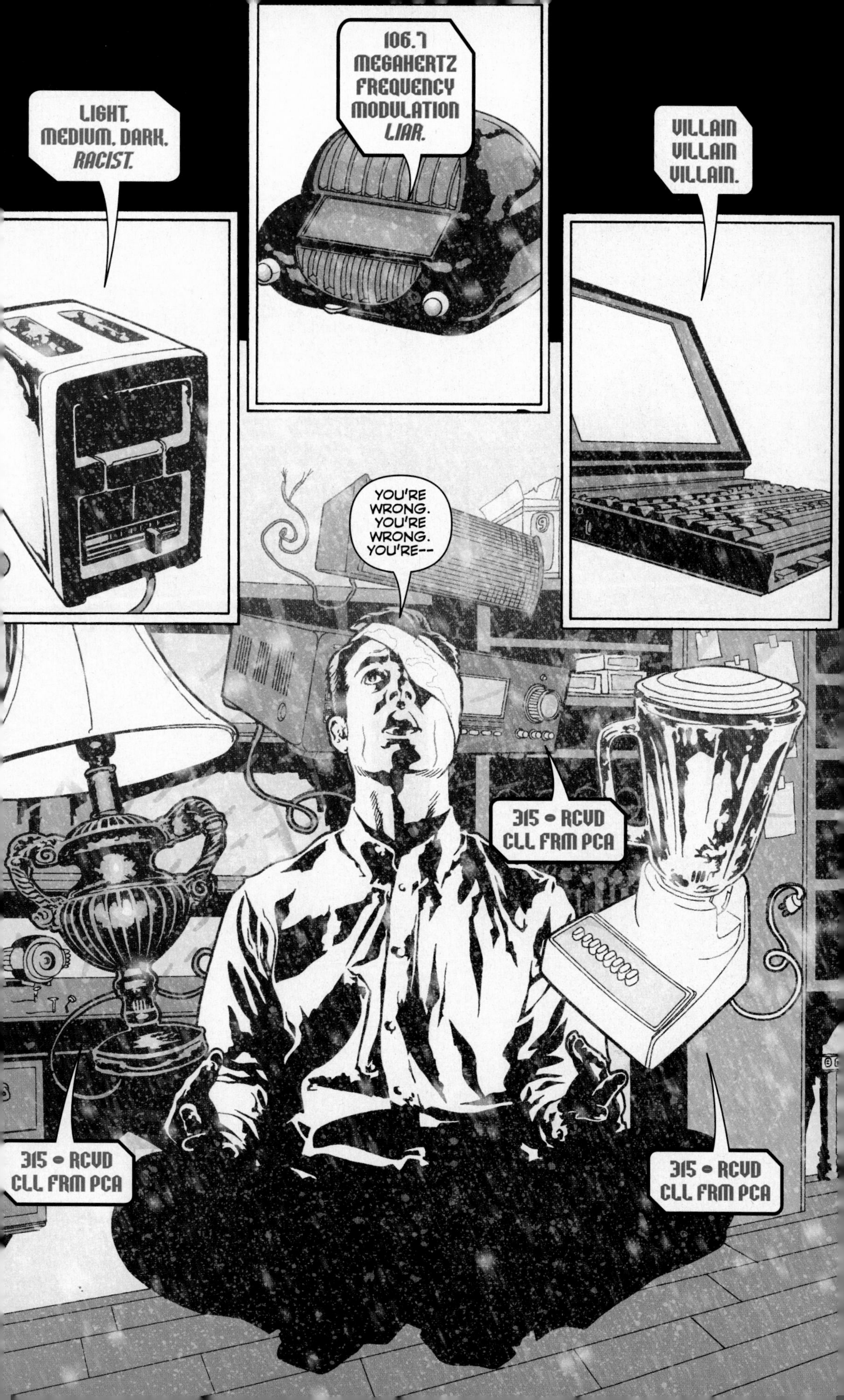
LIGHT. MEDIUM. DARK. RACIST.
106.7 MEGAHERTZ FREQUENCY MODULATION LIAR.
VILLAIN VILLAIN VILLAIN.
YOU'RE WRONG. YOU'RE WRONG. YOU'RE--
315 - RCVD CLL FRM PCA
315 - RCVD CLL FRM PCA
315 - RCVD CLL FRM PCA

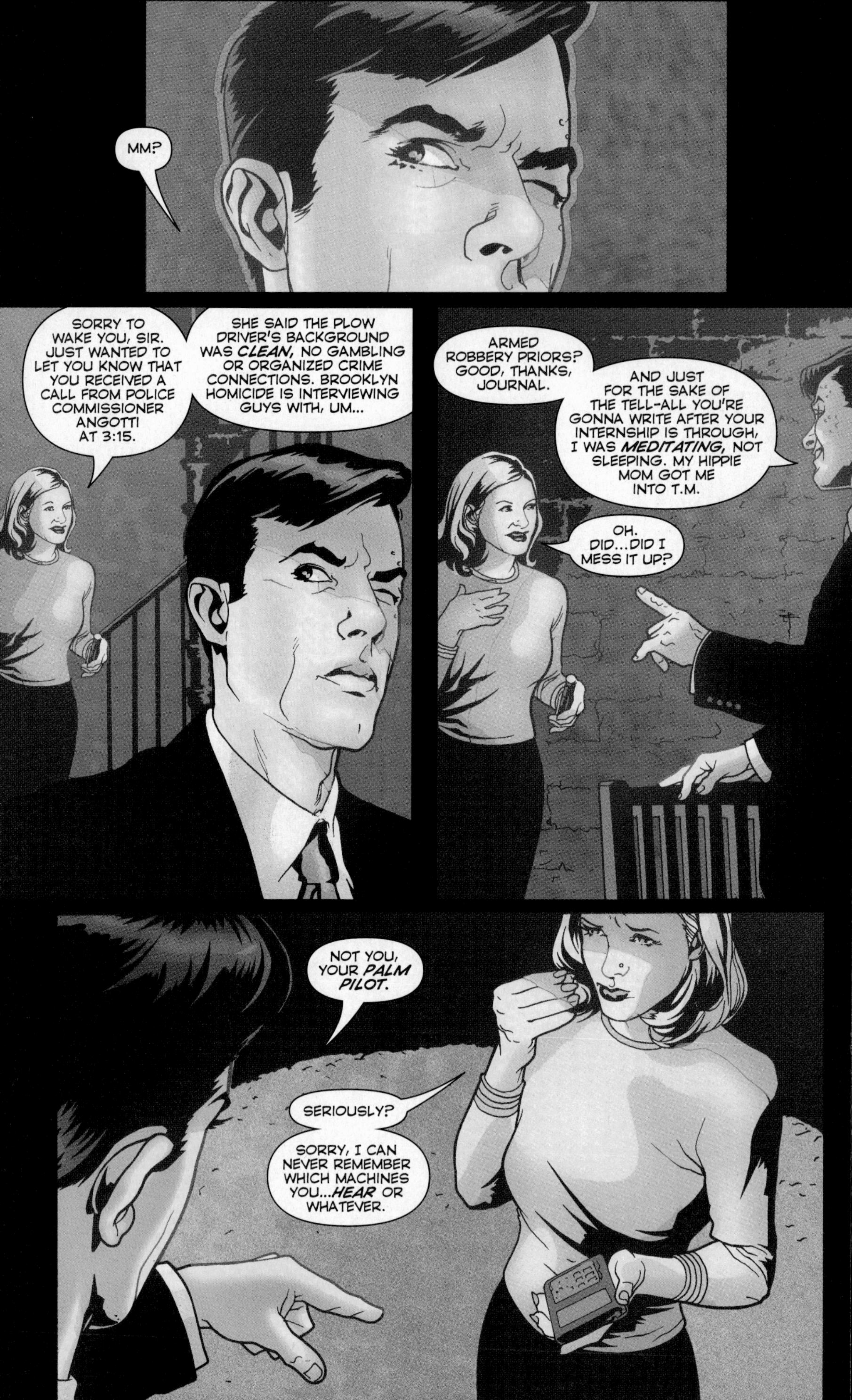
MM?
SORRY TO WAKE YOU, SIR. JUST WANTED TO LET YOU KNOW THAT YOU RECEIVED A CALL FROM POLICE COMMISSIONER ANGOTTI AT 3:15.
SHE SAID THE PLOW DRIVER'S BACKGROUND WAS *CLEAN,* NO GAMBLING OR ORGANIZED CRIME CONNECTIONS. BROOKLYN HOMICIDE IS INTERVIEWING GUYS WITH, UM...
ARMED ROBBERY PRIORS? GOOD, THANKS, JOURNAL.
AND JUST FOR THE SAKE OF THE TELL-ALL YOU'RE GONNA WRITE AFTER YOUR INTERNSHIP IS THROUGH, I WAS *MEDITATING,* NOT SLEEPING. MY HIPPIE MOM GOT ME INTO T.M.
OH. DID...DID I MESS IT UP?
NOT YOU, YOUR *PALM PILOT*.
SERIOUSLY?
SORRY, I CAN NEVER REMEMBER WHICH MACHINES YOU...*HEAR* OR WHATEVER.

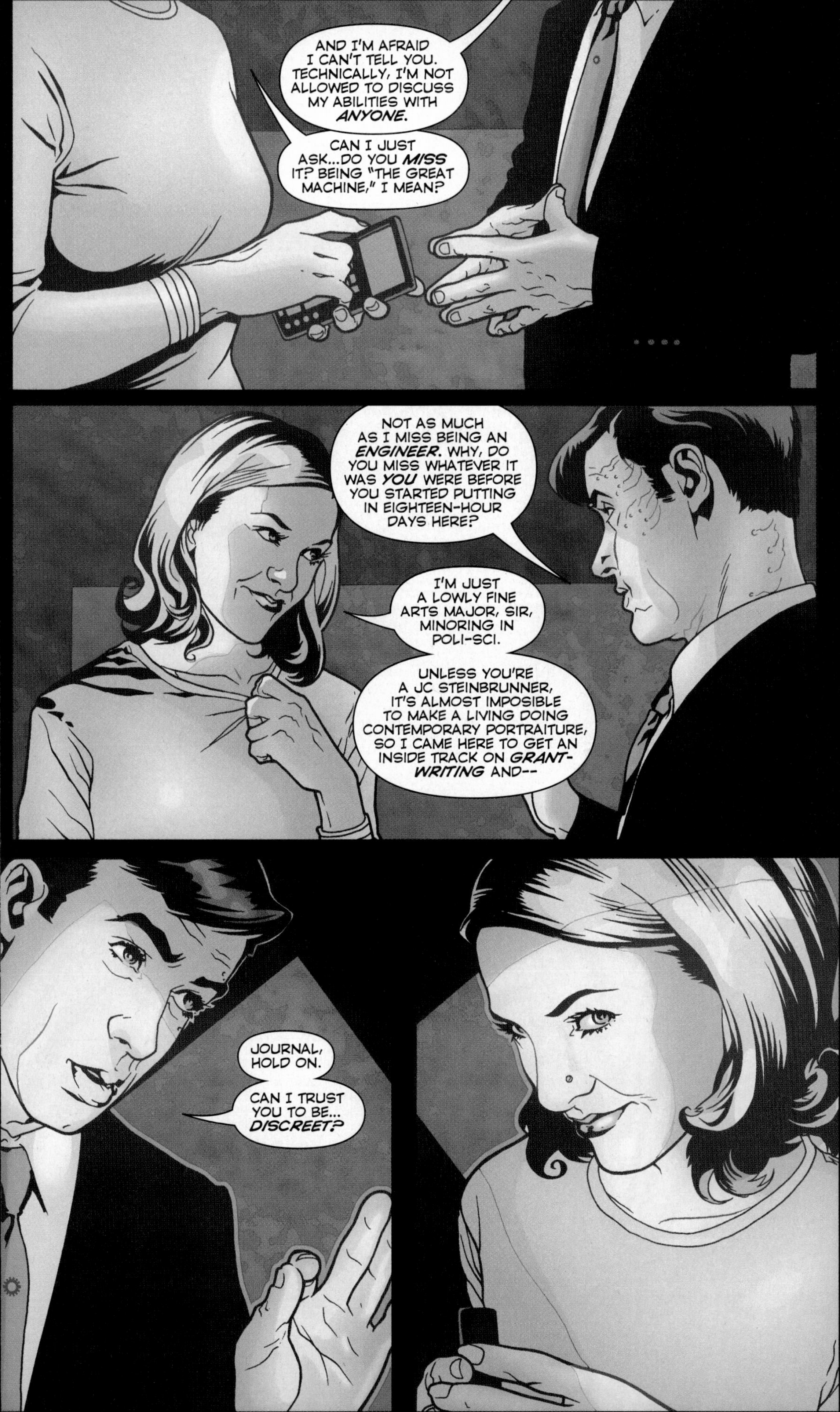
AND I'M AFRAID I CAN'T TELL YOU. TECHNICALLY, I'M NOT ALLOWED TO DISCUSS MY ABILITIES WITH ANYONE.
CAN I JUST ASK...DO YOU MISS IT? BEING "THE GREAT MACHINE," I MEAN?
NOT AS MUCH AS I MISS BEING AN ENGINEER. WHY, DO YOU MISS WHATEVER IT WAS YOU WERE BEFORE YOU STARTED PUTTING IN EIGHTEEN-HOUR DAYS HERE?
I'M JUST A LOWLY FINE ARTS MAJOR, SIR, MINORING IN POLI-SCI.
UNLESS YOU'RE A JC STEINBRUNNER, IT'S ALMOST IMPOSIBLE TO MAKE A LIVING DOING CONTEMPORARY PORTRAITURE, SO I CAME HERE TO GET AN INSIDE TRACK ON GRANT-WRITING AND--
JOURNAL, HOLD ON.
CAN I TRUST YOU TO BE... DISCREET?

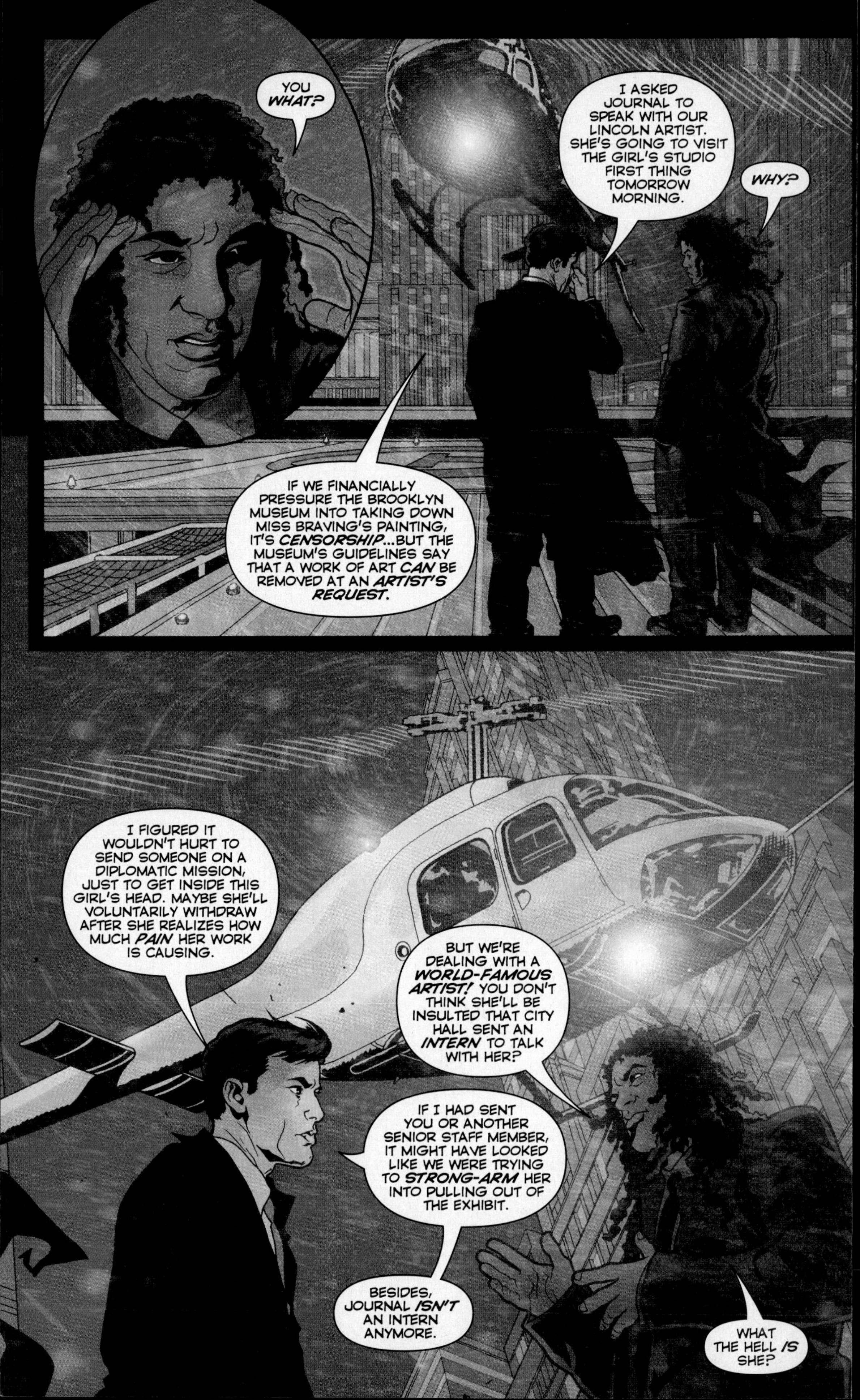
YOU *WHAT?*
I ASKED JOURNAL TO SPEAK WITH OUR LINCOLN ARTIST. SHE'S GOING TO VISIT THE GIRL'S STUDIO FIRST THING TOMORROW MORNING.
WHY?
IF WE FINANCIALLY PRESSURE THE BROOKLYN MUSEUM INTO TAKING DOWN MISS BRAVING'S PAINTING, IT'S *CENSORSHIP*...BUT THE MUSEUM'S GUIDELINES SAY THAT A WORK OF ART *CAN* BE REMOVED AT AN *ARTIST'S REQUEST*.
I FIGURED IT WOULDN'T HURT TO SEND SOMEONE ON A DIPLOMATIC MISSION, JUST TO GET INSIDE THIS GIRL'S HEAD. MAYBE SHE'LL VOLUNTARILY WITHDRAW AFTER SHE REALIZES HOW MUCH *PAIN* HER WORK IS CAUSING.
BUT WE'RE DEALING WITH A *WORLD-FAMOUS ARTIST!* YOU DON'T THINK SHE'LL BE INSULTED THAT CITY HALL SENT AN *INTERN* TO TALK WITH HER?
IF I HAD SENT YOU OR ANOTHER SENIOR STAFF MEMBER, IT MIGHT HAVE LOOKED LIKE WE WERE TRYING TO *STRONG-ARM* HER INTO PULLING OUT OF THE EXHIBIT.
BESIDES, JOURNAL *ISN'T* AN INTERN ANYMORE.
WHAT THE HELL *IS* SHE?

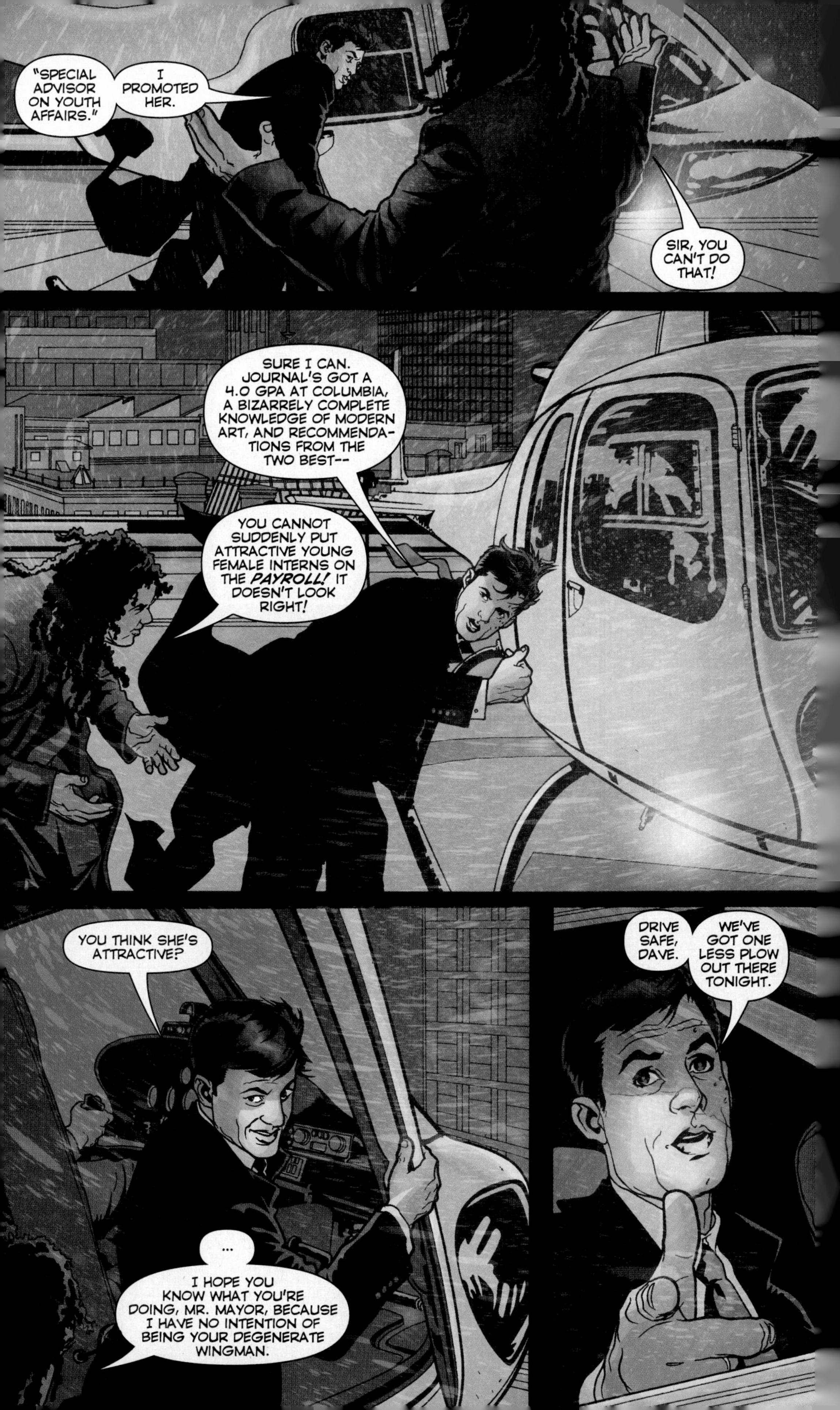
"SPECIAL ADVISOR ON YOUTH AFFAIRS."
I PROMOTED HER.
SIR, YOU CAN'T DO THAT!
SURE I CAN. JOURNAL'S GOT A 4.0 GPA AT COLUMBIA, A BIZARRELY COMPLETE KNOWLEDGE OF MODERN ART, AND RECOMMENDATIONS FROM THE TWO BEST--
YOU CANNOT SUDDENLY PUT ATTRACTIVE YOUNG FEMALE INTERNS ON THE *PAYROLL!* IT DOESN'T LOOK RIGHT!
YOU THINK SHE'S ATTRACTIVE?
...
I HOPE YOU KNOW WHAT YOU'RE DOING, MR. MAYOR, BECAUSE I HAVE NO INTENTION OF BEING YOUR DEGENERATE WINGMAN.
DRIVE SAFE, DAVE.
WE'VE GOT ONE LESS PLOW OUT THERE TONIGHT.

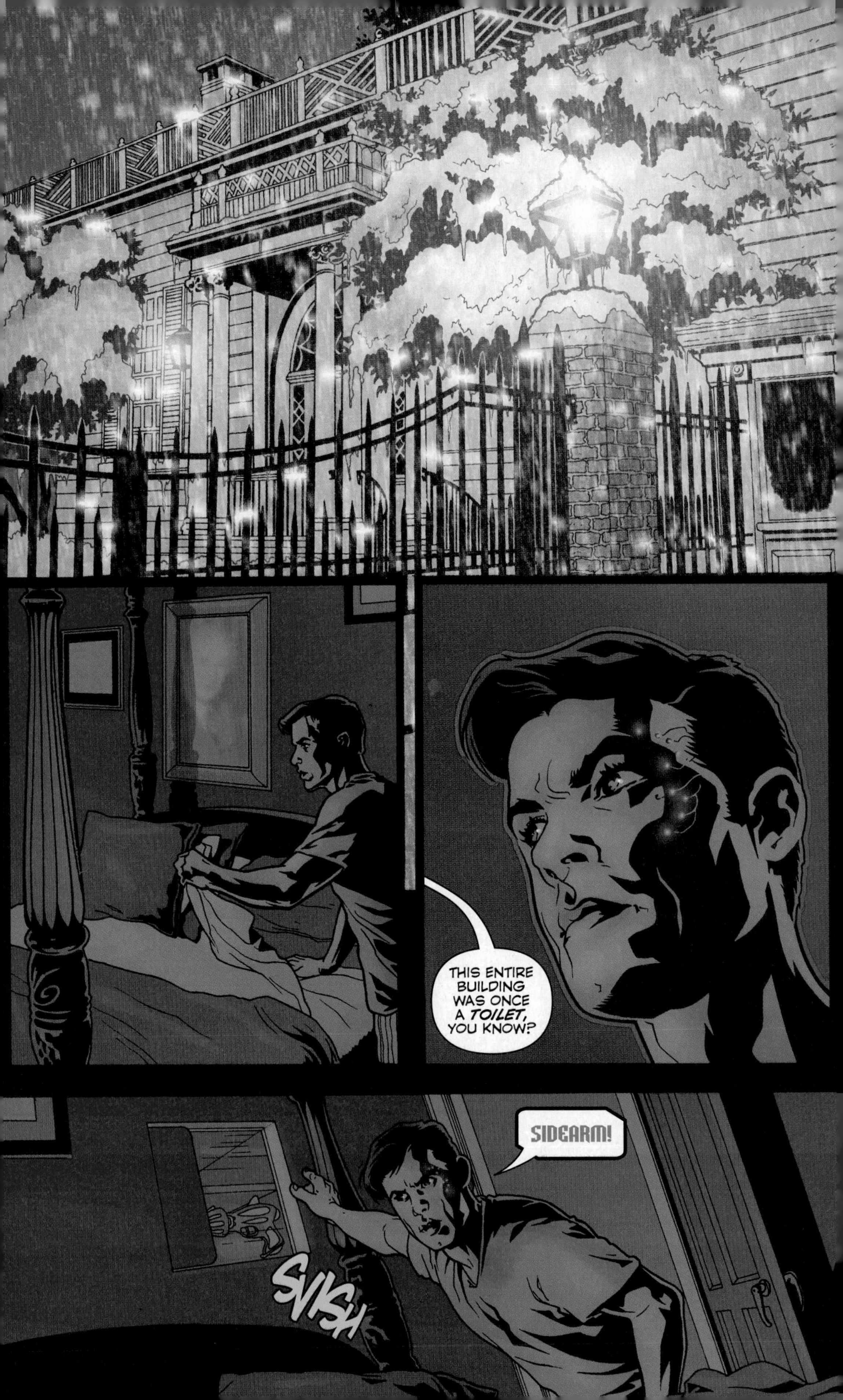
THIS ENTIRE BUILDING WAS ONCE A *TOILET*, YOU KNOW?
SIDEARM!
SVISH

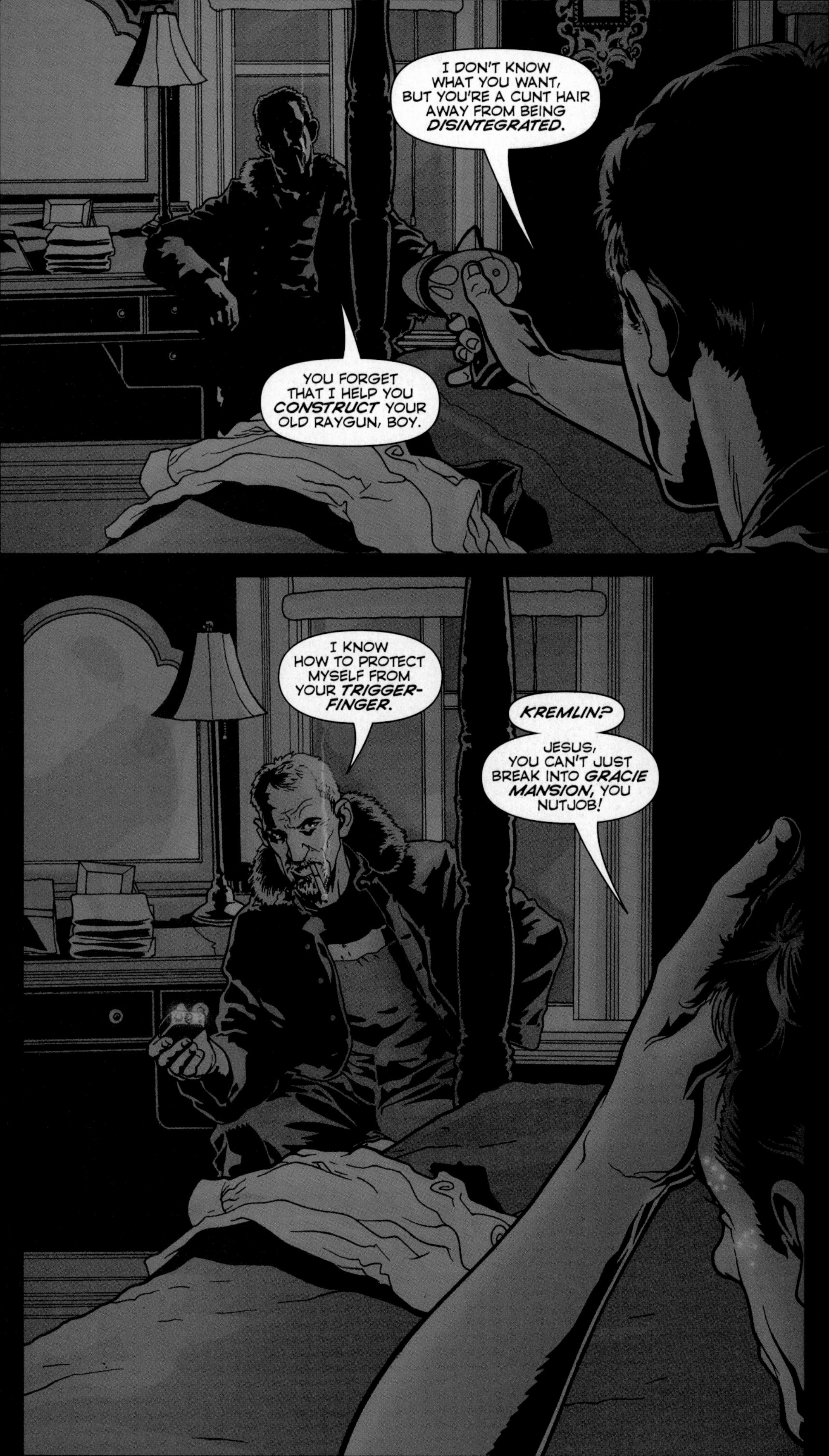

I DON'T KNOW WHAT YOU WANT, BUT YOU'RE A CUNT HAIR AWAY FROM BEING *DISINTEGRATED*.
YOU FORGET THAT I HELP YOU *CONSTRUCT* YOUR OLD RAYGUN, BOY.
I KNOW HOW TO PROTECT MYSELF FROM YOUR *TRIGGER-FINGER*.
KREMLIN?
JESUS, YOU CAN'T JUST BREAK INTO *GRACIE MANSION*, YOU NUTJOB!

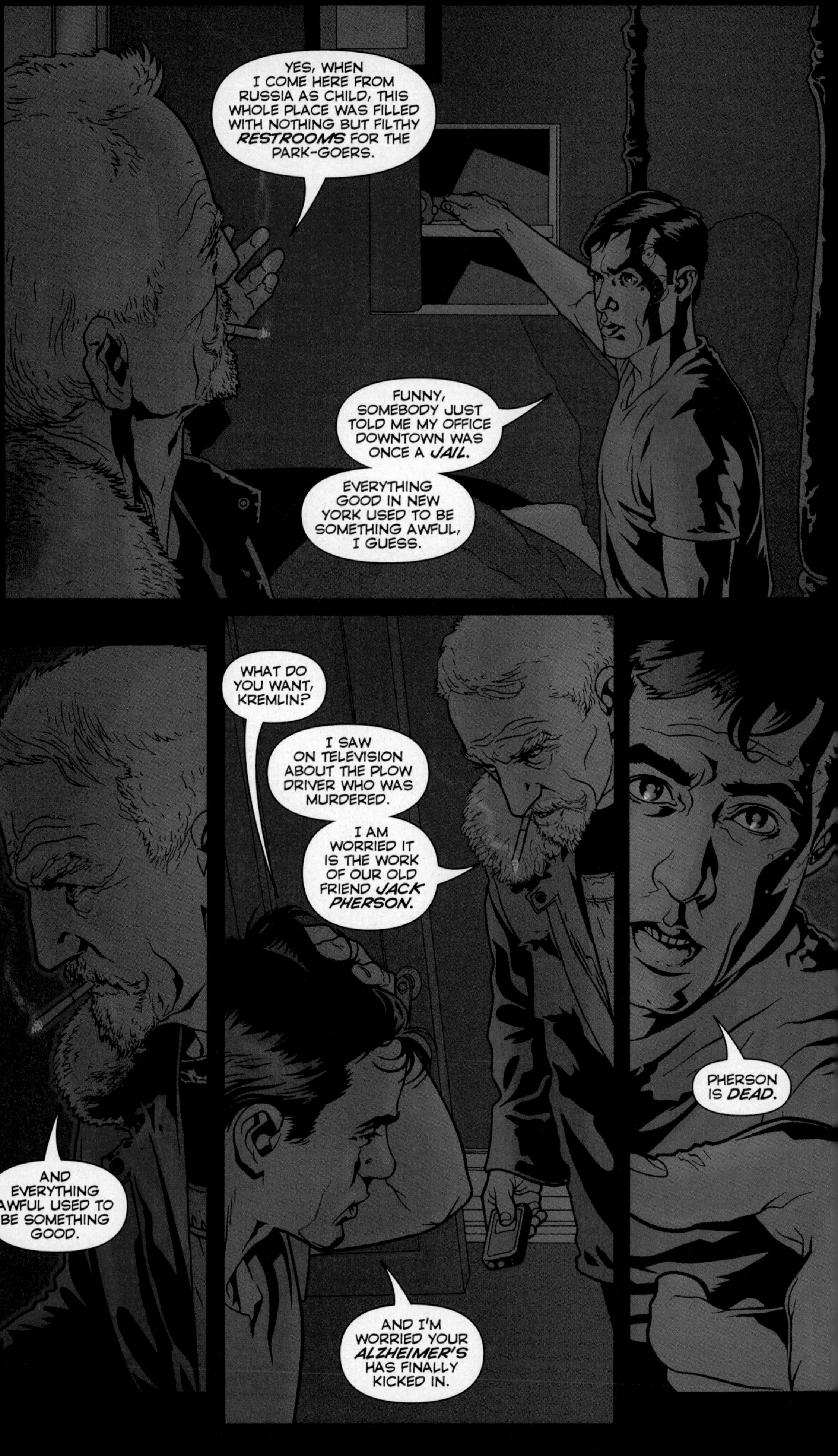
YES, WHEN I COME HERE FROM RUSSIA AS CHILD, THIS WHOLE PLACE WAS FILLED WITH NOTHING BUT FILTHY RESTROOMS FOR THE PARK-GOERS.
FUNNY, SOMEBODY JUST TOLD ME MY OFFICE DOWNTOWN WAS ONCE A JAIL.
EVERYTHING GOOD IN NEW YORK USED TO BE SOMETHING AWFUL, I GUESS.
AND EVERYTHING AWFUL USED TO BE SOMETHING GOOD.
WHAT DO YOU WANT, KREMLIN?
I SAW ON TELEVISION ABOUT THE PLOW DRIVER WHO WAS MURDERED.
I AM WORRIED IT IS THE WORK OF OUR OLD FRIEND JACK PHERSON.
AND I'M WORRIED YOUR ALZHEIMER'S HAS FINALLY KICKED IN.
PHERSON IS DEAD.

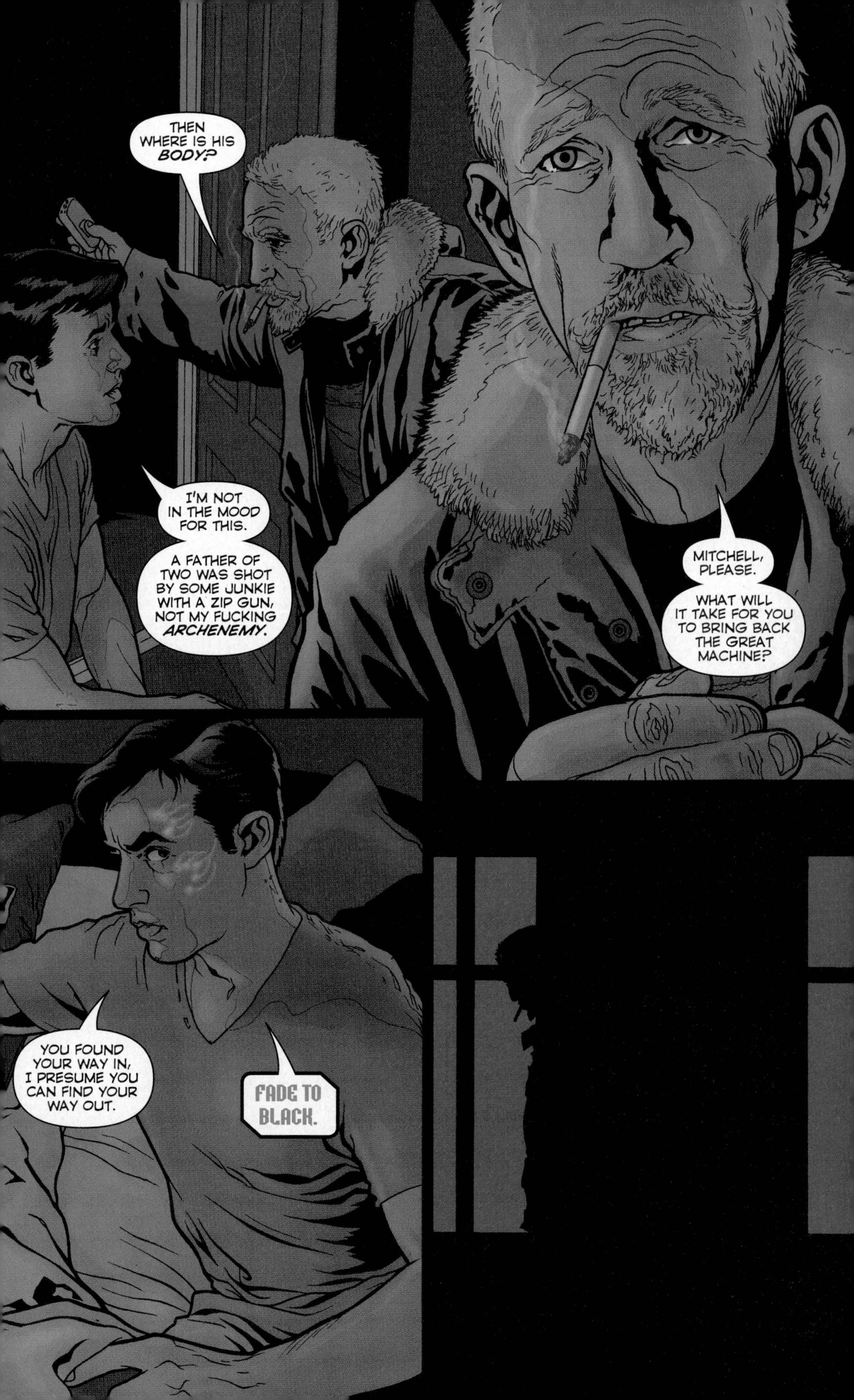
THEN WHERE IS HIS *BODY?*
I'M NOT IN THE MOOD FOR THIS.
A FATHER OF TWO WAS SHOT BY SOME JUNKIE WITH A ZIP GUN, NOT MY FUCKING *ARCHENEMY*.
MITCHELL, PLEASE.
WHAT WILL IT TAKE FOR YOU TO BRING BACK THE GREAT MACHINE?
YOU FOUND YOUR WAY IN, I PRESUME YOU CAN FIND YOUR WAY OUT.
FADE TO BLACK.

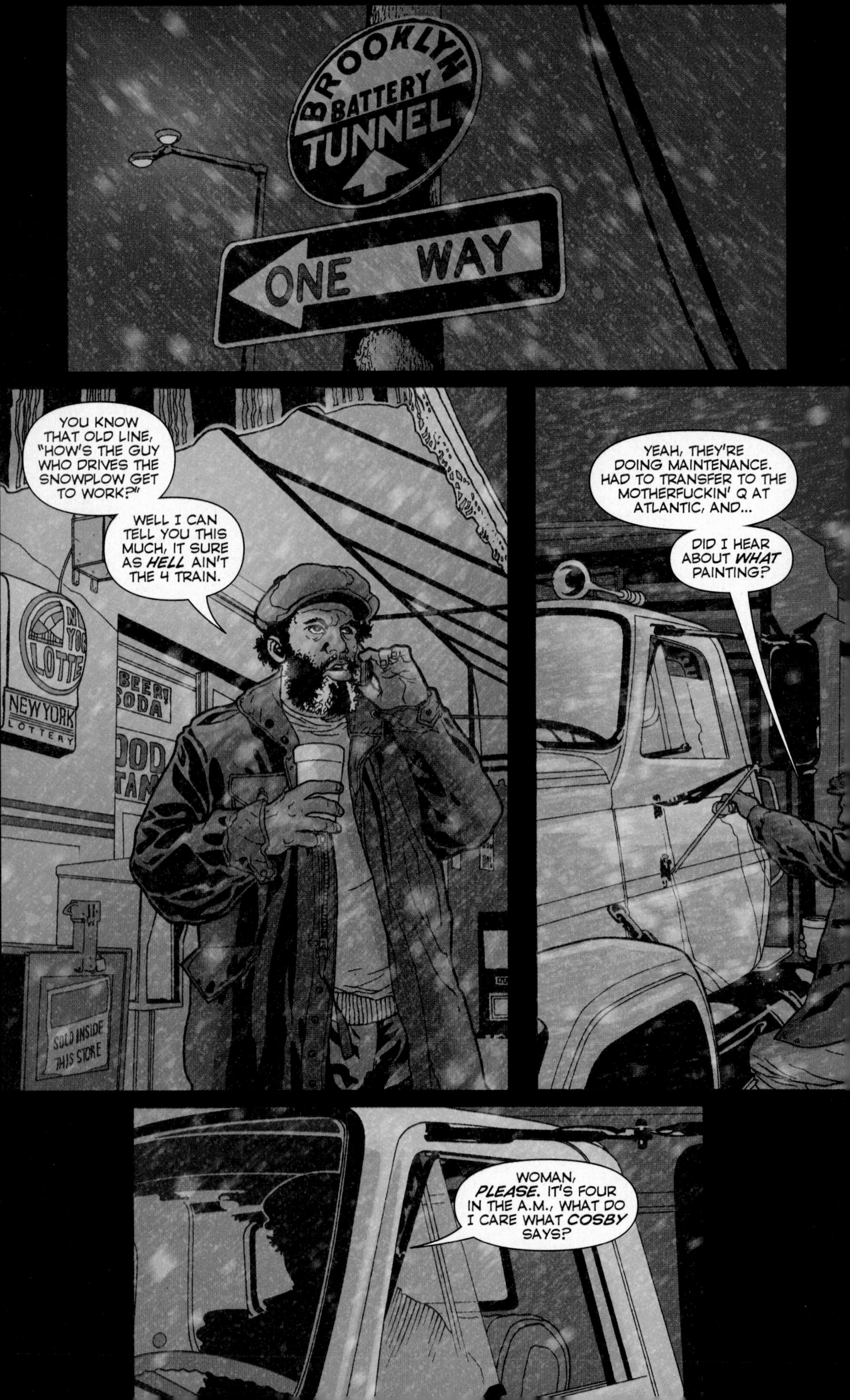
BROOKLYN BATTERY TUNNEL
ONE WAY
YOU KNOW THAT OLD LINE, "HOW'S THE GUY WHO DRIVES THE SNOWPLOW GET TO WORK?"
WELL I CAN TELL YOU THIS MUCH, IT SURE AS *HELL* AIN'T THE 4 TRAIN.
NEW YORK LOTTERY
BEER! SODA
SOLD INSIDE THIS STORE
YEAH, THEY'RE DOING MAINTENANCE. HAD TO TRANSFER TO THE MOTHERFUCKIN' Q AT ATLANTIC, AND...
DID I HEAR ABOUT *WHAT* PAINTING?
WOMAN, *PLEASE*. IT'S FOUR IN THE A.M., WHAT DO I CARE WHAT *COSBY* SAYS?

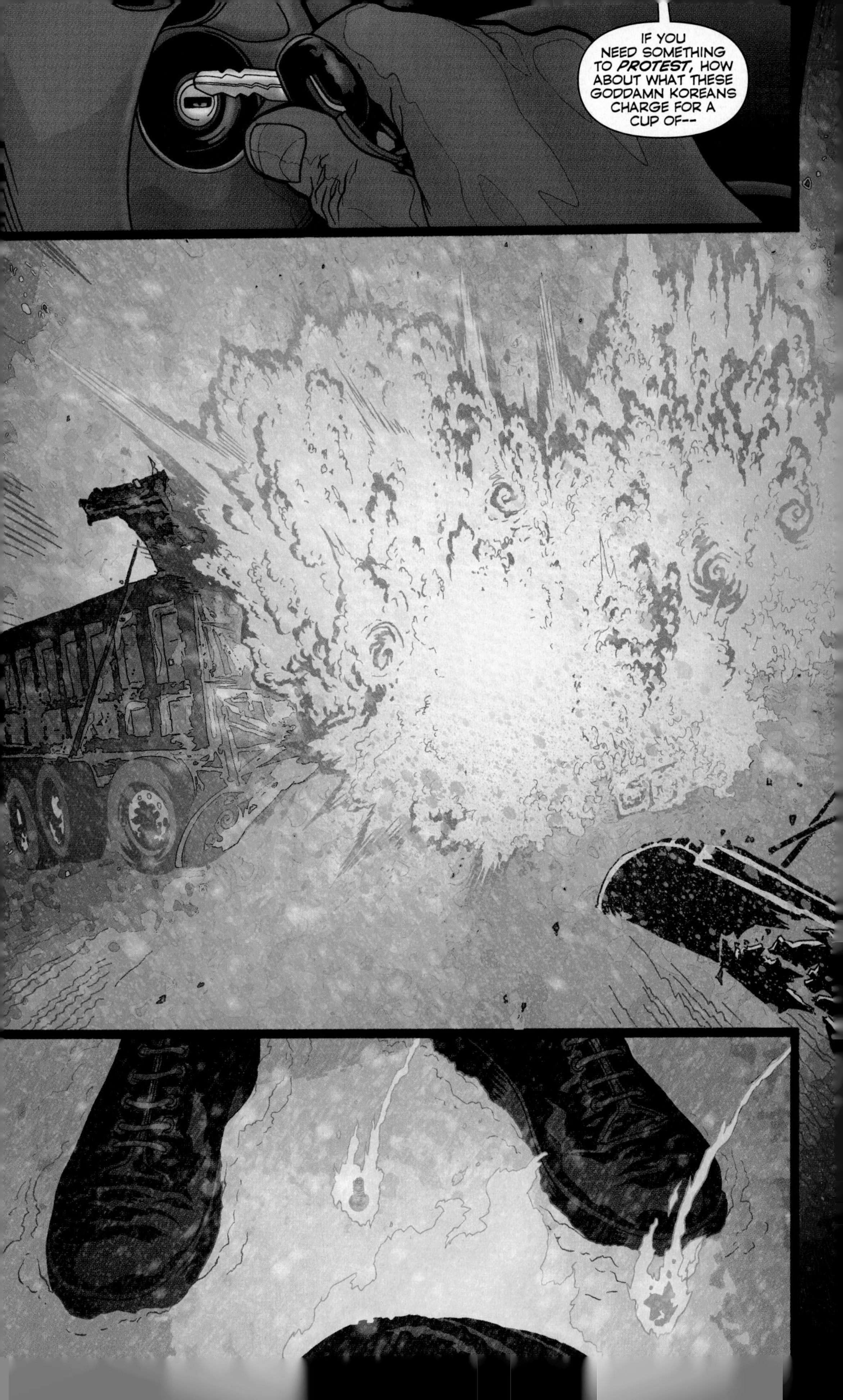
IF YOU NEED SOMETHING TO PROTEST, HOW ABOUT WHAT THESE GODDAMN KOREANS CHARGE FOR A CUP OF--

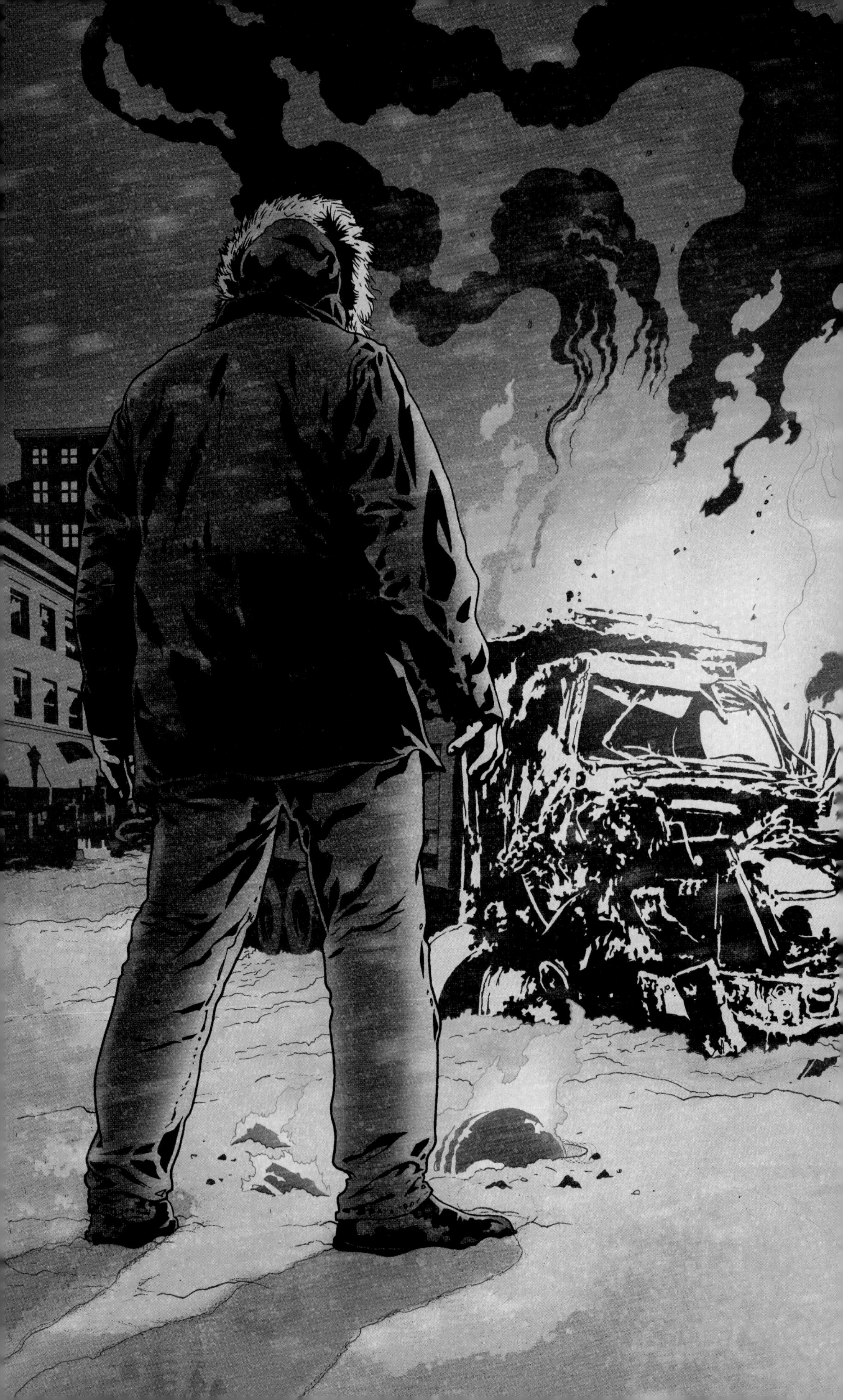

CHAPTER 4

Part 3

State of Emergency

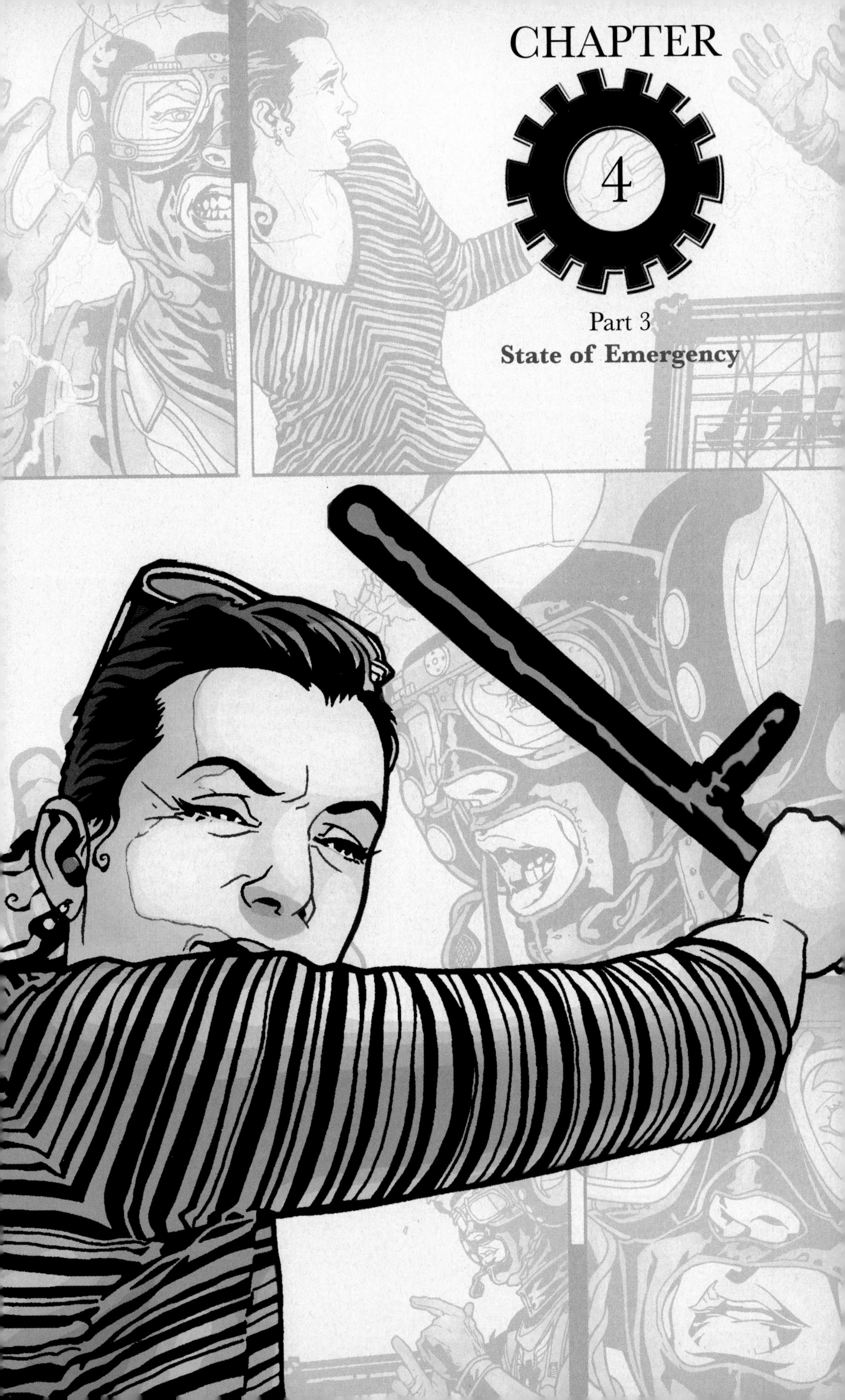

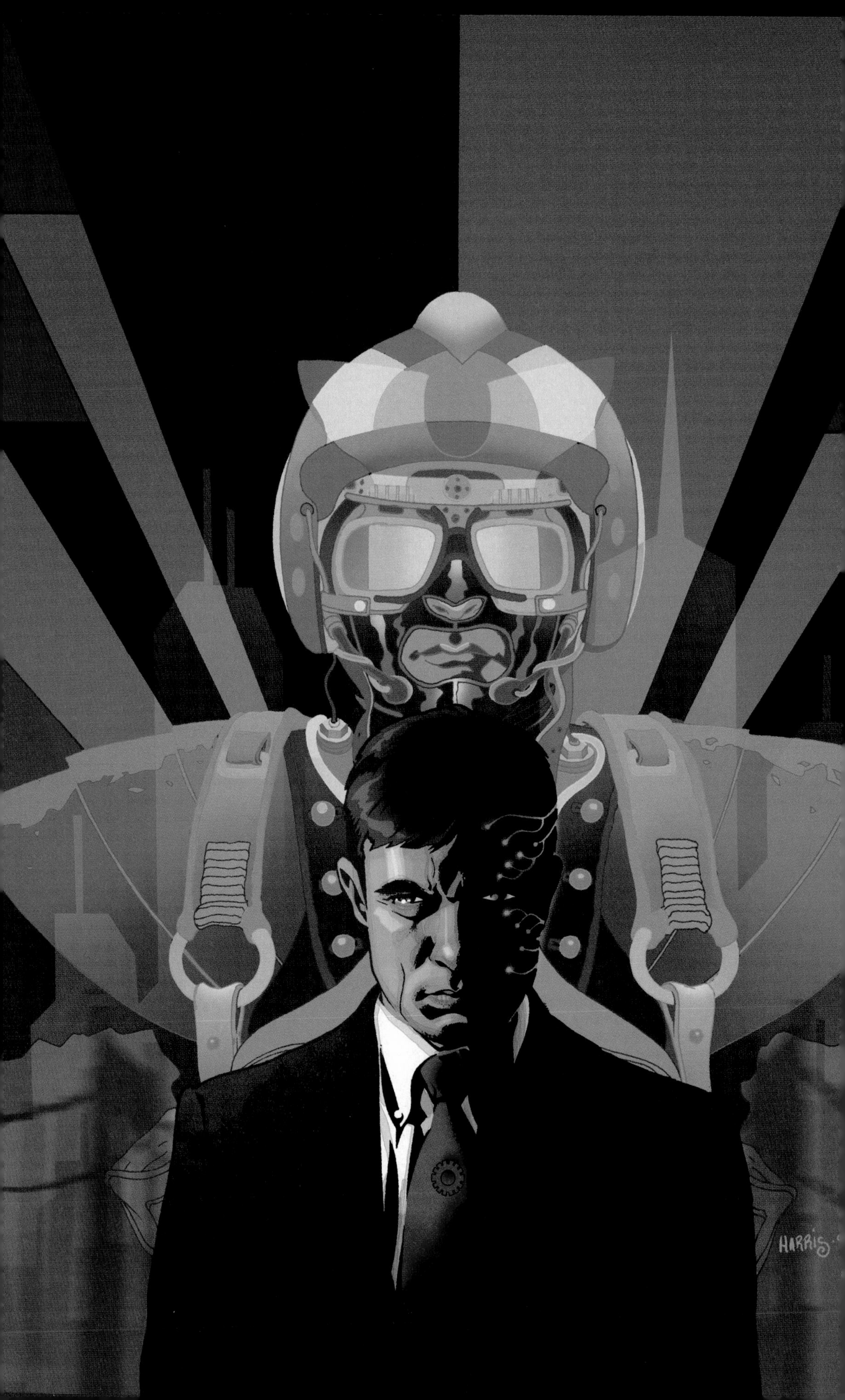
HARRIS

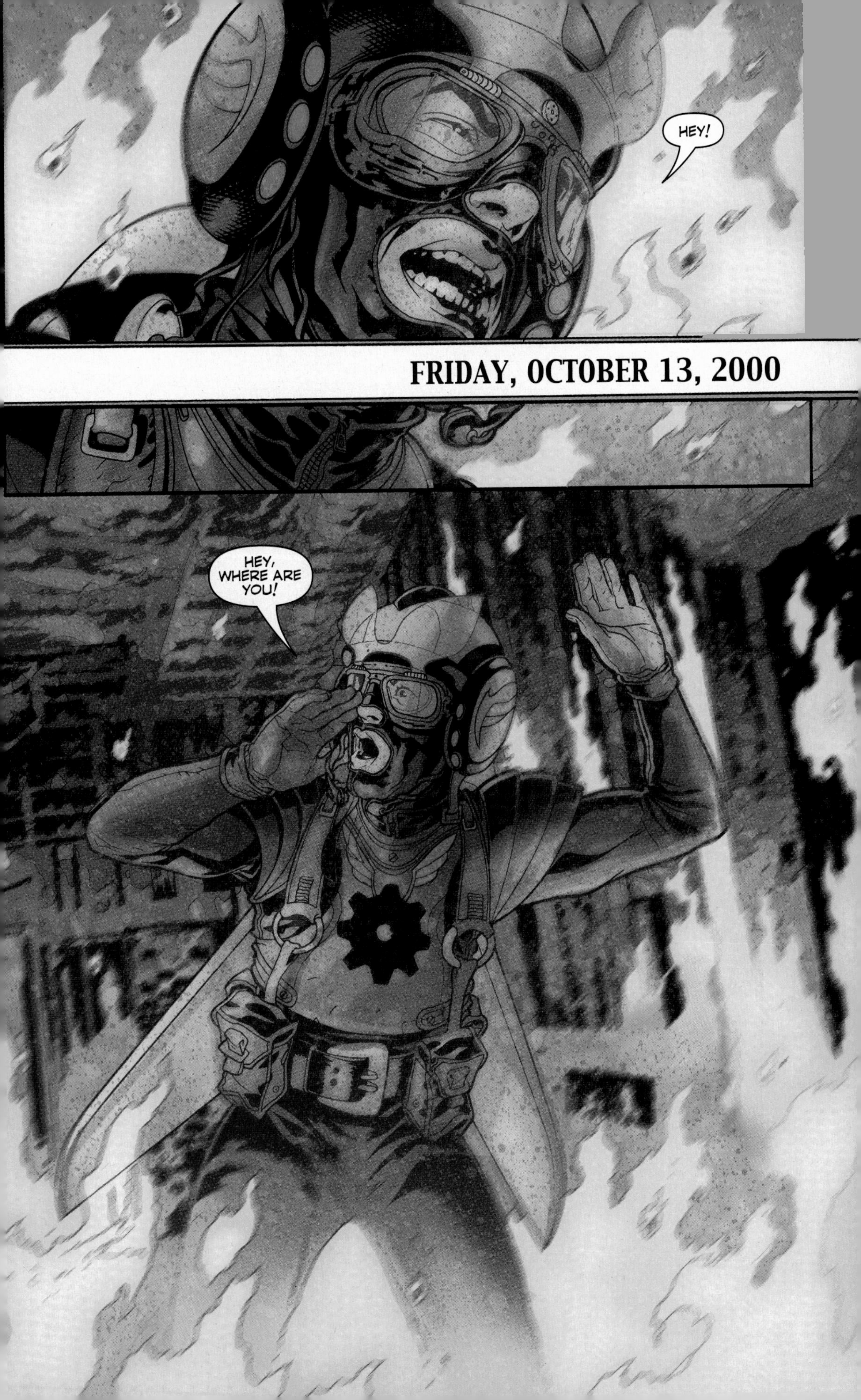
HEY!
FRIDAY, OCTOBER 13, 2000
HEY, WHERE ARE YOU!

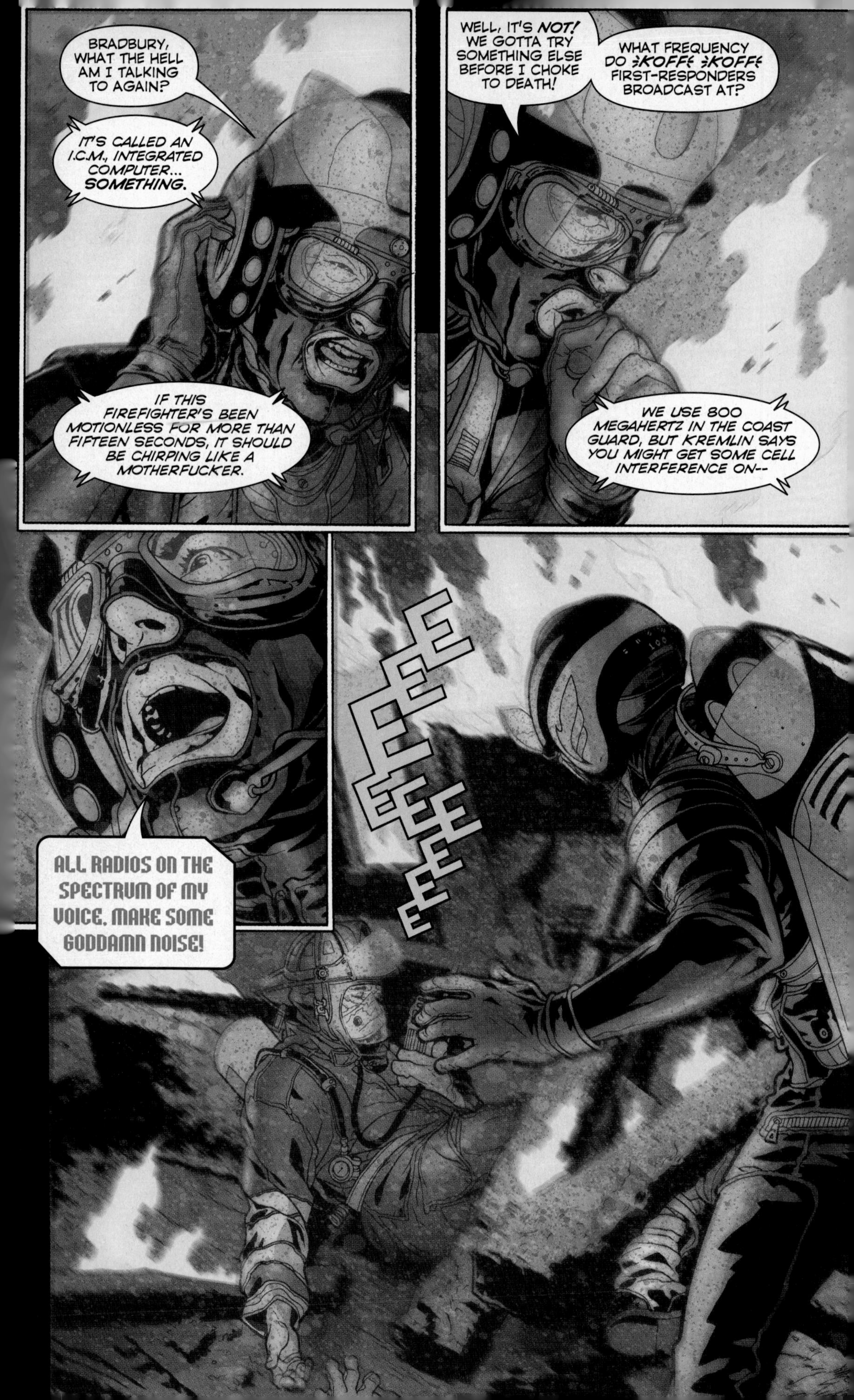
BRADBURY, WHAT THE HELL AM I TALKING TO AGAIN?
IT'S CALLED AN I.C.M., INTEGRATED COMPUTER... SOMETHING.
IF THIS FIREFIGHTER'S BEEN MOTIONLESS FOR MORE THAN FIFTEEN SECONDS, IT SHOULD BE CHIRPING LIKE A MOTHERFUCKER.
WELL, IT'S NOT! WE GOTTA TRY SOMETHING ELSE BEFORE I CHOKE TO DEATH!
WHAT FREQUENCY DO *KOFF* *KOFF* FIRST-RESPONDERS BROADCAST AT?
WE USE 800 MEGAHERTZ IN THE COAST GUARD, BUT KREMLIN SAYS YOU MIGHT GET SOME CELL INTERFERENCE ON--
ALL RADIOS ON THE SPECTRUM OF MY VOICE. MAKE SOME GODDAMN NOISE!
EEEEEEEEEEE

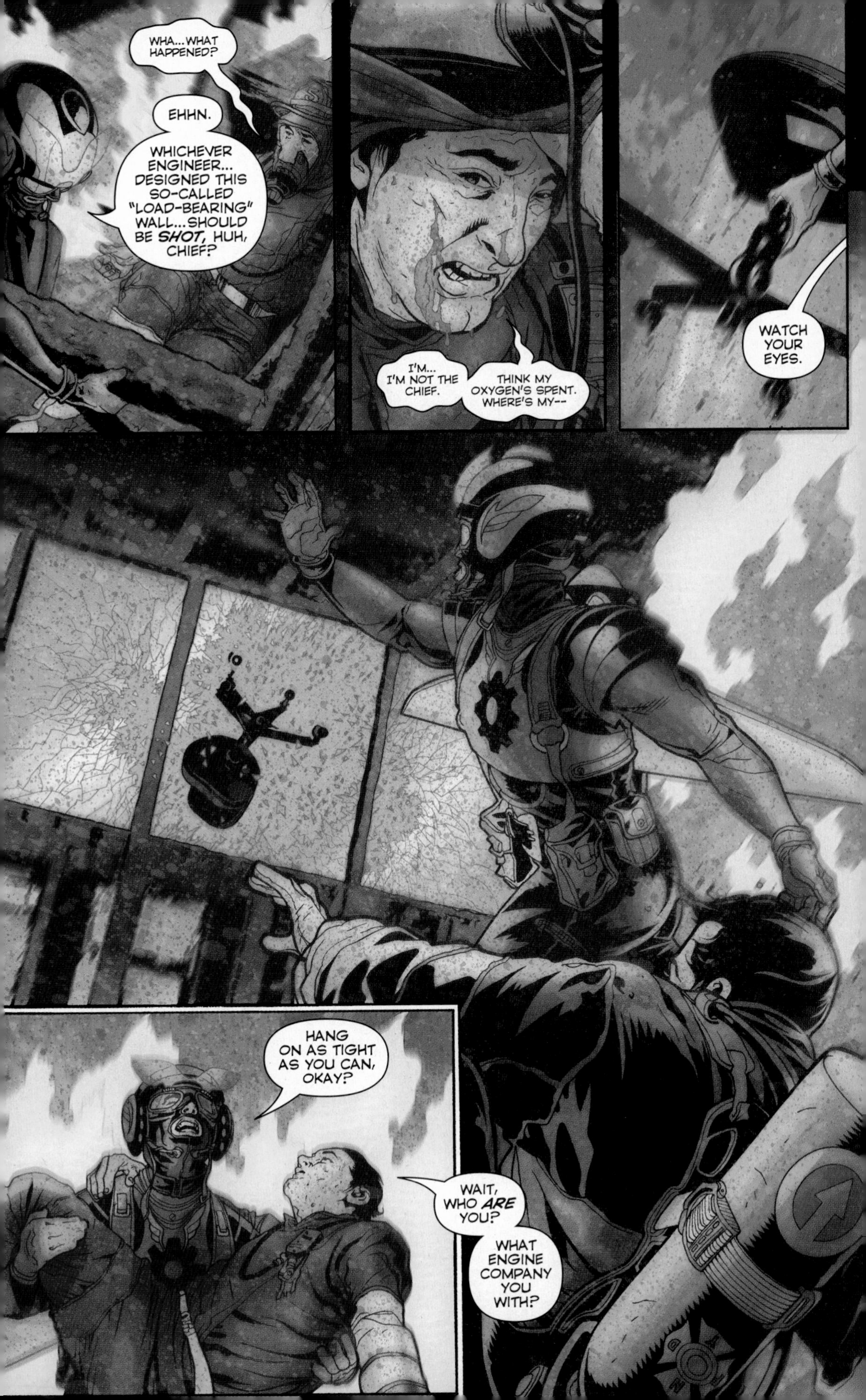
WHA...WHAT HAPPENED?
EHHN.
WHICHEVER ENGINEER... DESIGNED THIS SO-CALLED "LOAD-BEARING" WALL...SHOULD BE *SHOT,* HUH, CHIEF?
I'M... I'M NOT THE CHIEF.
THINK MY OXYGEN'S SPENT. WHERE'S MY--
WATCH YOUR EYES.
HANG ON AS TIGHT AS YOU CAN, OKAY?
WAIT, WHO *ARE* YOU?
WHAT ENGINE COMPANY YOU WITH?

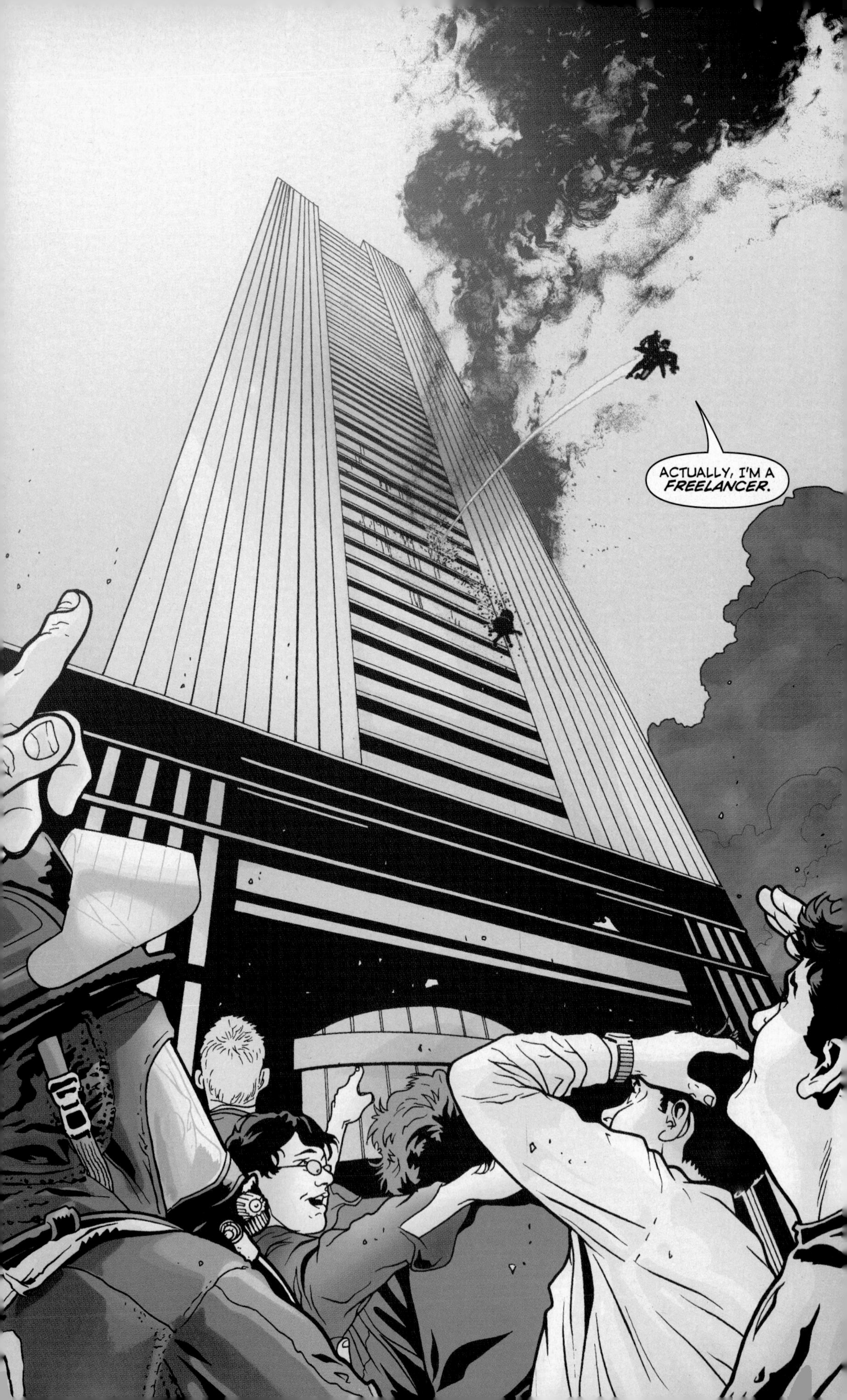
ACTUALLY, I'M A FREELANCER.

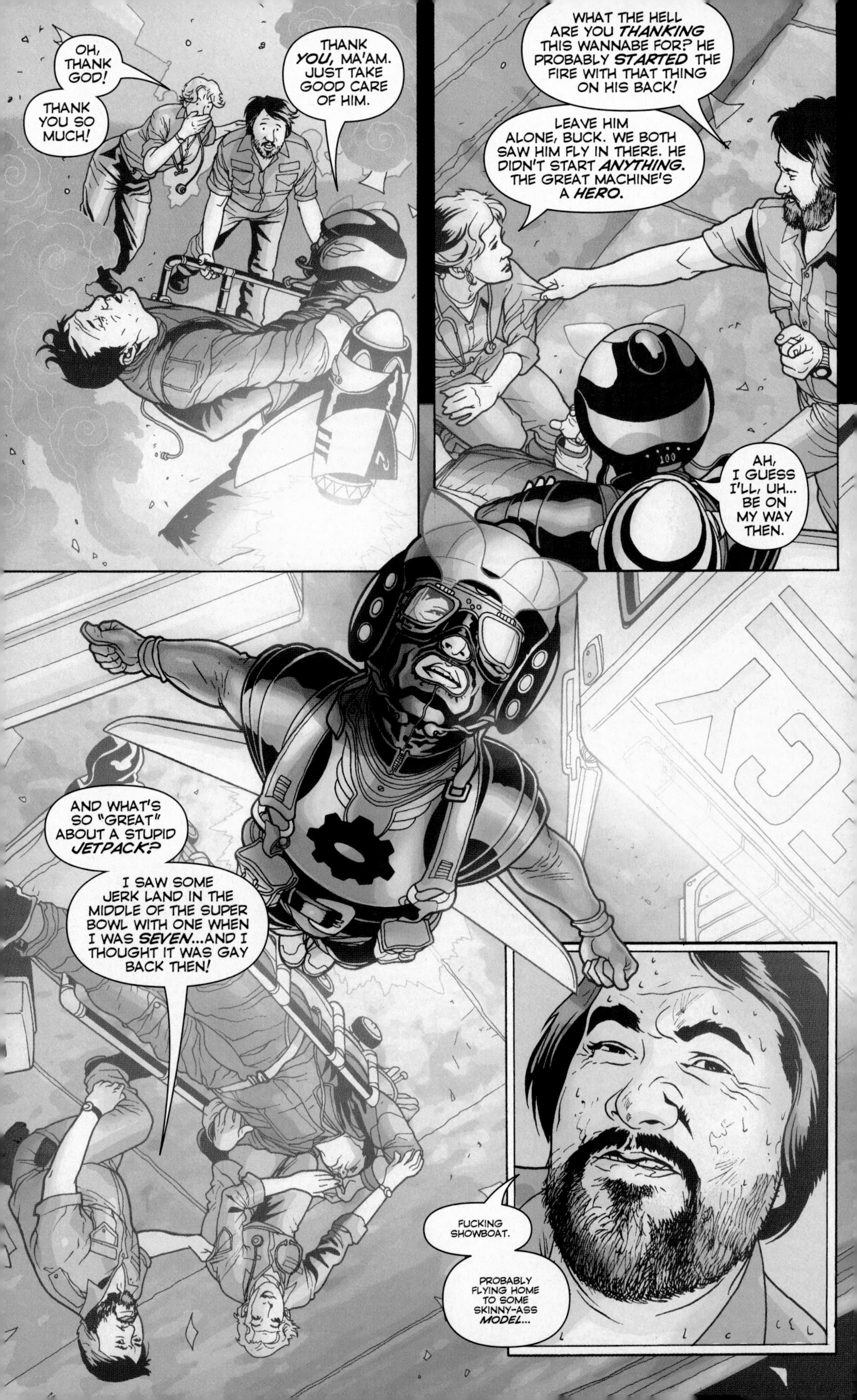

OH, THANK GOD!
THANK YOU SO MUCH!
THANK *YOU*, MA'AM. JUST TAKE GOOD CARE OF HIM.
WHAT THE HELL ARE YOU *THANKING* THIS WANNABE FOR? HE PROBABLY *STARTED* THE FIRE WITH THAT THING ON HIS BACK!
LEAVE HIM ALONE, BUCK. WE BOTH SAW HIM FLY IN THERE. HE DIDN'T START *ANYTHING*. THE GREAT MACHINE'S A *HERO*.
AH, I GUESS I'LL, UH... BE ON MY WAY THEN.
AND WHAT'S SO "GREAT" ABOUT A STUPID *JETPACK?*
I SAW SOME JERK LAND IN THE MIDDLE OF THE SUPER BOWL WITH ONE WHEN I WAS *SEVEN*...AND I THOUGHT IT WAS GAY BACK THEN!
FUCKING SHOWBOAT.
PROBABLY FLYING HOME TO SOME SKINNY-ASS *MODEL*...

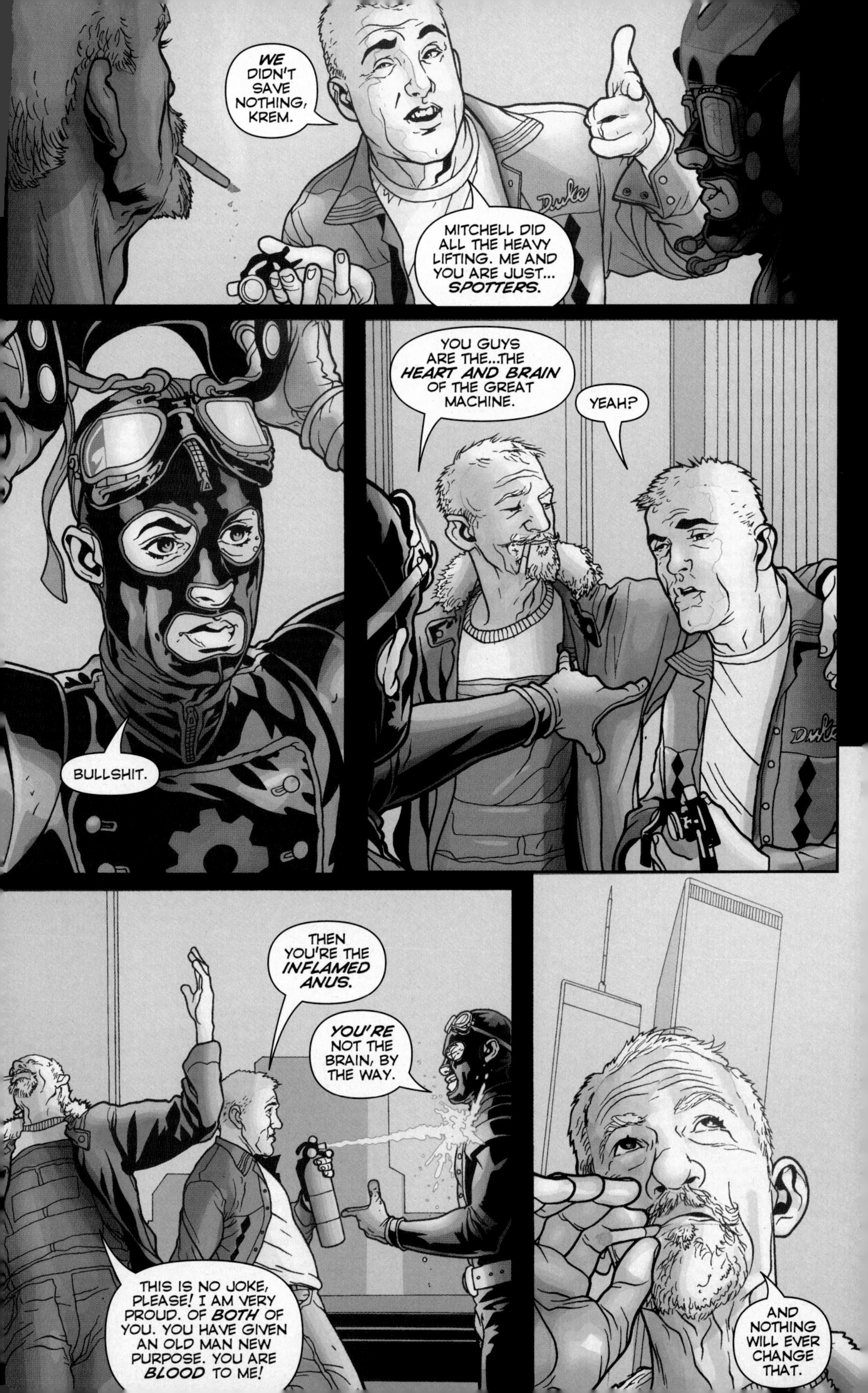

WE DIDN'T SAVE NOTHING, KREM.
MITCHELL DID ALL THE HEAVY LIFTING. ME AND YOU ARE JUST... *SPOTTERS*.
BULLSHIT.
YOU GUYS ARE THE...THE *HEART AND BRAIN* OF THE GREAT MACHINE.
YEAH?
THEN YOU'RE THE *INFLAMED ANUS*.
YOU'RE NOT THE BRAIN, BY THE WAY.
THIS IS NO JOKE, PLEASE! I AM VERY PROUD. OF *BOTH* OF YOU. YOU HAVE GIVEN AN OLD MAN NEW PURPOSE. YOU ARE *BLOOD* TO ME!
AND NOTHING WILL EVER CHANGE THAT.

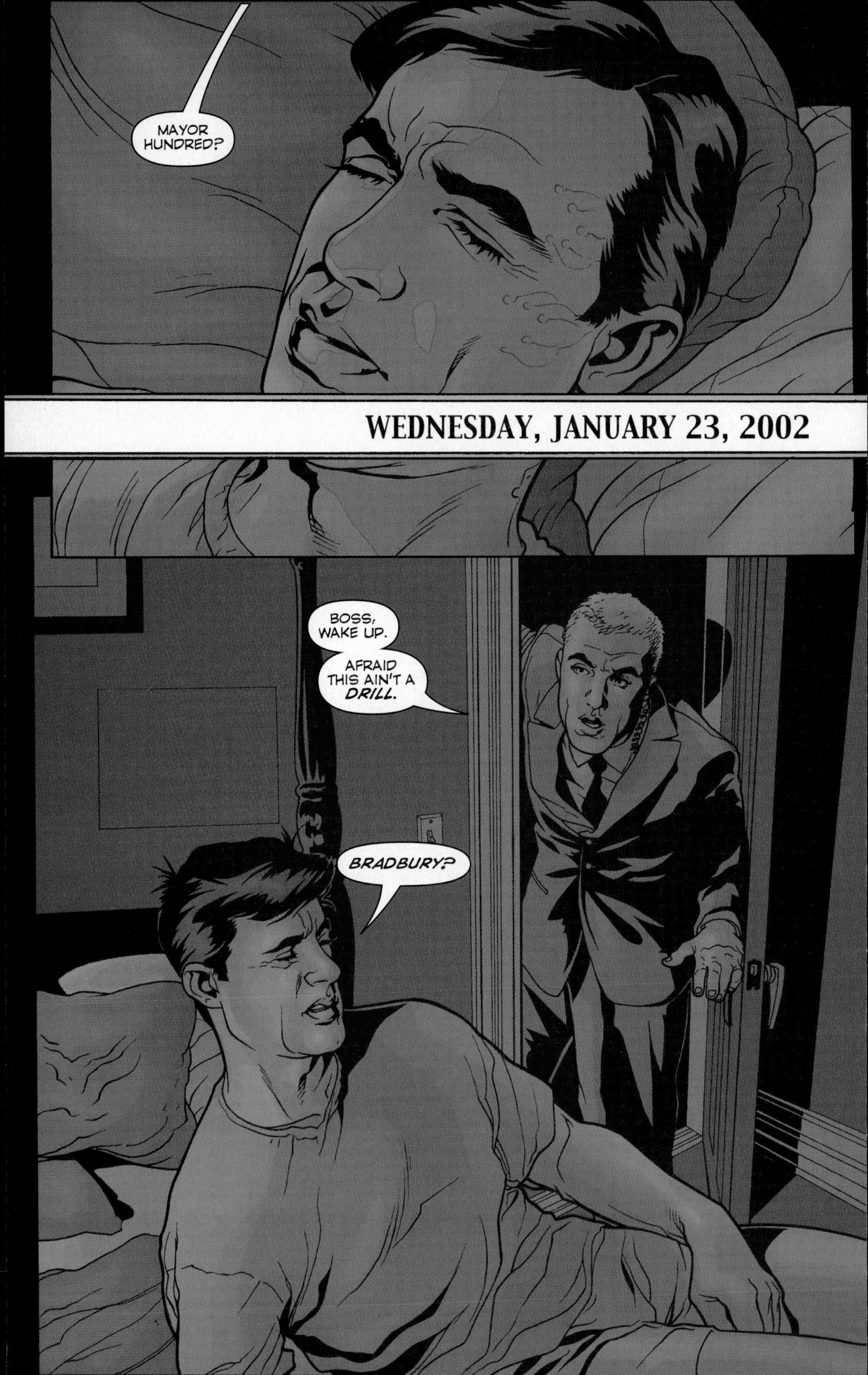
MAYOR HUNDRED?
WEDNESDAY, JANUARY 23, 2002
BOSS, WAKE UP.
AFRAID THIS AIN'T A DRILL.
BRADBURY?

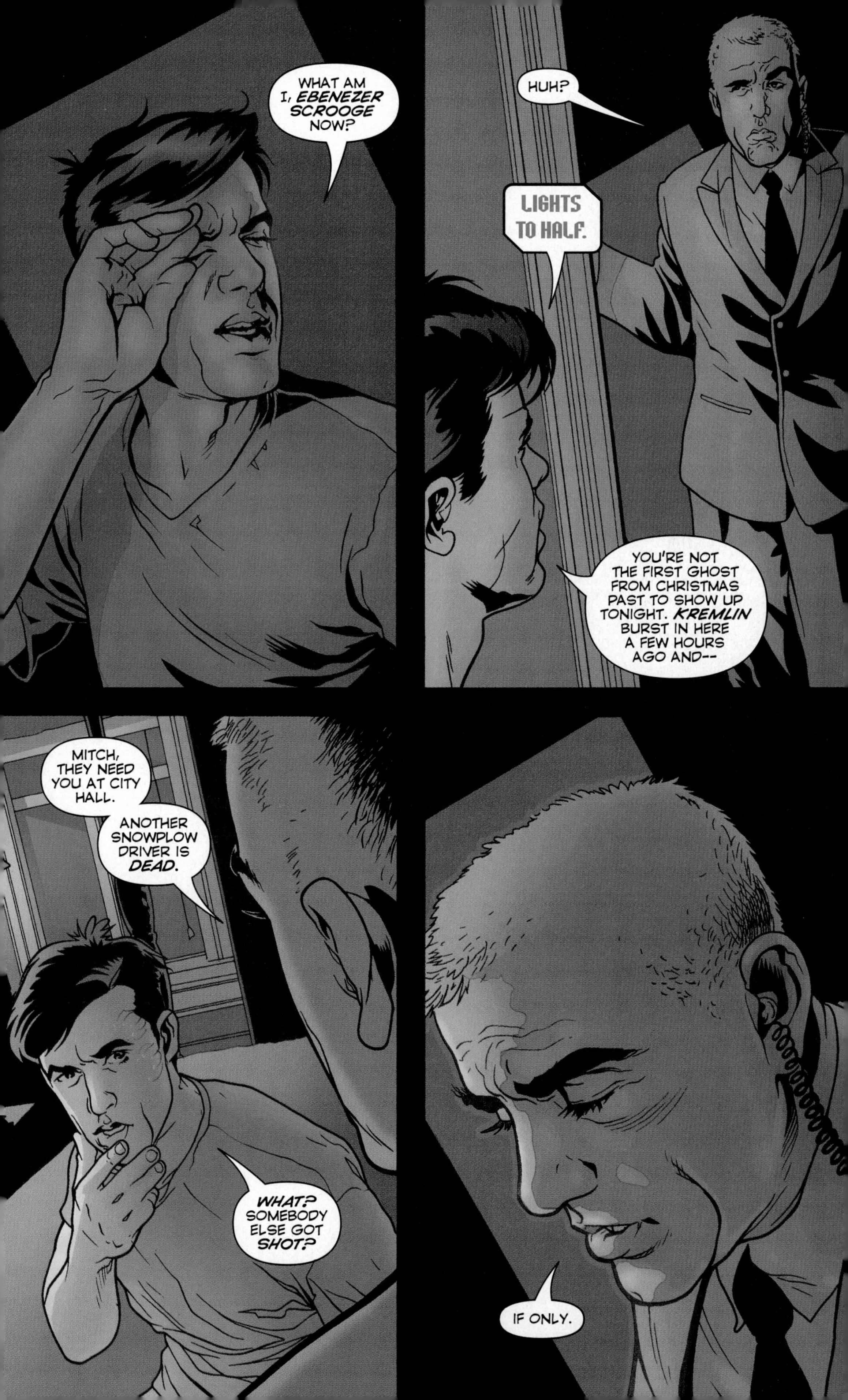
WHAT AM I, EBENEZER SCROOGE NOW?
HUH?
LIGHTS TO HALF.
YOU'RE NOT THE FIRST GHOST FROM CHRISTMAS PAST TO SHOW UP TONIGHT. KREMLIN BURST IN HERE A FEW HOURS AGO AND--
MITCH, THEY NEED YOU AT CITY HALL.
ANOTHER SNOWPLOW DRIVER IS DEAD.
WHAT? SOMEBODY ELSE GOT SHOT?
IF ONLY.

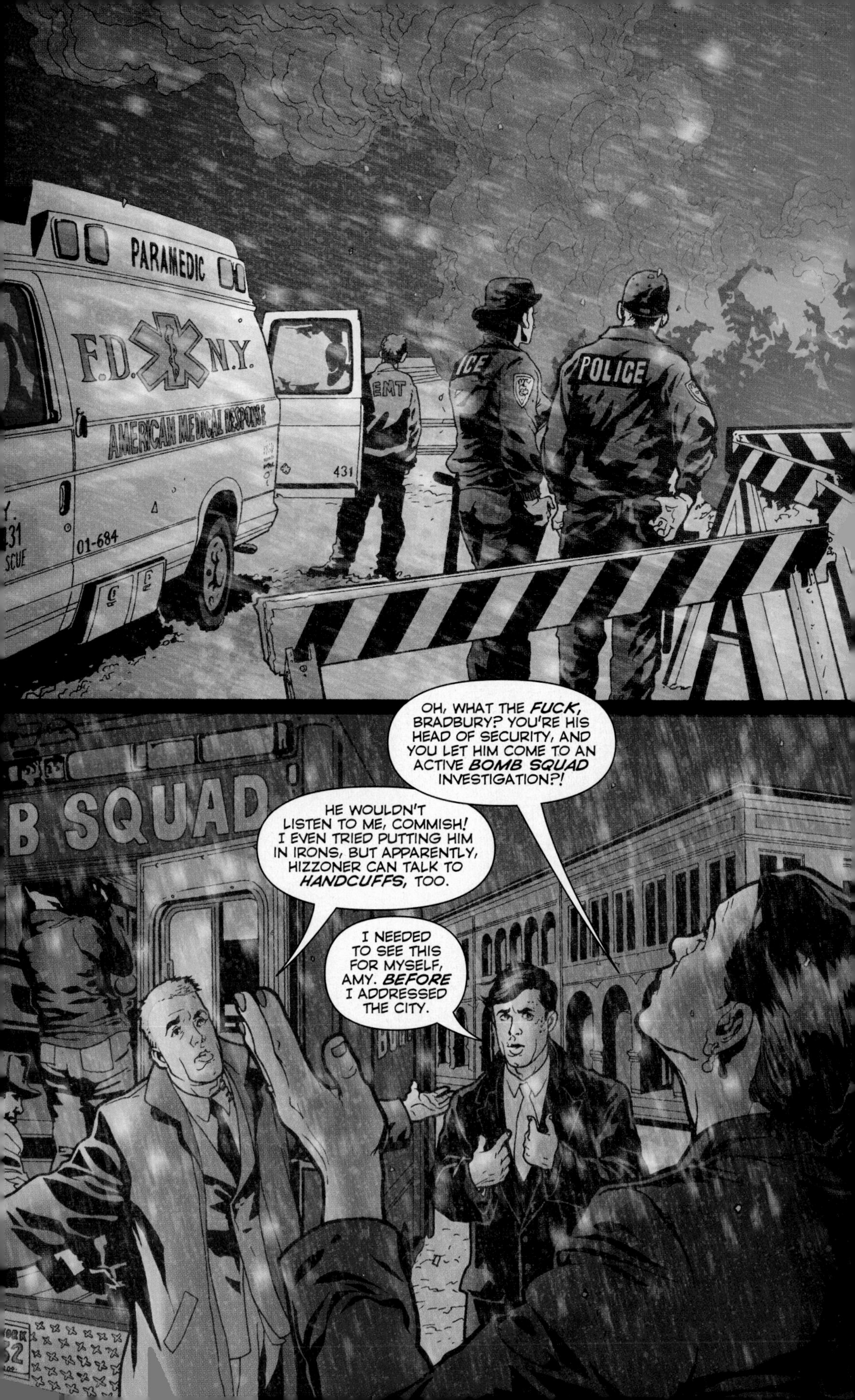
PARAMEDIC
F.D. N.Y.
AMERICAN MEDICAL RESPONSE
431
01-684
EMT
POLICE
B SQUAD
OH, WHAT THE *FUCK*, BRADBURY? YOU'RE HIS HEAD OF SECURITY, AND YOU LET HIM COME TO AN ACTIVE *BOMB SQUAD* INVESTIGATION?!
HE WOULDN'T LISTEN TO ME, COMMISH! I EVEN TRIED PUTTING HIM IN IRONS, BUT APPARENTLY, HIZZONER CAN TALK TO *HANDCUFFS*, TOO.
I NEEDED TO SEE THIS FOR MYSELF, AMY. *BEFORE* I ADDRESSED THE CITY.

TRISTA, NO ONE IS GOING TO *DESTROY* YOUR ARTWORK.

BUT THE TAXPAYERS *ARE* PARTIALLY FUNDING ITS DISPLAY, AND IF MAYOR HUNDRED IS GOING TO CONVINCE THEM THAT IT'S A WORTHWHILE USE OF THEIR MONEY, HE COULD USE YOUR HELP.

CAN YOU TELL ME WHAT YOUR *INTENTION* WAS WITH THE PIECE? WHAT YOU WERE TRYING TO SAY?

IT'S NOT MY JOB TO *EXPLAIN* MY PAINTINGS. THEY SPEAK FOR THEMSELVES.

OUR GENERATION'S BEEN RUINED BY CLIFFS NOTES AND... AND *DIRECTOR'S COMMENTARIES.* PEOPLE SHOULD LEARN TO COME TO THEIR *OWN* GODDAMN CONCLUSIONS ABOUT ART.

I MEAN, I KNOW YOU'RE JUST SOME GLORIFIED INTERN, BUT IF YOUR PARENTS WERE FRUITY ENOUGH TO NAME YOU *JOURNAL,* THEY PROBABLY TAUGHT YOU *SOMETHING* ABOUT CULTURE, RIGHT?

WHAT DO *YOU* THINK WHEN YOU LOOK AT THIS?

HONESTLY?

I THINK IT'S A JOKE.

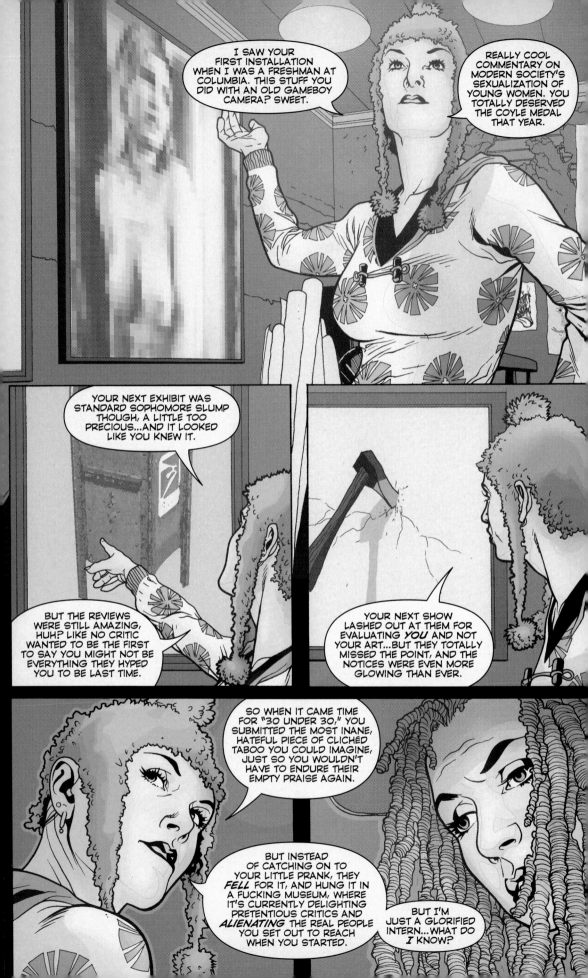

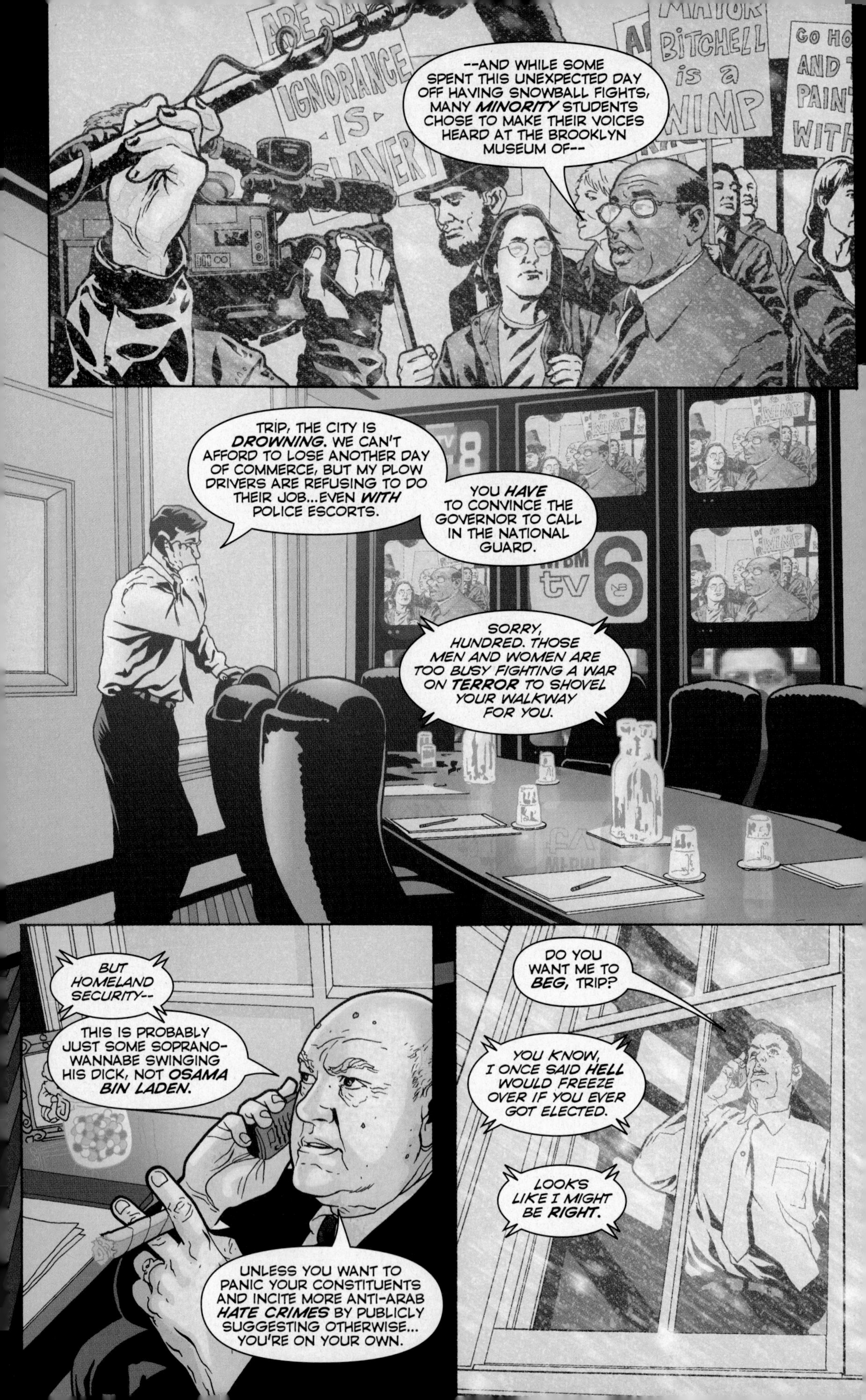
IGNORANCE IS
--AND WHILE SOME SPENT THIS UNEXPECTED DAY OFF HAVING SNOWBALL FIGHTS, MANY *MINORITY* STUDENTS CHOSE TO MAKE THEIR VOICES HEARD AT THE BROOKLYN MUSEUM OF--
TRIP, THE CITY IS *DROWNING*. WE CAN'T AFFORD TO LOSE ANOTHER DAY OF COMMERCE, BUT MY PLOW DRIVERS ARE REFUSING TO DO THEIR JOB...EVEN *WITH* POLICE ESCORTS.
YOU *HAVE* TO CONVINCE THE GOVERNOR TO CALL IN THE NATIONAL GUARD.
SORRY, HUNDRED. THOSE MEN AND WOMEN ARE TOO BUSY FIGHTING A WAR ON *TERROR* TO SHOVEL YOUR WALKWAY FOR YOU.
BUT HOMELAND SECURITY--
THIS IS PROBABLY JUST SOME SOPRANO-WANNABE SWINGING HIS DICK, NOT *OSAMA BIN LADEN*.
UNLESS YOU WANT TO PANIC YOUR CONSTITUENTS AND INCITE MORE ANTI-ARAB *HATE CRIMES* BY PUBLICLY SUGGESTING OTHERWISE... YOU'RE ON YOUR OWN.
DO YOU WANT ME TO *BEG*, TRIP?
YOU KNOW, I ONCE SAID *HELL* WOULD FREEZE OVER IF YOU EVER GOT ELECTED.
LOOKS LIKE I MIGHT BE *RIGHT*.

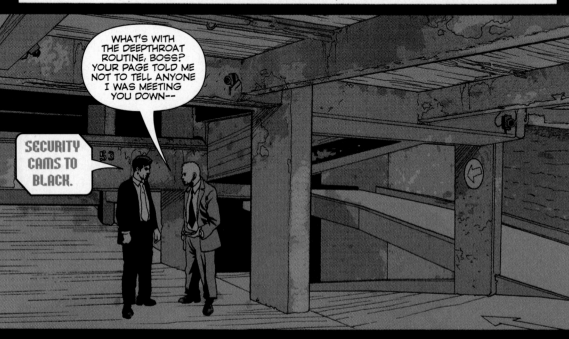

WHAT'S WITH THE DEEPTHROAT ROUTINE, BOSS? YOUR PAGE TOLD ME NOT TO TELL ANYONE I WAS MEETING YOU DOWN--

SECURITY CAMS TO BLACK.

BRADBURY, IT'S KREMLIN.

KREMLIN HAS THIS COAT.

YEAH, SO DO A MILLION OTHER PEOPLE WITH NO TASTE.

KREMLIN OWNS A GUN. HE KNOWS HOW TO MAKE BOMBS.

AND IT WAS JUST A FEW HOURS BEFORE THE *EXPLOSION* WHEN HE VISITED ME LAST NIGHT.

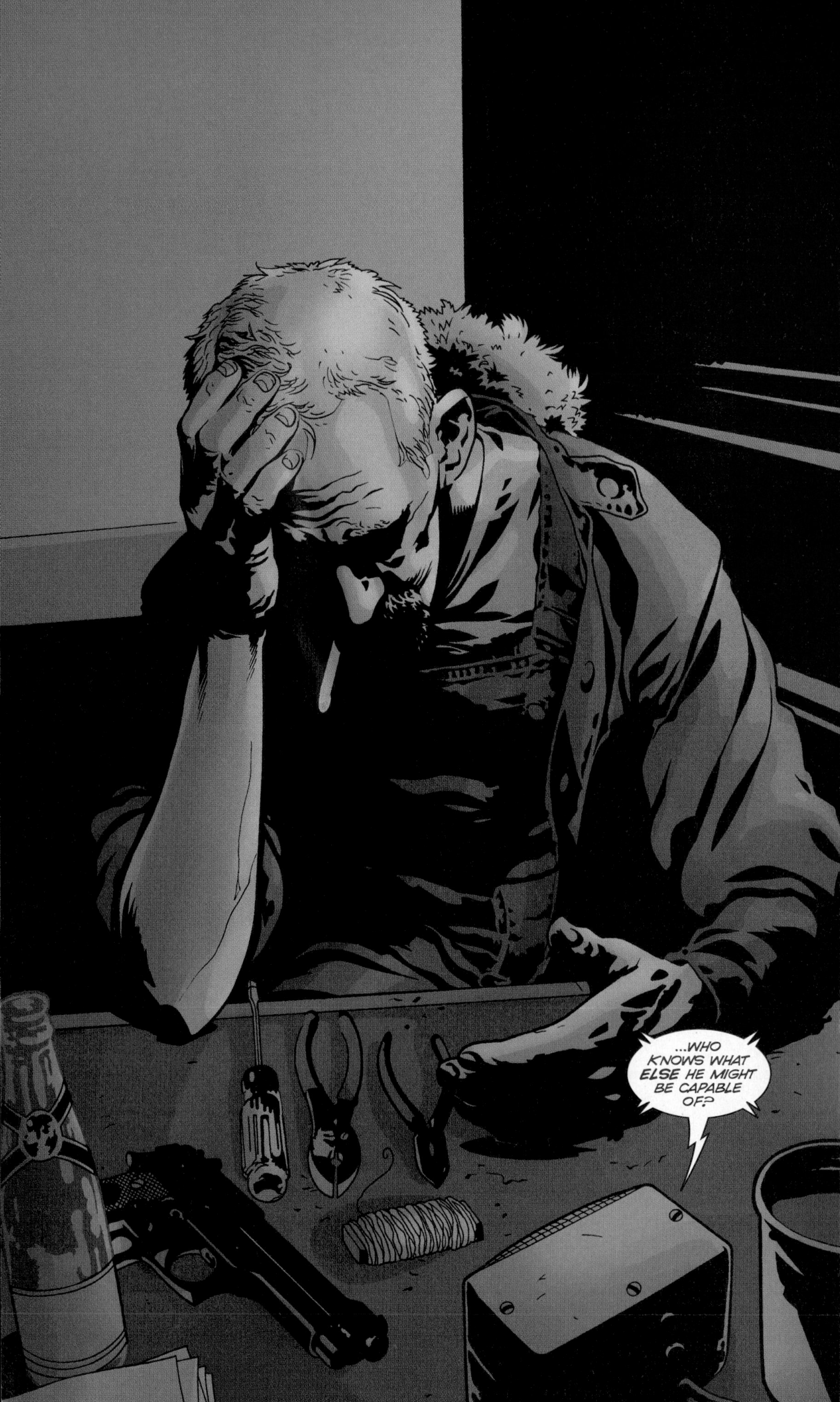
...WHO KNOWS WHAT ELSE HE MIGHT BE CAPABLE OF?

CHAPTER 5

Part 4
State of Emergency

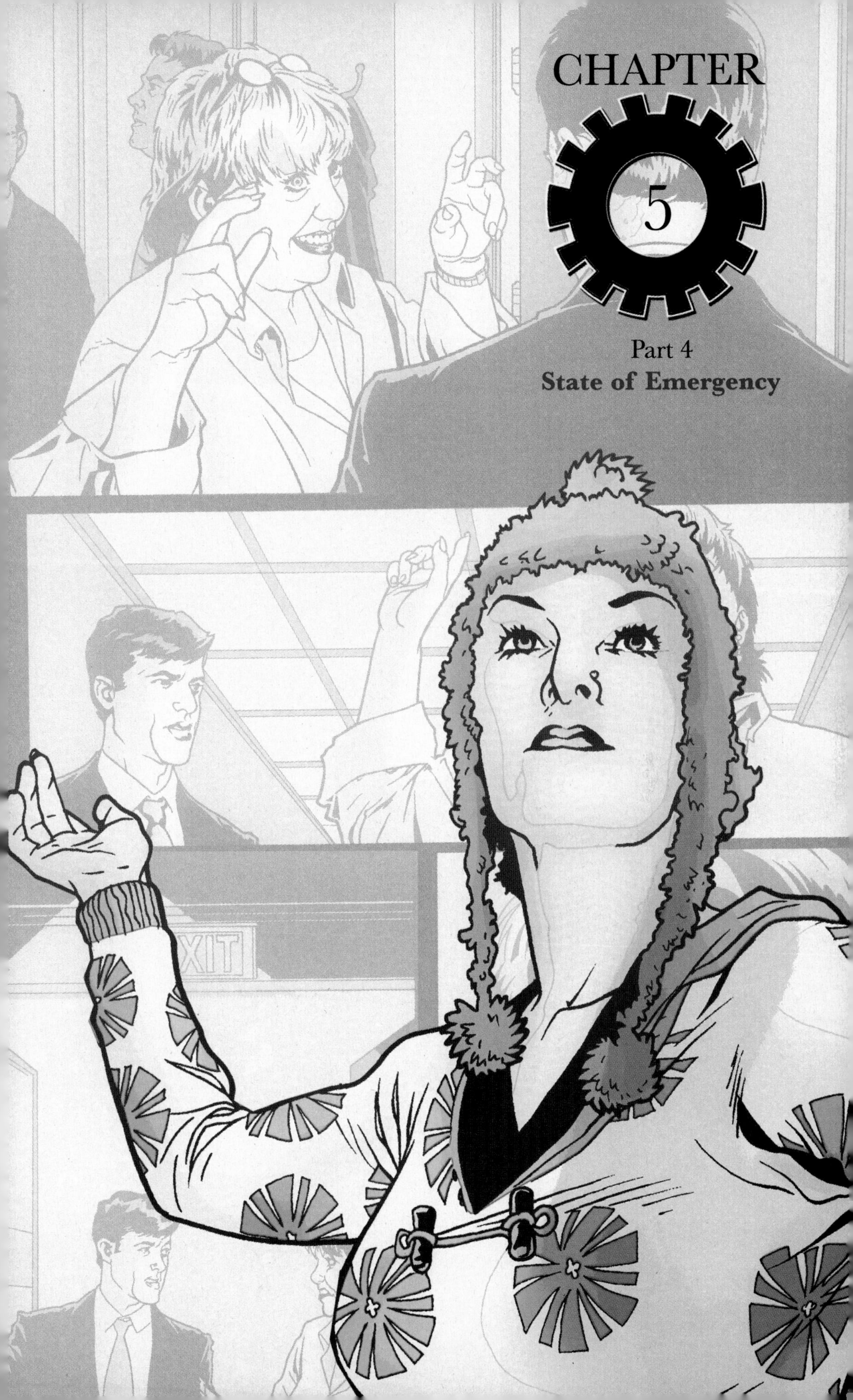

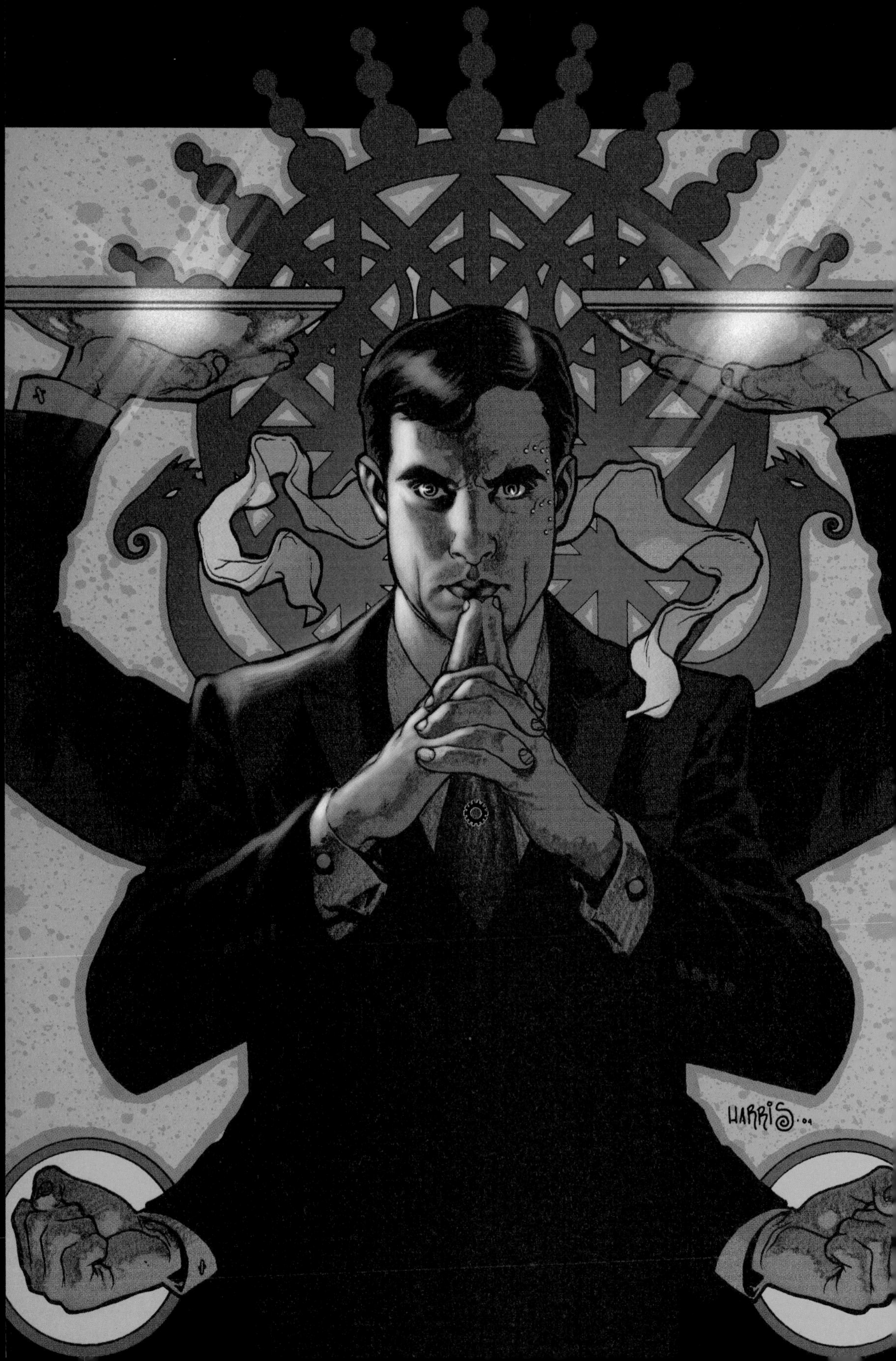
HARRIS .04

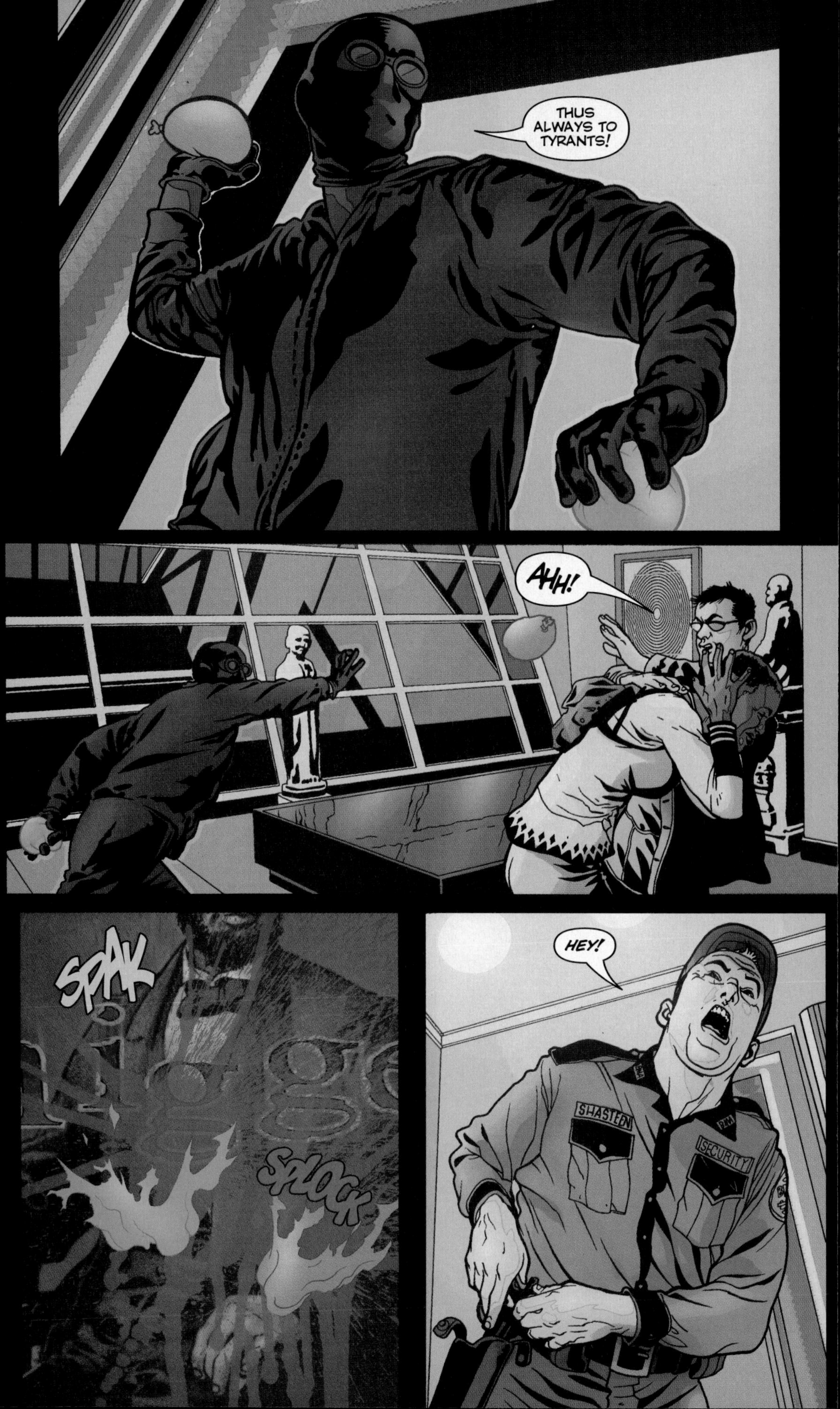
THUS ALWAYS TO TYRANTS!
AHH!
SPAK
SPLOCK
HEY!
SHASTEEN
SECURITY

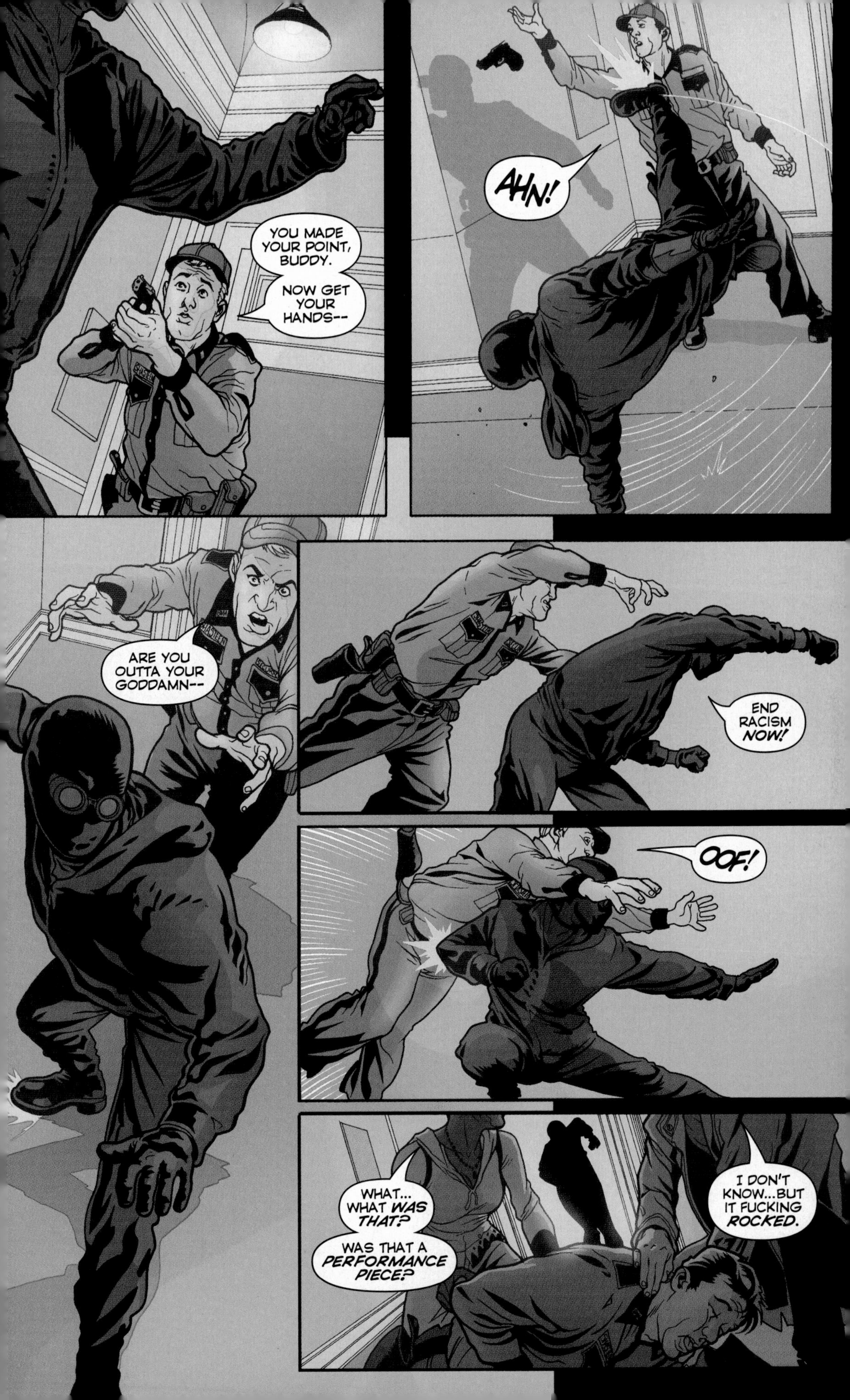
YOU MADE YOUR POINT, BUDDY.
NOW GET YOUR HANDS--
AHN!
ARE YOU OUTTA YOUR GODDAMN--
END RACISM NOW!
OOF!
WHAT... WHAT WAS THAT?
WAS THAT A PERFORMANCE PIECE?
I DON'T KNOW...BUT IT FUCKING ROCKED.

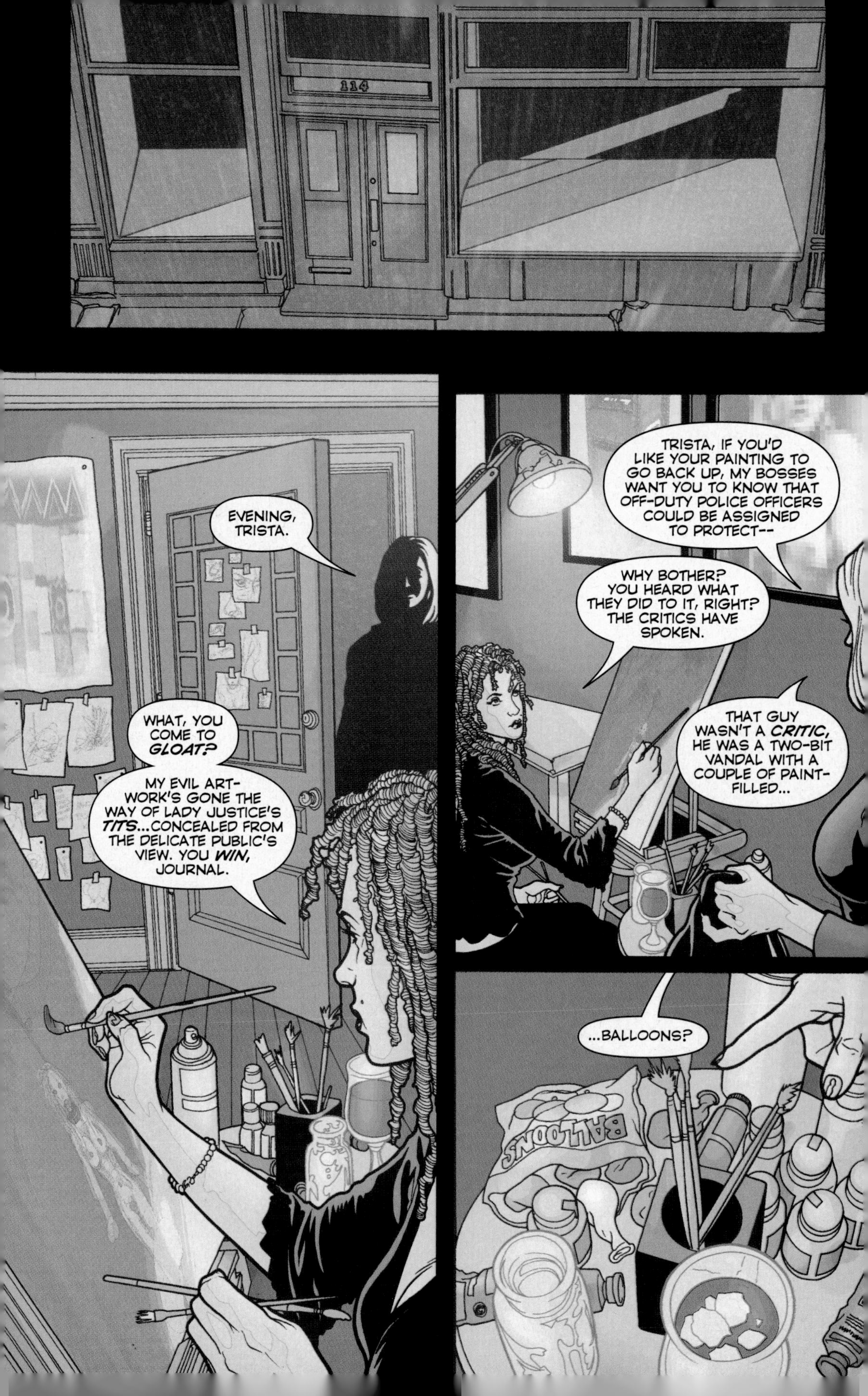
114
EVENING, TRISTA.
WHAT, YOU COME TO GLOAT?
MY EVIL ART-WORK'S GONE THE WAY OF LADY JUSTICE'S TITS...CONCEALED FROM THE DELICATE PUBLIC'S VIEW. YOU WIN, JOURNAL.
TRISTA, IF YOU'D LIKE YOUR PAINTING TO GO BACK UP, MY BOSSES WANT YOU TO KNOW THAT OFF-DUTY POLICE OFFICERS COULD BE ASSIGNED TO PROTECT--
WHY BOTHER? YOU HEARD WHAT THEY DID TO IT, RIGHT? THE CRITICS HAVE SPOKEN.
THAT GUY WASN'T A CRITIC, HE WAS A TWO-BIT VANDAL WITH A COUPLE OF PAINT-FILLED...
...BALLOONS?
BALLOONS

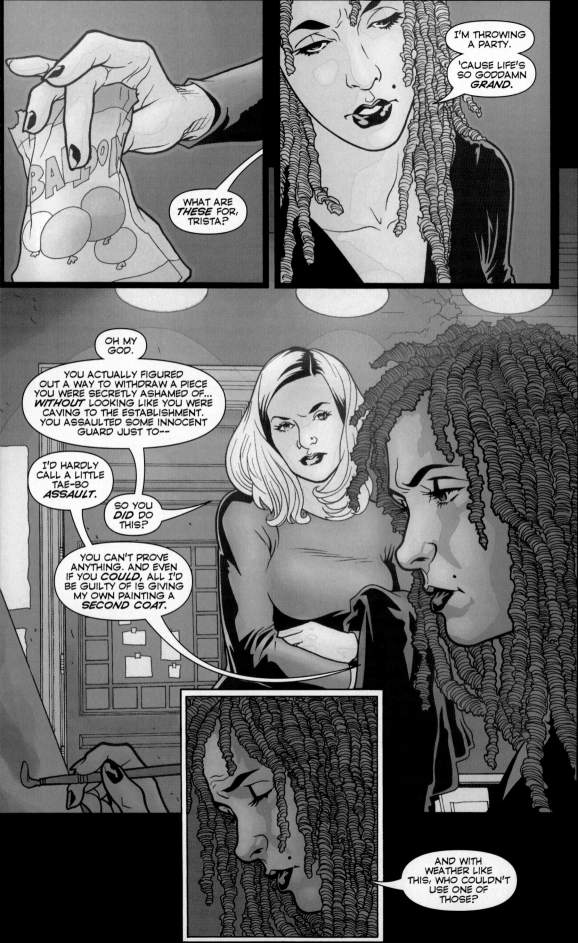

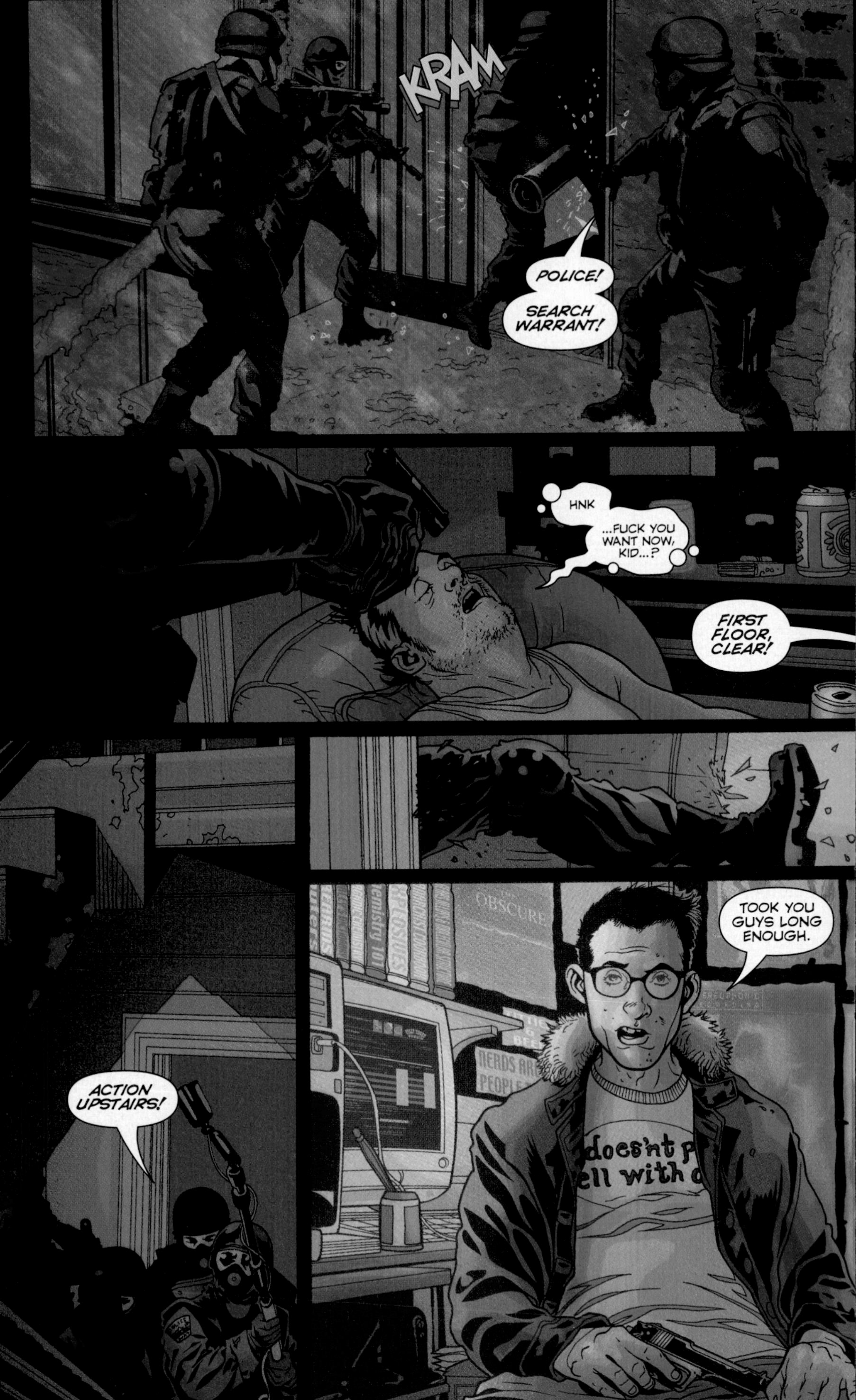
KRAM
POLICE!
SEARCH WARRANT!
HNK
...FUCK YOU WANT NOW, KID...?
FIRST FLOOR, CLEAR!
ACTION UPSTAIRS!
TOOK YOU GUYS LONG ENOUGH.

TUESDAY, MAY 8, 2001

CAST OF CHARACTERS

JIMMY HILL
AS: MITCHELL HUNDRED

DOODLE GRUB
AS: TRIP

ERIC O'DELL
AS: BRADBURY

MARNIE HILL
AS: JOURNAL MOORE

GRETA O'DELL
AS: COMMISSIONER ANGOTTI
AND TRISTA BRAVING

ENZO HARRIS
AS: YOUNG MITCHELL

LARRY BRANTLEY
AS: KREMLIN

STACIE HARRIS
AS: MITCHELL'S MOTHER

TONY HARRIS
AS: VARIOUS

PAT GRAHAM
AS: CANDY WATSON

JIMMY CLARK
AS: JACKSON GEORGES

EDDIE THOMAS
AS: CHIEF OF PATROL KURSON

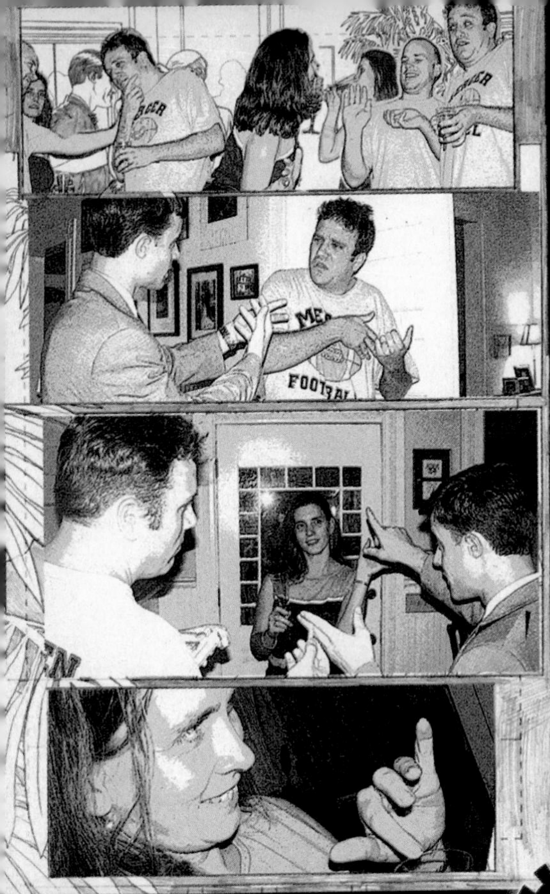

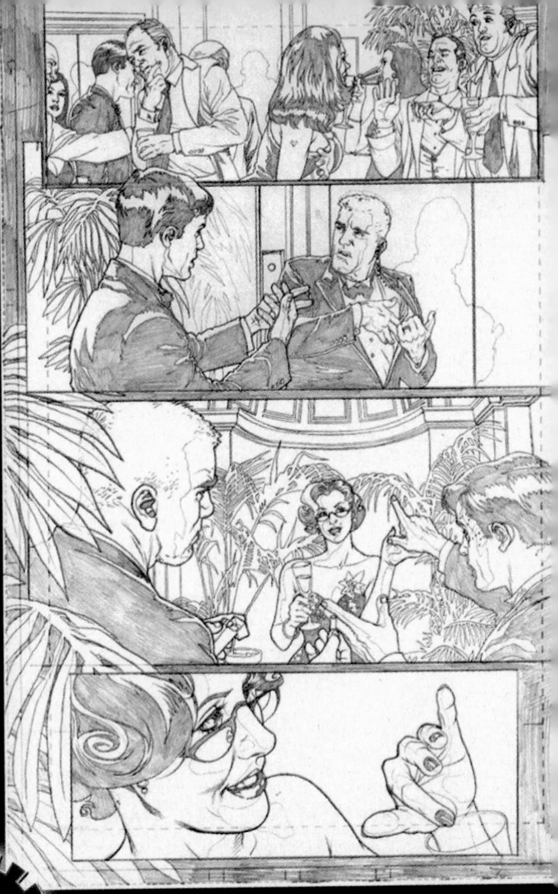

FROM REFERENCE TO FINISH PAGES

PAGE 1

BY HARRIS, FEISTER AND METTLER

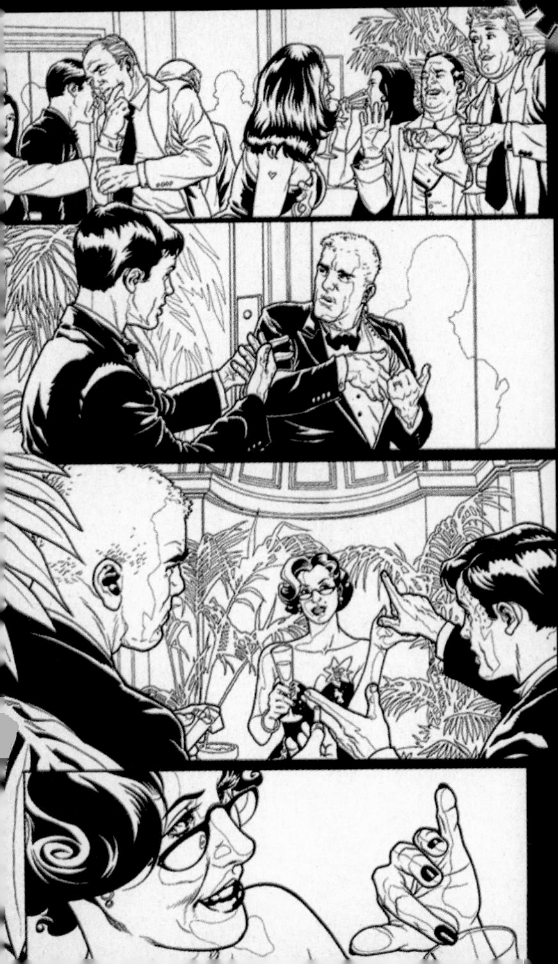

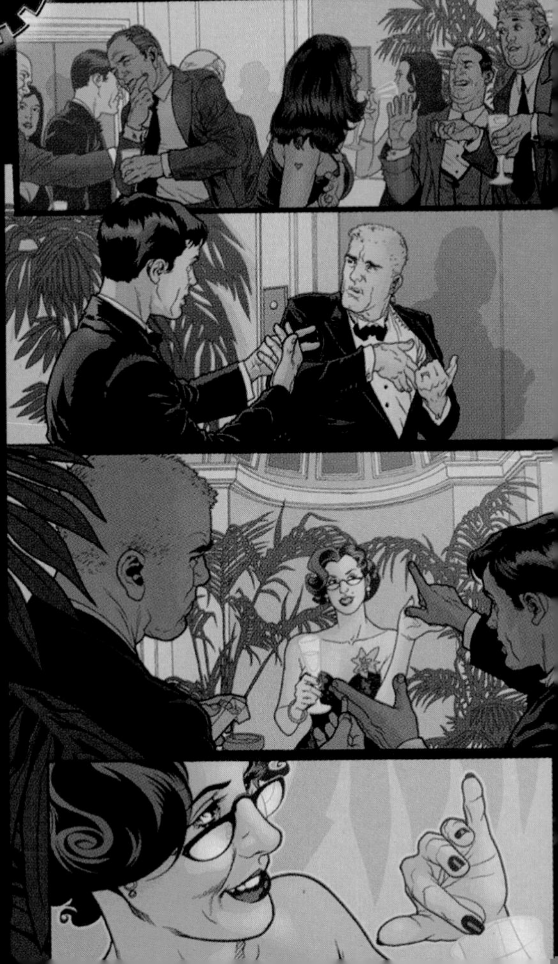

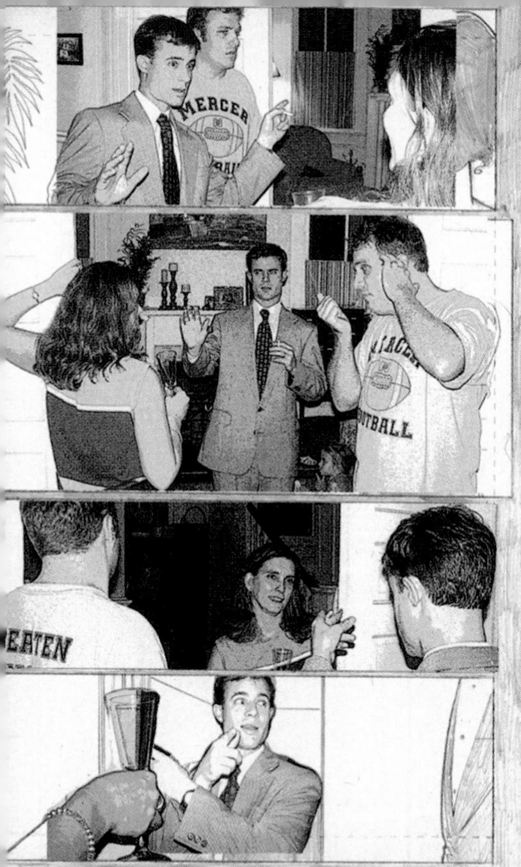
MERCER

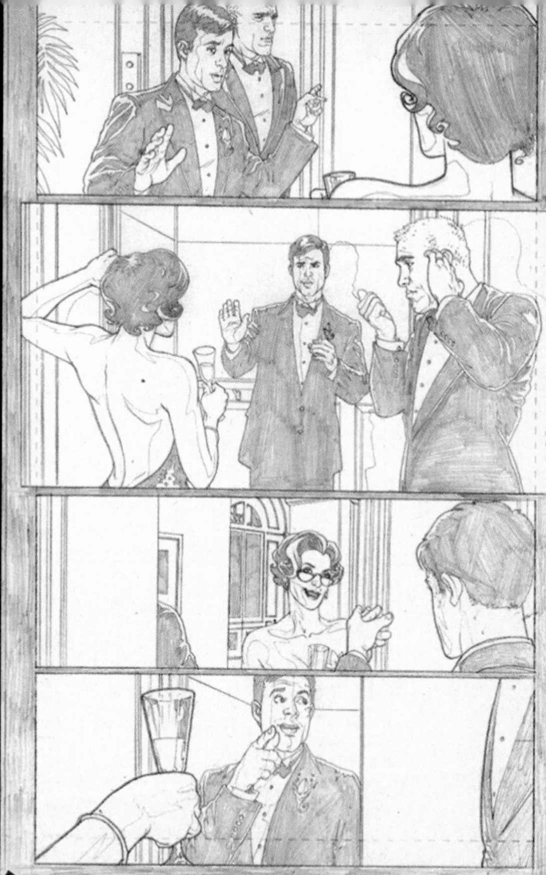

FROM REFERENCE TO FINISH PAGES

PAGE 2

BY HARRIS, FEISTER AND METTLER

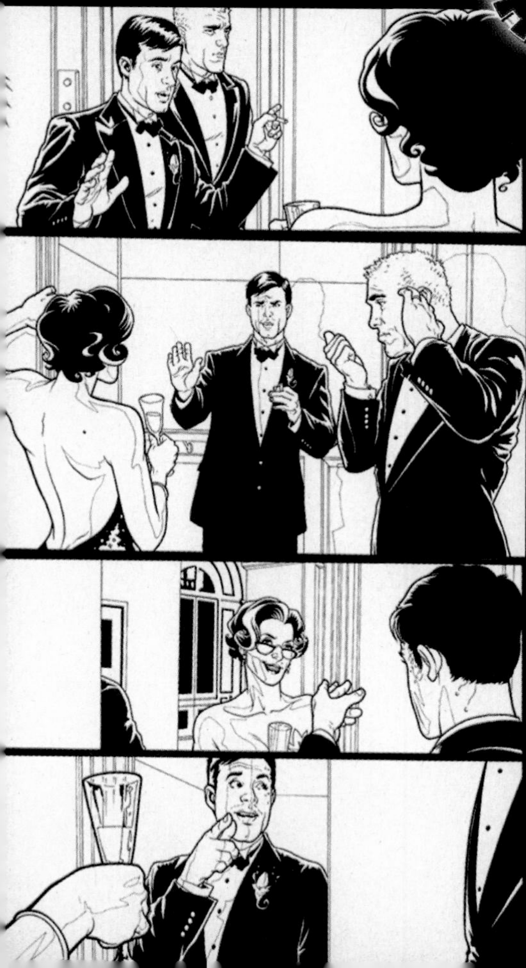

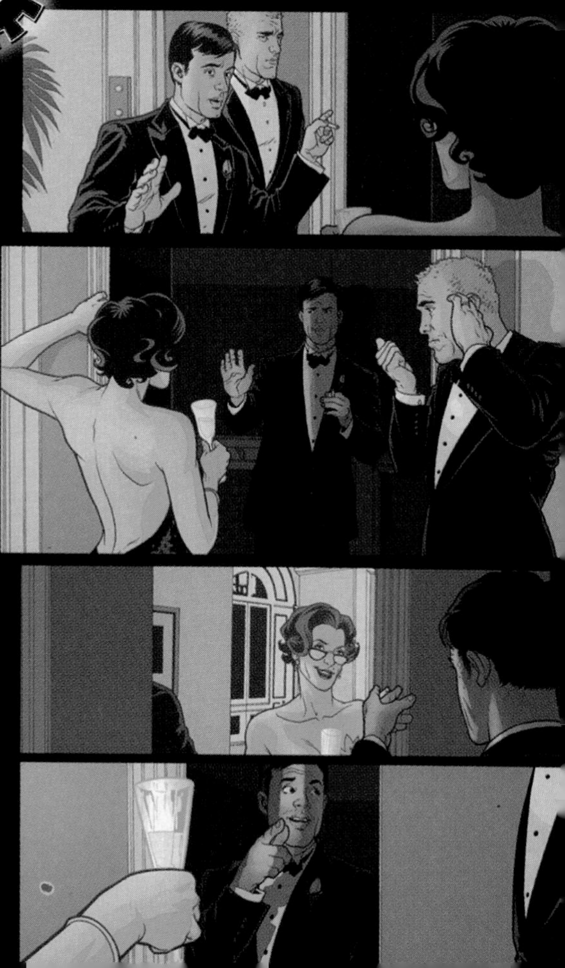

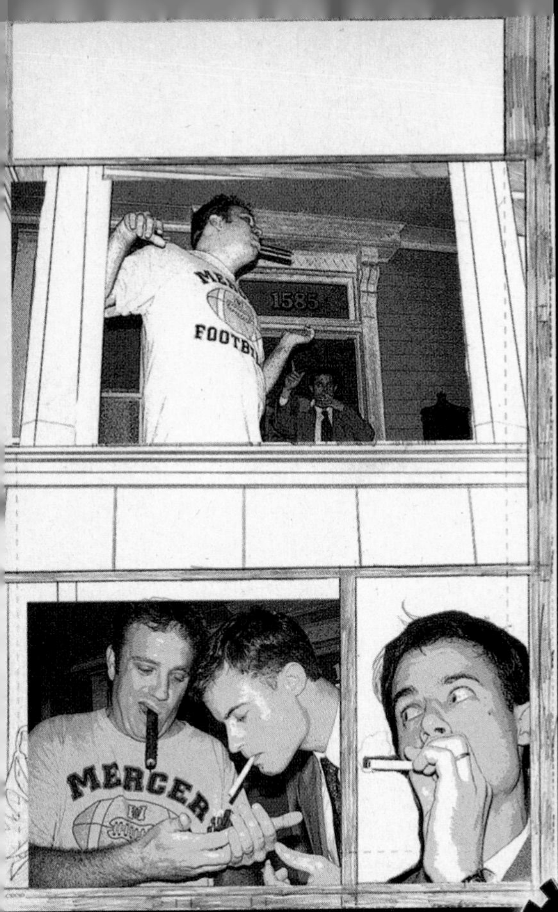
1585
MERCER

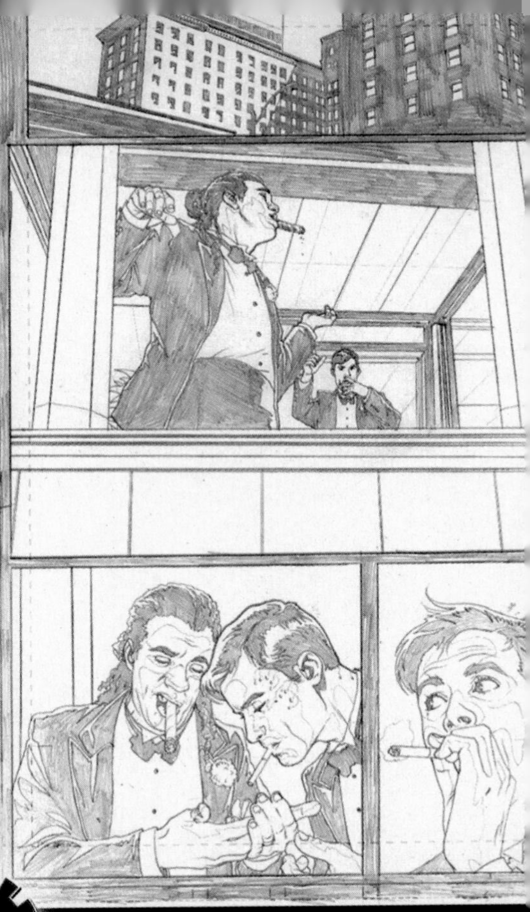

FROM REFERENCE TO FINISH PAGES

PAGE 3

BY HARRIS, FEISTER AND METTLER

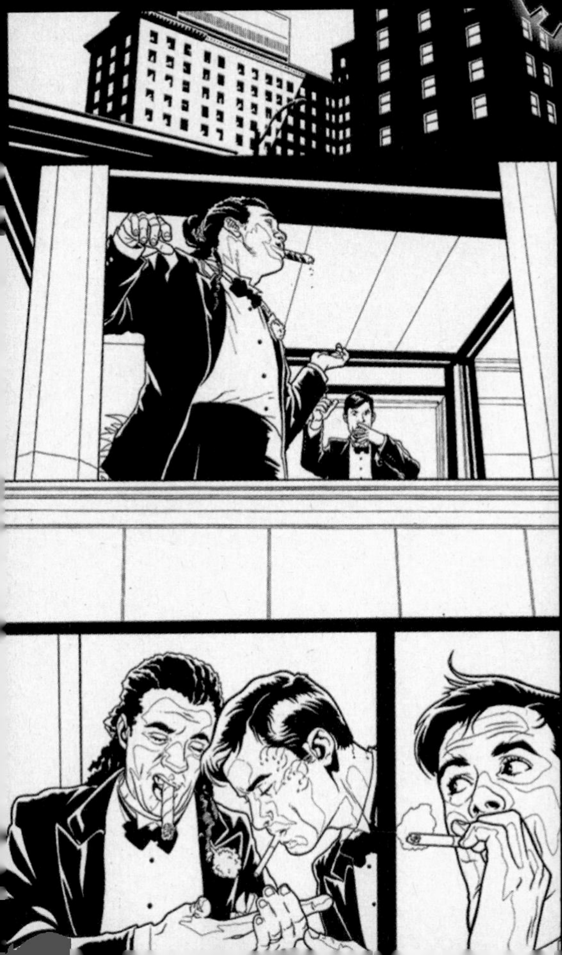

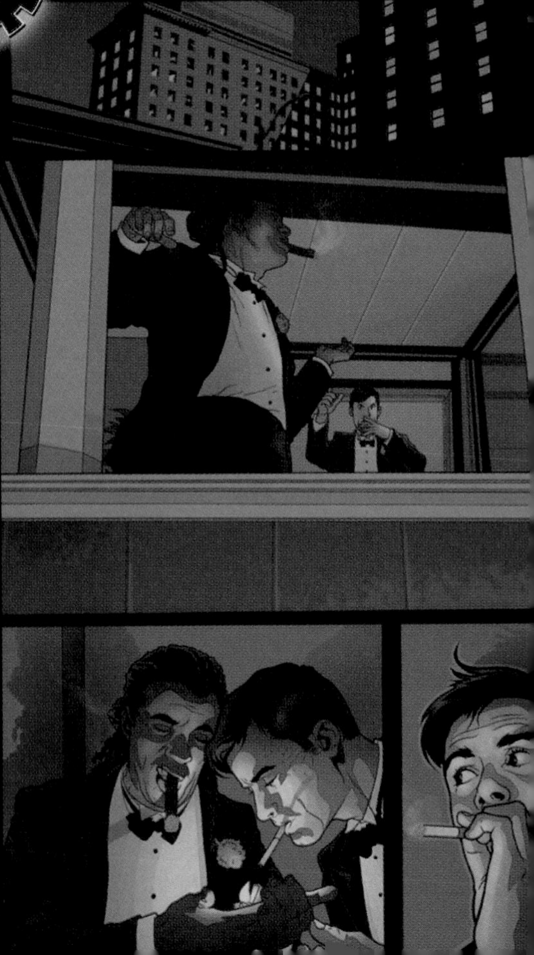

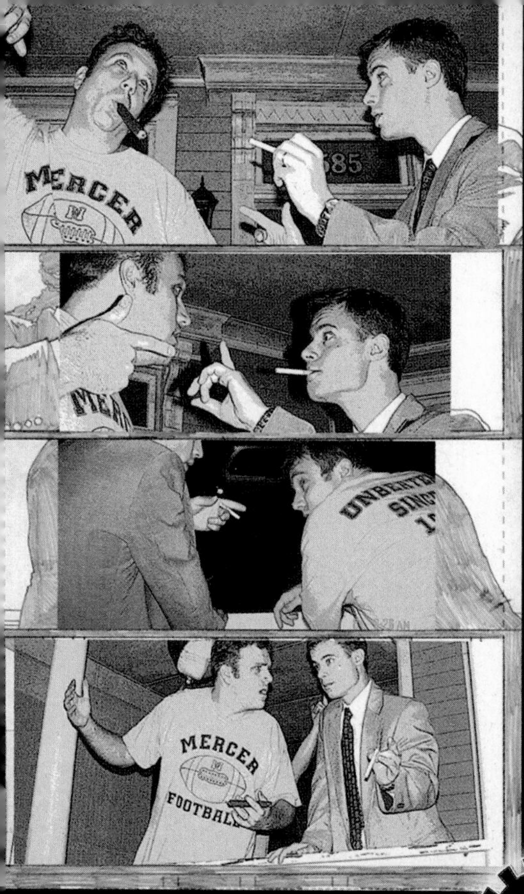
MERCER
MERCER
FOOTBALL

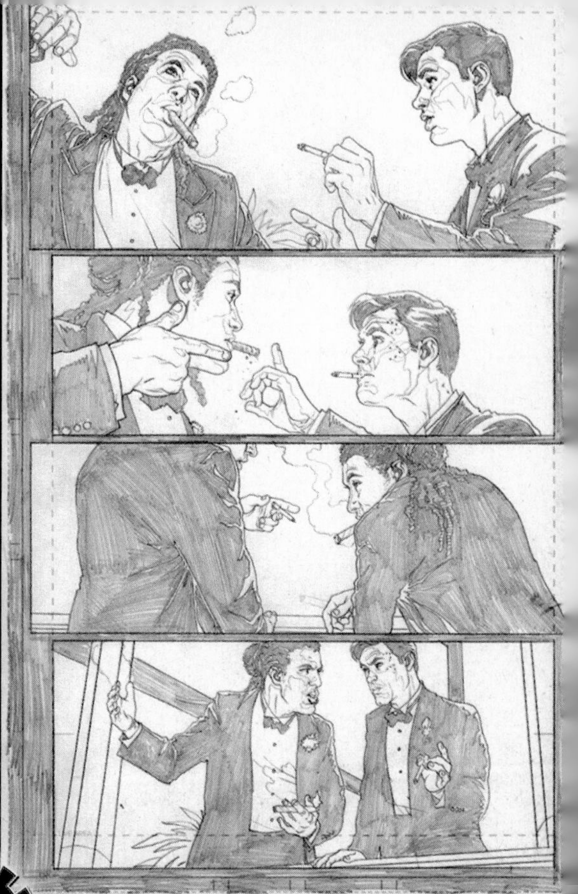

FROM REFERENCE TO FINISH PAGES

PAGE 4

BY HARRIS, FEISTER AND METTLER

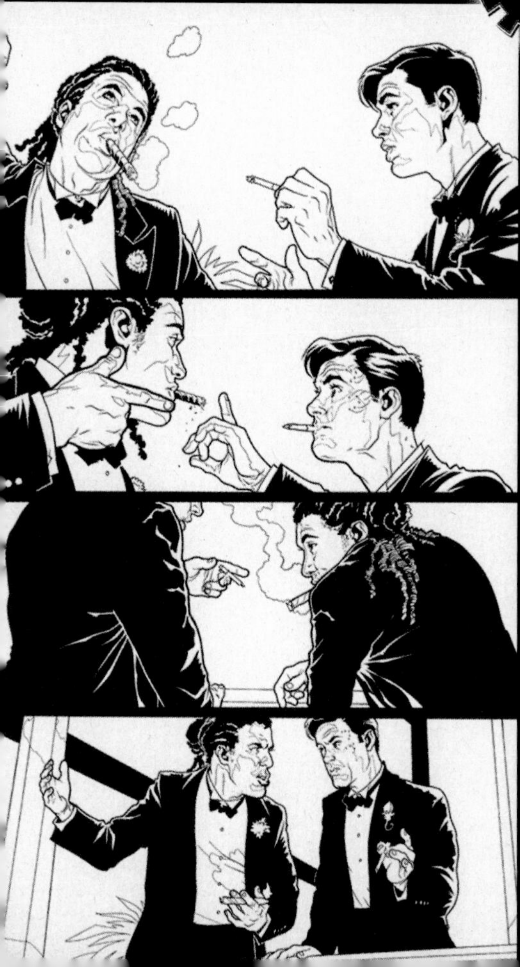

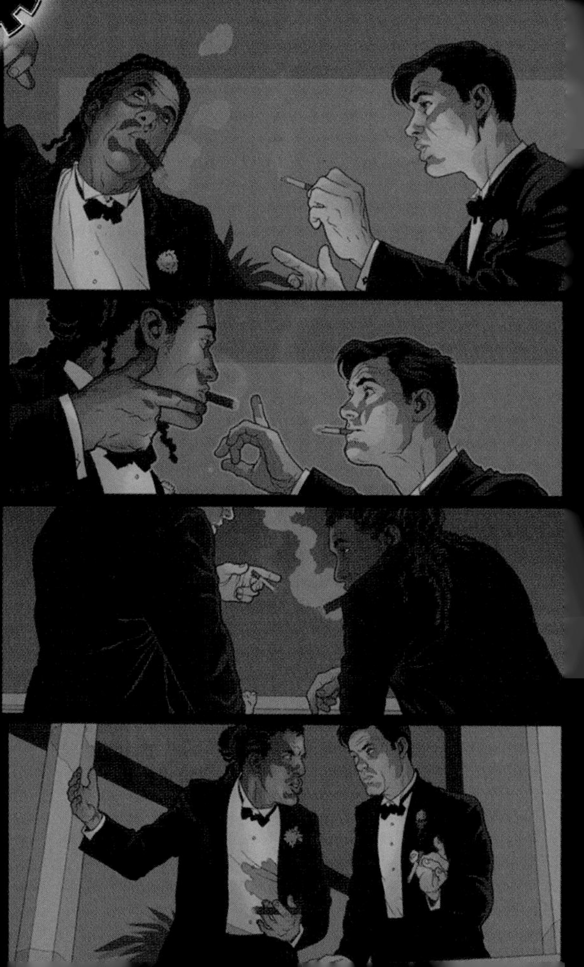

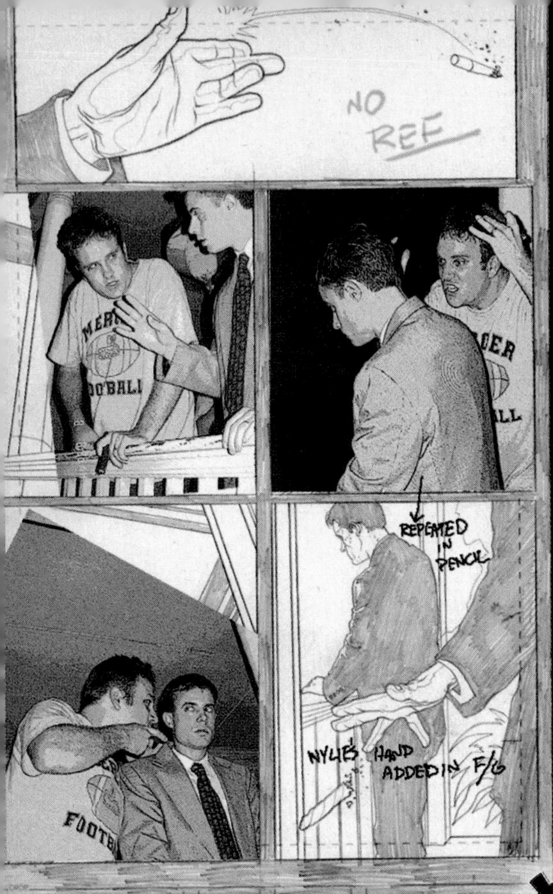
NO REF
REPEATED IN PENCIL
NYLE'S HAND ADDED IN F/G

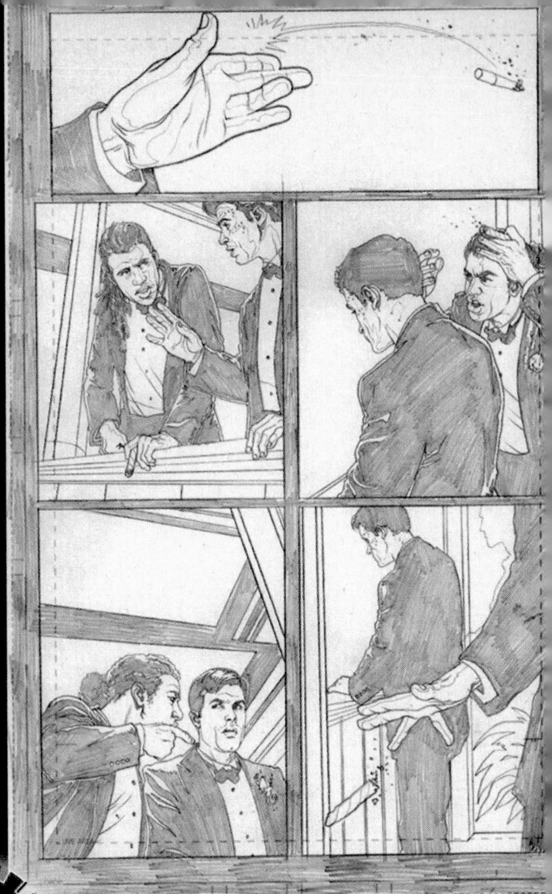

FROM REFERENCE TO FINISH PAGES

PAGE 5

BY HARRIS, FEISTER AND METTLER

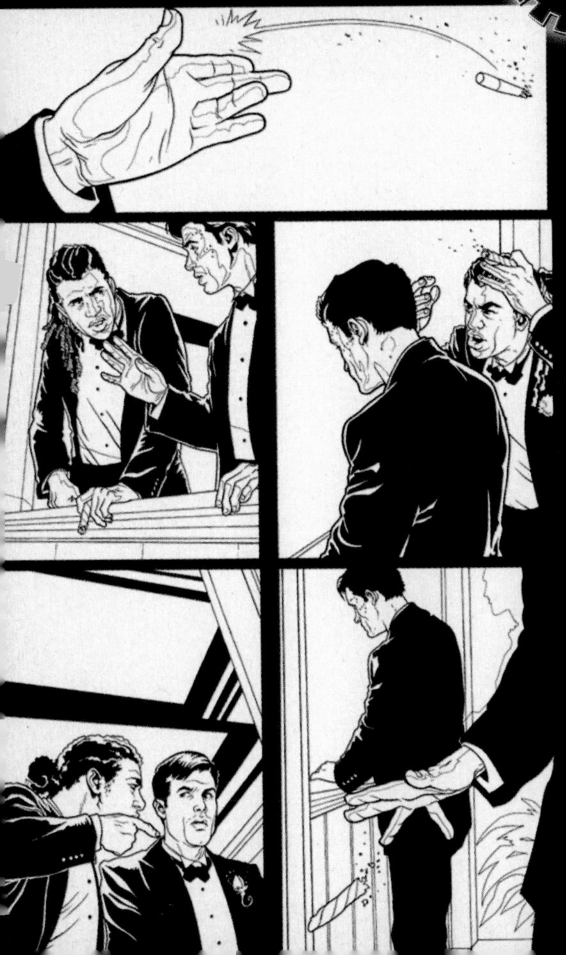

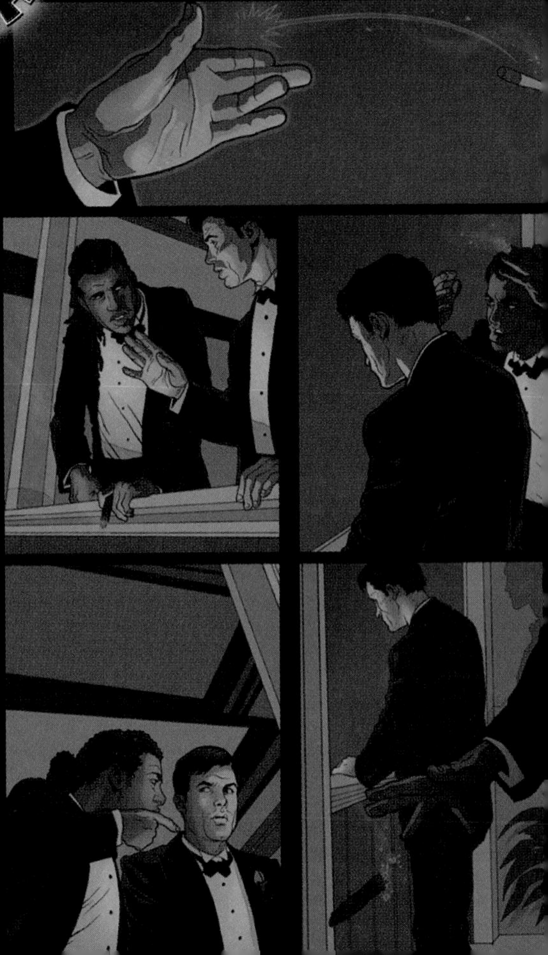

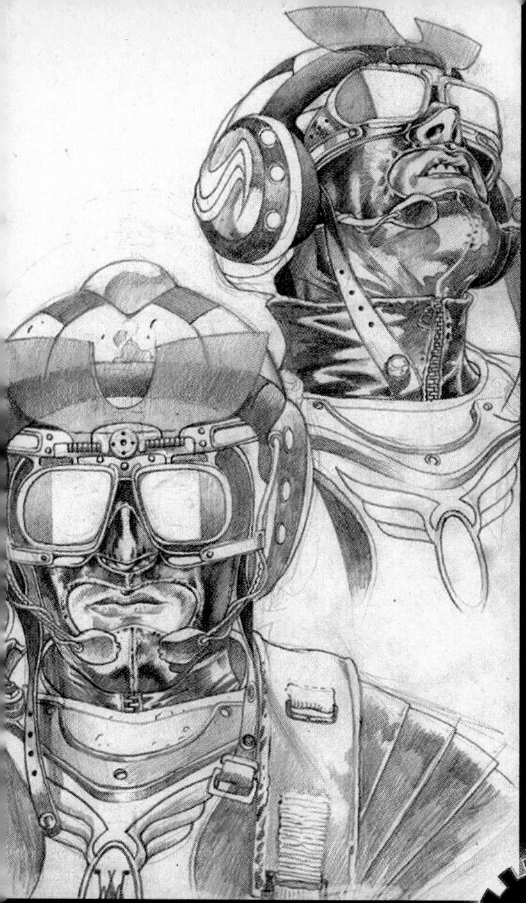

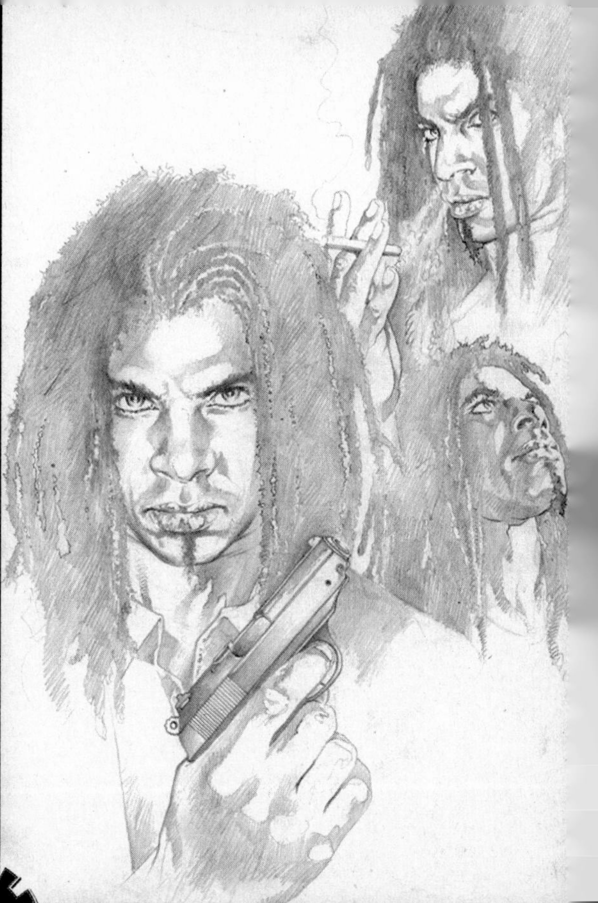

EXTRA SKETCHES

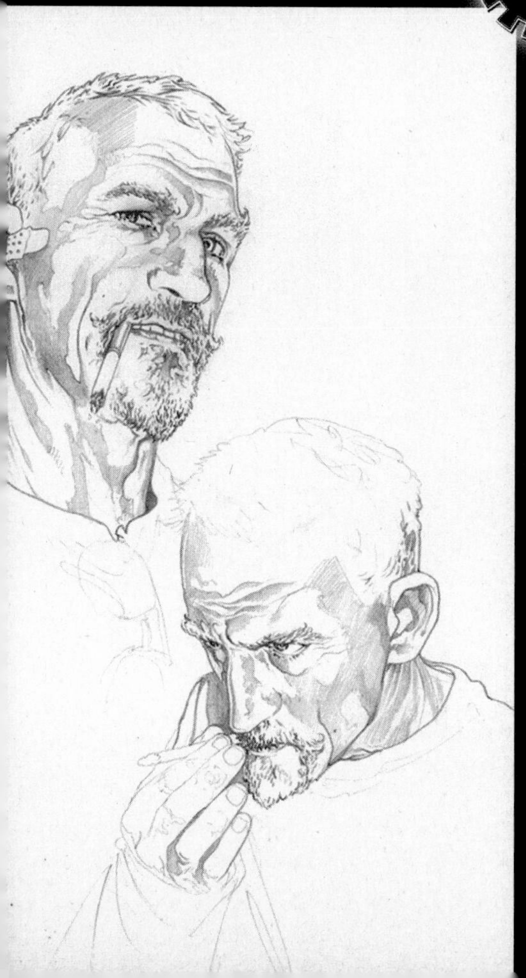

MJOB!!! : Tidy Bowl Killer leaves another Floater!

COLD-SNAP: Winter ain't over till the Fat Lady sings!

NEW ★ ★ ★ ★ YORK

DAILY WIRE

New York's Most Respected Newspaper

★ EXCLUSIVE ★

CRAZED WINGMAN
Shuts Down Subways for Eleven Hours!

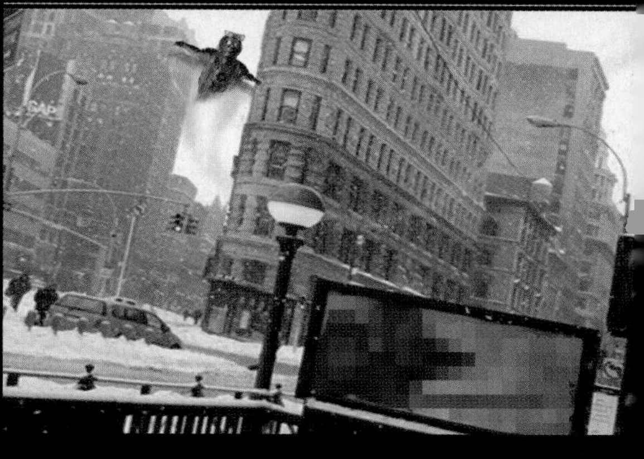

BACKLIST

Y: THE LAST MAN
BOOKS 1–4

VAUGHAN/GUERRA/VARIOUS

JSA:
THE LIBERTY FILES

JOLLEY/HARRIS/SNYDER

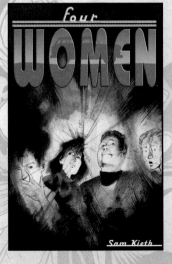

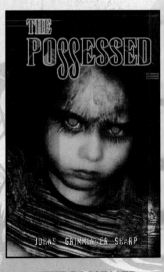

GLOBAL FREQUENCY
BOOKS 1 & 2

ELLIS/VARIOUS

FOUR WOMEN

KIETH

THE POSSESSED

JOHNS/GRIMMINGER/SHARP

Search the Graphic Novels section of
wildstorm.com for art and info on every one
of our hundreds of books!

TO FIND MORE COLLECTED EDITIONS AND MONTHLY COMIC BOOKS FROM
WILDSTORM AND DC COMICS, CALL 1-888-COMIC BOOK FOR THE NEAREST COMIC
SHOP OR GO TO YOUR LOCAL BOOK STORE.